CW01021811

This book was donated by SAGE

# Sociology of
# the Sacred

# Theory, Culture & Society

*Theory, Culture & Society* caters for the resurgence of interest in culture within contemporary social science and the humanities. Building on the http://thenarrowboatpub.com/ch this tradition has been reshaped by a new generation of theorists. It also publishes theoretically informed analyses of everyday life, popular culture, and new social and intellectual movements.

EDITOR: Mike Featherstone, *Goldsmiths College, University of London*

SERIES EDITORIAL BOARD
Roy Boyne, *University of Durham*
Nicholas Gane, *University of Warwick*
Scott Lash, *Goldsmiths College, University of London*
Couze Venn, *Goldsmiths College, University of London*

The *Theory, Culture & Society* book series, the journals *Theory, Culture & Society* and *Body & Society*, and related conference, seminar and postgraduate programmes now operate from the Department of Sociology at Goldsmiths College, University of London. For further details of the TCS Centre's activities please contact:

*Theory, Culture & Society*
Department of Sociology
Goldsmiths, University of London
Floors 8–11 Warmington Tower
New Cross, London SE14 6NW, UK
e-mail: tcs@sagepub.co.uk
web: www.theoryculturesociety.org

*Recent volumes include:*

**Cosmopolitanism**
Zlatko Skrbis and Ian Woodward

**The Body and Social Theory 3e**
Chris Shilling

**Immaterial Bodies**
Lisa Blackman

**French Post-War Social Theory**
Derek Robbins

**The Domestic Economy of The Soul**
John O'Neill

Philip A Mellor and Chris Shilling

# Sociology of the Sacred

*Religion, Embodiment and Social Change*

Los Angeles | London | New Delhi
Singapore | Washington DC

Los Angeles | London | New Delhi
Singapore | Washington DC

SAGE Publications Ltd
1 Oliver's Yard
55 City Road
London EC1Y 1SP

SAGE Publications Inc.
2455 Teller Road
Thousand Oaks, California 91320

SAGE Publications India Pvt Ltd
B 1/I 1 Mohan Cooperative Industrial Area
Mathura Road
New Delhi 110 044

SAGE Publications Asia-Pacific Pte Ltd
3 Church Street
#10-04 Samsung Hub
Singapore 049483

© Philip A. Mellor and Chris Shilling 2014

First published 2014

Apart from any fair dealing for the purposes of research or private study, or criticism or review, as permitted under the Copyright, Designs and Patents Act, 1988, this publication may be reproduced, stored or transmitted in any form, or by any means, only with the prior permission in writing of the publishers, or in the case of reprographic reproduction, in accordance with the terms of licences issued by the Copyright Licensing Agency. Enquiries concerning reproduction outside those terms should be sent to the publishers.

Editor: Mila Steele
Assistant editor: James Piper
Production editor: Imogen Roome
Copyeditor: Kate Harrison
Proofreader: Leigh C. Timmins
Indexer: Debbie Shilling
Marketing manager: Michael Ainsley
Cover design: Wendy Scott
Typeset by: C&M Digitals (P) Ltd, Chennai, India
Printed in India at Replika Press Pvt Ltd

**Library of Congress Control Number: 2013957371**

**British Library Cataloguing in Publication data**

A catalogue record for this book is available from the British Library

MIX
Paper from
responsible sources
FSC
www.fsc.org    FSC® C016779

ISBN 978-1-4462-7223-7

At SAGE we take sustainability seriously. Most of our products are printed in the UK using FSC papers and boards. When we print overseas we ensure sustainable papers are used as measured by the Egmont grading system. We undertake an annual audit to monitor our sustainability.

# Contents

# 1

## Introduction

This book explores the relationship between religion and secularization in the contemporary global era. In so doing, it seeks to advance sociological debates about how an increasing range of phenomena have come to be constructed and experienced as sacred, or extraordinary, and thereby contain the potential to shape social action in significant ways. These debates characteristically treat the category of the sacred as unitary, typically reflecting religious or quasi-religious processes. In contrast, we argue that there exist distinct, competing and interacting modalities of the sacred; a position attentive to the existence of this-worldly (secular) as well as the other-worldly (religious) manifestations of objects, relationships and ideas that are set apart from the mundane. Introducing what we identify as socio-religious, transcendent, bio-political and bio-economic modalities of the sacred, we seek to re-structure discussions of secularization by focusing on the variable capacities of these very different extraordinary forces to enframe and shape people's embodied experiences. These modalities are especially important for our concerns because of their implications for the corporeal and cognitive terrain on which forms of religious habitus are nurtured or impeded, and it is the future of these forms of habitus that remain vital for, yet are marginalized within, recent debates about secularization and the revitalization of religion.

In broad terms, these debates about religion and secularization appear for many to have been settled. Most recent analysts agree that there has, during the last few decades, been a global resurgence of particular religions, as well as a growth in social and cultural phenomena designated sacred. It is now common, indeed, to regard previously influential sociological models of secularization as fundamentally mistaken, with visions of a 'post-secular' age promoted as preferable bases from which to assess these issues (e.g. Berger, 1999; Habermas, 2008, 2010). Opposing this growing consensus, we suggest that processes of secularization remain central to the extraordinary power and status accorded to bio-economic and bio-political forces affecting the world today.[1] Before developing this argument, though, it is necessary to disentangle the claims and analytical conflations characteristic of discussions in this area in order to show why they are problematic.

Secularization is commonly understood in existing debates as a process of change wherein the expanding scope and importance of non-religious aspects of social and cultural life marginalize both religion *and* the sacred. Conversely, de-secularization is frequently depicted as a reassertion of the significance of religion *and* the sacred relative to the secular (Demerath, 2000, 2007). The problem with such conceptions, however, is not only that 'the sacred' is assumed always to be in opposition to 'the secular', but also that it is regularly conflated with 'religion'. Insofar as religion is distinguished from the sacred, it tends to be seen as a particular institutional form of, or pattern of regulation relative to, experiences, beliefs, objects and practices that have an extraordinary character. Within this formulation, there is no space for recognizing that the sacred can assume secular as well as religious or quasi-religious manifestations.

These conceptions of religion, the sacred and the secular, are common, but do not help us understand the varied relationships that exist between these phenomena. In addressing this situation, we seek to enhance understandings of secularization, in terms of the declining social significance of religion, by examining how such processes can include the colonization of religious forms and identities by bio-economic and bio-political modalities of the sacred. Here, we view religion specifically as forms of belief and practice oriented towards other-worldly forms of sacred authority that have implications for this-worldly existence. Thus, while particular religions operationalized on the basis of strong conceptions of the sacred have endured and expanded, we also identify circumstances wherein *secularizing modalities of the sacred* threaten to marginalize religion.

In developing our understanding of religion and secularization processes, we also highlight the significance of embodiment (i.e. the socially shaped, organic foundations associated with human frailties, capabilities and proficiencies). There has been much recent interest in the body and religion, but this is seldom evident in secularization debates. Yet religious and secular modalities of the sacred enframe embodied experiences in diverse ways. The significance of this is that such enframings can shape people's practices and beliefs, thereby structuring the terrain on which dispositional orientations towards religion (what we refer to as forms of religious habitus) are created or obstructed. The widely contrasting ways in which lived experience can be shaped means that we should not expect there to be a unitary experience of any of these modalities (in terms, for example, of a universal, phenomenological encounter with the 'numinous' [Otto, 1958; Eliade, 1959; James, 1983]). Nevertheless, the parameters in which particular forms of religious habitus can be forged are context specific, and are threatened by a secular colonization of experience.

The following chapters develop these introductory comments by examining how religious and secular modalities of the sacred enframe and shape embodied experiences in distinctive and sometimes radically opposed ways. Chapter 2 explicates the main features of these socio-religious, transcendent, bio-political and bio-economic modalities, before Chapters 3 to 6 focus on how they shape key areas of embodied experience identified within classical sociological theory as offering potential bridges into religious forms of life. Chapter 7 then explores the general terrain on which experience can nurture or impede forms of religious habitus in the contemporary era. Here, we suggest that people's unprecedented knowledge about, and experience of, coexisting and competing religious and secular modalities of the sacred (as a result of the global extension of capitalism, accelerated flows of information through digital media, and large scale migration) has *undermined* the traditional means through which forms of religious habitus are constructed, but *opens up* opportunities for the reflexive instauration of religious modes of being (Latour, 2011).

The aim of this first chapter, however, is to contextualize our approach within sociological theories of secularization, religion and the sacred. We begin by suggesting that common conceptions of the relationship between modernization and secularization actually *under-estimate* the importance of contemporary secularizing processes, before arguing that there is a tendency for analyses of social differentiation to overlook how segmentation not only constrains the exercise of religious authority, but also creates space for the expansion of *non-religious* modalities of sacred authority. Finally, we engage with the 'turn to the body' in sociological studies of religion by emphasizing the importance of *embodiment as a whole* (body and mind, feeling and cognition) for the construction of religious experiences, while also highlighting the capacity of contrasting modalities of the sacred to reinforce or undermine the grounds on which forms of religious habitus are created.

## Modernization and Secularization

For much of the twentieth century, discussions about the fate of religion were contextualized within secularization narratives. There were dissenting voices, and debates about the variability of such processes (Martin, 1966, 1978, 1991), but the secularization thesis was unquestionably dominant, reflecting a broader socio-logical view that modernity was corrosive of religious identities and institutions. The central theoretical and methodological foun-dations for this thesis were established by sociology's founding figures, yet mirrored wider cultural assumptions: the declining significance of religion in technologically advanced societies was generally held to be self-evident. During the 1980s and 1990s, however, the public view of religion in the West began to change, and there also occurred a reorientation of the sociology of religion that resulted in the development of four ostensibly distinct positions regarding secularization.

The first, 'revitalization of religion', approach forcefully *rejects* the secularization thesis. Arguments concerning the revival of religion – including the renewed global prominence of religious conflict and the increasing use of religion in struggles for cultural recognition and citizenship – are here associated with theoretically oriented claims about humans' enduring religious needs. Whereas secularization theories argued that scientific knowledge and an emergent market of competing life-worlds 'disenchanted' the world, this approach emphasizes how such developments can *reinforce* religious identifi-cations in contexts of rapid change. In assessing the influence of this argument, the volte-face of Berger (1999: 2) on the secularization thesis is particularly noteworthy. Previously one of its most influen-tial exponents, Berger concluded that the world remains 'as furiously religious as ever' (see also Stark and Bainbridge, 1985, 1987; Warner, 1993; Riesebrodt, 2000, 2001).

A second position *moderates* rather than rejects secularization nar-ratives, assessing them as useful insofar as they signal contingent, culturally and geographically partial and inherently reversible trends. From this perspective the secularization thesis was mistaken not in identifying elements of modernization that could corrode religion, but in assuming these resulted in *irreversible* and *uniform* change. The idea that secular elements *inevitably* marginalize, transform and undermine religious beliefs, practices and identities is, therefore, rejected. Norris and Inglehart (2004) provide a powerful articulation of this argument, exhibiting attentiveness to patterns of extensive and limited secularization across the globe, *and* to contexts wherein rapid modernization has provoked significant de-secularization (see also Martin, 1966, 1978, 2005; Beyer, 2007; Demerath, 2007; Gorski and Altinordu, 2008).

While these 'revitalization of religion' and 'moderate secularization' positions focus on evolving relationships between religious and secular phenomena, a third, 'resurgence of the sacred', approach redirects attention away from the boundaries of the religious and the secular. Here, 'the sacred' is expanded to such a degree that it is understood to include, or transcend, both terms, while questions about secularization appear to be rendered irrelevant by this perspective. This is not because it holds that religion has necessarily been revitalized, but because of its identification of an increasingly significant and broad range of secular as well as 'spiritual' sacred phenomena. Lynch's (2012) outline of a 'sociology of the sacred' distinct from the 'sociology of religion' is one example of this argument: since the sacred is associated with a 'communicative structure' of non-contingent norms and values expressed through symbols, cognitive orientations and bodily emotions, recurrent patterns of sacralization become important *regardless* of whether these are categorized or experienced as secular or religious (see also Alexander, 1988; Knott, 2005; Knott and Franks, 2007; Nynäs et al., 2012).

A fourth position, in contrast, continues to espouse a 'strong secularization thesis'. This re-emphasizes a correlation between modernization and secularization with regard to the corrosive effects on religious belief and practice of post-traditional patterns of individualism. It also highlights the diminishing social and cultural significance of religion that follows from the structural and functional differentiation of modern societies. Supported by empirical data strongly indicative of a decline in explicit religious commitments in Europe and the US, alongside ambiguous but suggestive data in terms of secularization patterns across other parts of the globe, Bruce (2003, 2006) is a key exponent of this argument. This is evident in his scepticism concerning whether instances of religious revival or growth necessarily call into question a correlation between modernization and secularization, and in his criticisms of scholarly attempts to displace questions about secularization by renaming as 'religious' or 'sacred' an increasing range of secular phenomena (Inglehart, 1997; Norris and Inglehart, 2004).

These 'revitalization of religion', 'moderate secularization', 'resurgence of the sacred' and 'strong secularization' positions are often understood to be incommensurate, yet we suggest that, despite appearances, they exhibit *considerable convergences* in recognizing the *advance of secularization*. Indeed, the correlation between modernization and secularization prominent in strong secularization accounts (viewed as setting these against their competitors [Berger, 1999; Bruce, 2006: 35; Davie, 2010]) is actually *presupposed* in numerous accounts of revitalized religion, as well as in moderate secularization accounts. This is evident in their acknowledgement of a global trend for modern societies to become structurally differentiated into a number of semi-autonomous spheres – the political, religious, economic, etc. – each possessed of their own character and rationality (Parsons, 1960; Bell, 1977; Martin, 1978; Luhmann, 1985; Mouzelis, 2012). The suggestion here is that religion is increasingly located – at least within the 'macro' level of society – in a distinctive institutional space, constraining its capacity to structure other institutions, and existing as one life sphere within an economy of others that shape human experience in diverse ways (Bruce, 2011; Mouzelis, 2012: 208–10). Indeed, Martin (2005, 2011), a long-standing critic of strong versions of secularization theory, has nonetheless argued that structural differentiation and the consequent institutional segmentation of religion is one aspect of secularization that is, ultimately, *irreversible* (Mouzelis, 2012: 213).

Accounts of the resurgent sacred appear to offer a greater challenge to claims of a correlation between modernization and secularization. This is again questionable, though, as evident in two key manifestations of this approach. First, following Durkheim's (1995) focus on the role of the sacred in incorporating individuals into symbolic and experiential communities, a distinction is frequently drawn between orthodox, institutional forms of religion, *increasingly incapable of fulfilling this role*, and forms of heterodox spirituality or sacred norms and experiences of resurgent significance. Here, rather than being decisively rejected, the focus on the resurgent sacred cannot conceal the implicit acceptance of a correlation between modernization and secularization with regard to institutional religion. This mirrors Luckmann's (1967) distinction between 'visible' and 'invisible' forms of religion, recapitulating his argument that secularization undermines the former in favour of the latter (Heelas and Woodhead, 2005; Heelas, 2006: 53; Lynch, 2012: 3–4, 17). In consequence, it might be said that such accounts actually *accept* key features of strong accounts of secularization, despite rejecting the idea that the sacred has been undermined.

A second manifestation of this resurgent sacred approach might be seen as more radical. This rejects the terms 'religion' and the 'secular', and thus the notion that there exists a structural differentiation between them, on the basis that these reflect the 'epistemic hegemony' of a Western and Christian world-view and history, possessing little applicability to non-Western societies (Asad, 1993; Gorski and Altinordu, 2008; Turner, 2010a: xiv; Casanova, 2012: 253; King, 2013; see also Beckford, 2003). The problem with this stance, however, is that ignores the political *reality* of conflicts over the differentiation of the religious and the secular in contexts such as Eastern Europe, Afghanistan, Iran, Turkey, North Africa, Egypt, Israel, South East Asia and China (Demerath, 2007: 64). It also fails to grasp how differentiation has spread throughout globalized societies (even if non-Western regions of the world have appropriated it in a 'glocalizing' form, particularizing it according to local circumstances [Beyer, 2007: 110]). Casanova (2012: 41), for example, accepts that for Western *and* non-Western societies:

> the cosmic order is increasingly defined by modern science and technology; the social order is increasingly defined by the interlocking of citizenship, 'democratic' states, market economies, and mediatic public spheres; and the moral order is increasingly defined by the calculations of rights-bearing individual agents, claiming human dignity, equality, and the pursuit of happiness.

In short, the four positions outlined are less distinct than they appear to be when it comes to acknowledging (even if only implicitly) the considerable importance of secularization, while there is also a tendency within them to elide the sacred with religion. The limited convergences between them, indeed, suggest that we need to interrogate further whether there exists a secularizing 'socio-logic' to modern societal changes (Bruce, 2006: 35), and what the precise role of the sacred is in such developments. Of immediate significance in this regard is the importance of social differentiation and de-differentiation, recognized variously in the above positions, for the scope of *worldly* and *other-worldly* authorities.

### Differentiation, De-Differentiation and Other-Worldly Authority

We have already noted that, despite ostensibly rejecting a correlation between secularization and modernization, accounts of the revitalization of religion tend to acknowledge a global trend for modern societies to become structurally differentiated into a number of semi-autonomous spheres. In this respect, theorists espousing this position have mostly avoided pitching their arguments with reference to its 'macro-level' institutional location, focusing instead on 'meso-level' developments. It is *beneath* the institutional structures of society – but manifest variously in the civic sphere, social movements, local and regional groups, families, and the life-worlds of individuals – that religious resurgence is discovered (Martin, 1978, 2011; Riesebrodt, 2001; Norris and Inglehart, 2004; Beyer, 2007; Demerath, 2007; Gorski and Altinordu, 2008). The acknowledgement of a significant divide between macro- and meso-levels, however, has major implications for the scope and influence of religious authority.

This is clear in the writings of those rational choice theorists who argue for the revitalization of religion on the basis of a strong differentiation of macro- from meso-level. They identify the proliferation of religious options in the modern era as evidence of people's essential religiosity, explaining away *apparent* secularization as a 'supply-side' failure of religious organizations, largely within monopoly situations, to provide what consumers need (Warner, 1993; Stark, 1999; Gorski and Altinordu, 2008: 58). Nonetheless, rational choice theorists still accept that the differentiation of modern societies has reduced the power and social authority of churches: 'the primary aspects of public life' are no longer 'suffused with religious symbols, rhetoric or ritual' (Stark, 1999: 4–5; Demerath, 2007: 63).

A similar use of macro- and meso-level differentiation is made in relation to those contrasting claims regarding the revitalization of religion within an emergent 'post-secular' modernity (see Harrington, 2007; Boeve, 2008; Braidotti, 2008; Dalferth, 2010; Davie, 2010; Lyon, 2010; McLennan, 2010; Nynäs et al., 2012). Thus, Habermas's (2008) declaration of the arrival of a 'post-secular age' co-exists with his ongoing emphasis on the functional differentiation of religion at the macro-level of modern societies (Beckford, 2012: 8). Taylor (2007), similarly, identifies a powerful 'yearning for transcendence' in modern societies but recognizes the pervasive macro-level constraints upon it within the 'immanent frame' of modernity (Warner et al., 2010: 6). Sources of formal religious authority are, again, circumscribed within the differentiated spheres of polity and economy, if not in relation to the views and actions of private individuals.

This distinction between macro-level structural differentiation and meso-level religious vitality usefully enables us to identify distinctive religious trajectories within society and acknowledge the significance of patterns of de-secularization *within certain limits*.

Casanova (1994, 2006, 2012) exemplifies this when observing how macro-level secularization can actually encourage meso-level de-secularization. Shorn of its overarching legitimating role for society, 'religions can become movements and pressure groups that vie with rivals in the public sphere', with religious authority becoming increasingly efficacious *outside* the state (Dobbelaere, 1988, 1989; Gorski and Altinordu, 2008: 58). Nonetheless, while this distinction entails recognizing emergent 'levels' within society, and how the contrasting religious trajectories with which they may be associated can interact and change each other over time, these patterns of change are heavily weighted in one direction. There seems little scope for meso-level religious vitality to *enhance* the institutional reach of religious authority at a macro-level (Casanova, 2012: 30).

Contrary to how they are often perceived, then, accounts of the revitalization of religion and religious authority at the meso-level often *reinforce* conclusions about macro-level secularization. Nonetheless, as recent events in Egypt suggest, strong religious convictions can contest macro-level differentiation rather than exhibit passive acceptance of its irreversibility. As such, it would be wrong to assume that questions of the social significance of religious authority relative to patterns of differentiation are settled. It is equally questionable to exclude the possibility that the capacities of secularizing processes to spread in a de-differentiating manner are necessarily constrained by the meso-level resurgence of religion. Here, questions concerning the problematization of religious authority that is, in variable degrees, evident at macro-, meso-, and micro-levels of social life suggest a need for a more flexible understanding of how patterns of differentiation and de-differentiation shape the relationship between secularizing and de-secularizing processes.

In this respect, Chaves (1994: 751) has drawn upon contrasting assessments of differentiation in order to emphasize the contingent, political, and often conflict-ridden relationships between separate societal spheres (see Luhmann, 1982, 1990; Alexander, 1990; Coleman, 1990; Friedland and Alford, 1991). Utilizing Dobbelaere's (1981, 1985, 1987) multi-dimensional model of secularization, he identifies three levels at which declining religious authority can, but does not necessarily, occur. At the macro-level, it can be seen in the increasing inability of religious elites to exercise influence over other institutional sectors. At the meso-level, its evidence is manifest in the increasing tendency of many religious organizations to conform to, or reshape themselves in the light of, distinctively secular social, cultural or political concerns. At the micro-level, it emerges through the degree to which individual choices and actions are increasingly free of religious control (Chaves, 1994: 757).

On this basis, it is possible to distinguish between high levels of macro-level secularization characteristic of Western societies, and low levels characteristic of societies such as Iran, where religious authority has been re-exerted over other institutional spheres, while also being attentive to intra-society variations. In certain areas of US culture, for example, meso- as well as micro-level secularization can be weak (e.g. among conservative Protestant and African American communities), though in the culture as a whole religion tends to operate restrictedly as a *cultural resource*, that is, as symbols or rhetorical sources which can be drawn upon voluntarily for various purposes (Chaves, 1994: 761). This is quite different from Iran, a country in which religious authorities control meso- and micro-level activities, though there are limits to this even in such a context. Beyer's (1993) account of how internal conflicts surrounding de-differentiation became apparent after the 'theocratic triumph' of the mullahs in the Iranian revolution, and continue to be evident, is relevant here. As Chaves (1994: 766) puts it, 'there seem to be structural limits to religious authority's capacity to impose itself in a society that participates at all in a global institutional environment that is highly secularized'.

These analyses of social differentiation helpfully contextualize debates about secularization in relation to the variable distribution of religious authority, but their focus on the relationship between religious and non-religious authority either conflates religion with the sacred, or makes the latter a residual category. Rather than being explored as important in their own right, sacred phenomena that effect a displacement of other-worldly referents by secular agents of various sorts (e.g. much of the 'civil religion' of the US) are simply judged to be *not religious* (Chaves, 1994: 771). This limitation is evident in Chaves's (1994: 750–2) proposal that studies of secularization should focus purely on religious authority (defined as control of access via *other-worldly legitimations* to certain cultural goods of a positive [e.g. eternal life] or negative [e.g. meaninglessness] nature). His suggestion envisages a neatly delineated field for analysis, but if we wish to comprehend the wider character of the world we should note Fenn's (1978, 1982) interest in how the decline of religious authority has been accompanied by an increase in the visibility and significance of *non-religious forms* of *sacred authority*. These forms have been manifest variously in secular agencies, and 'occult' spiritualities, that borrow the authority of sacred symbols for their own ends (Fenn, 1978: 25, 36–7).

Fenn is here pointing towards the possibility that secularization can be accompanied by both a shrinkage of religious forms of authority and an *expansion* of the scope of non-religious forms of sacred authority (see also Demerath, 2000: 3).

This concern with religious authority reinforces the importance of disentangling the sacred from the religious, yet if we are to extend further our understanding of debates about secularization we need to recognize how the issues we have been exploring are themselves grounded in contrasting embodied experiences, practices and cognitive orientations. Those who have written about the contemporary fate of religion and the sacred have tended to adopt one of two major approaches towards this grounding: one that focuses on cognitive issues of belief, the other on more obviously 'enfleshed' matters of sensation and emotion.

## Embodiment(s) of Religion and of the Sacred

In accounting for the inherently corrosive impact of modern life upon religion, exponents of secularization have focused frequently on issues of cognition, particularly in their explorations of the plausibility of religious *beliefs*. Berger (1967), for example, suggested that religion loses its capacity in increasingly differentiated societies to provide an overarching *meaningful* order, as its belief systems are relativized by a plurality of others and undermined by science. Similarly, Bruce's (2010: 135) explorations of the political, structural and economic aspects of secularization identify the modern undermining of the plausibility of religious belief as 'the bottom line' in debates about the issue.

This focus on cognition highlights the importance of other-worldly belief systems for religious life, but others who share this concern for belief have drawn opposing conclusions about its sustainability in the contemporary era. The suggestion that modernity's intellectual pluralism creates market conditions that allow religious certitudes to flourish is one example of this (Stark and Bainbridge, 1985, 1987; Warner, 1993, 1997; Iannaccone, 1995, 1997). A similarly cognitive focus informs Habermas's post-secular view of religion as a source of *epistemic content* that can, under certain conditions, shape public debate and communicative interaction (Braeckman, 2009: 284). So too does it influence Giddens's (1991) and Norris and Inglehart's (2004) association of revitalized religion with *propositional certainties* that can shield people from the existential insecurities engendered by rapid social change. Here, religious belief offers a cognitive prophylactic against societies characterized by accelerated rationalization and differentiation.

In contrast to this focus on belief, the second approach to questions concerning the persistence or diminution of religious or sacred forces within society adopts a more 'carnal' orientation. Here, conceptions of 'religion as belief' are judged to be predicated on early-modern Protestant models of religiosity, to some extent replicated in the Catholic Counter-Reformation, wherein enfleshed forms of religious life gave way to those 'in the head' (Asad, 1993; Taylor, 2007: 554). Taking issue with this specificity, sociological and anthropological analyses of the ritual diversity, and the sensual and emotional experiences inherent to immersion within forms of sacred life, have focused on material culture (Morgan, 2010), 'aesthetic formations' (Meyer, 2010a, 2010b), and bodily and affectual reconstruction (Turner, 1984, 1991; Feder et al., 1989; Csordas, 1990, 1994; McGuire, 1990; Bell, 1992; Coakley, 1997; Vásquez, 2011). These approaches usefully highlight a broader range of enfleshed phenomena central to experiences of the sacred, religious or otherwise, than those characteristic of cognitively-focused secularization narratives. Nevertheless, they tend to underplay the importance of people's reflexive engagements with doctrinal considerations, and at times overlook the constraints that rationalization and differentiation can place upon the social significance of bodily sensations of the religious or the sacred.

Rather than simply opposing the cognitive orientation of much secularization theory to the focus on sensory and sensual forms of religious or sacred life, we suggest it is necessary to adopt a broader view of the embodied, experiential grounding for religious and secular phenomena. Some religious forms are clearly more cognitively oriented than others, for example, but even those that exhibit a strong intellectual focus on regulating, domesticating or repressing certain emotional orientations can nonetheless be understood to be engaged in attempted *re-formations* of the embodied nature and experience of religious life (Mellor and Shilling, 1997). As constituted and enacted by embodied human beings, even religions of 'the head' are necessarily embodied (Taylor, 2007: 554; Strhan, 2012). Relatedly, while certain religions engage very directly with emotional and sensation forms, they nonetheless seek to enframe human feelings, thoughts and actions within other-worldly orientations, codified within systems of orthodoxy and orthopraxy.

In moving towards a broader view of embodied experience, we adopt here a simple but flexible approach that encompasses the above concerns with both mind/belief and body/sensation. Developed and deployed in various ways within sociological writings on the socio-natural characteristics of human embodiment (e.g. Elias, 1991, 2000; Frank, 1995; Burkitt, 1999; Shilling, 2005a, 2012; Freund, 2006, 2011), this approach recognizes that our experiences are shaped culturally, and through individual reflection, while also acknowledging their underpinning and co-constitution by an organic stratum. Specifically, embodied experiences of both religious and secular life involve the mutual interactions and co-constitutions that occur among our *physiological responses* to stimuli, the culturally variable manner in which we *feel* those responses, and our own *interpretive classification* of and *reflections* on such feelings, as well as on our existence in the world and cosmos more generally.

We can illustrate this approach through the example of being threatened physically as a result of one's religious affiliation and practices. This experience is associated typically with a physiological response referred to as the 'fight or flight' mechanism (that prepares the body to respond through an increase in adrenaline which raises heart rate and blood pressure). Provoked instantaneously by the presence of threat, this stimulus is felt ordinarily in terms of fear or aggression, and can be reflected on (if often only quickly before acting) variously via concepts and impressions associated with ideas such as injustice, revenge, sorrow, and concern for one's safety. These are individual reflections, but use a language common to a wider group, and vary normatively depending on our cultural, gendered, religious and other upbringing, as well as the interdependencies in which we are enmeshed. Thus, the experience of being threatened may result in similar physiological responses between people belonging to very different religions, but these responses can be felt and reflected on very differently if the religion to which one is affiliated demands robust defensive response or forgiveness.

Reflecting upon an inspiring passage in a holy book provides us with a contrasting illustration of these distinctive components, one that shows how experience can be looked at from the starting point of deliberation and not just physiological stimuli. Acquiring renewed insight through such contemplative activity can produce feelings of elation, feelings that stimulate the nervous systems and lend physiological impetus to the intensity of this experience (Damasio, 2000: 59–60). Taking seriously the importance of reflexive activities such as these, indeed, implies that experiences can be at least potentially modified through a deliberative process wherein feelings are stimulated by, and directed towards, objects and situations on the basis of their having been *appraised* as meaningful (Papoulias and Callard, 2010; Leys, 2011).[2]

This account can be employed to investigate broad swathes of human life. In the context of debates about secularization and the modern world, however, it has particular utility in helping us grasp the nature and variable social consequences of phenomena that are encountered, designated and experienced as being of extraordinary importance.[3] Sociology, religious studies and anthropology have long recognized the importance of the sacred for human experience. Etymologically rooted in ideas of 'making holy', consecrating or setting apart phenomena from mundane reality, Eliade's (1963) conception of *hierophany* raises the possibility of experiences of something 'wholly other' in this world that can possess religious consequences in terms of stimulus, feeling and thought. So too does James's (1983) interest in ineffable and noetic experiences provide insight into exceptional knowledge which can be reflected upon if not translated fully into cognitive conceptions. More foundational to sociology, Durkheim (1973, 1995) insists there are things considered sacred, 'set apart' from egoistic organic life, accessed through 'positive' and 'negative' rites that stimulate effervescent experiences possessed of the capacity to join to a collectivity imbued with forms of collective consciousness otherwise egoistic beings. Weber also explores how phenomena encountered as sacred, enchanted and charismatic stimulate in people an experience of a socially creative distance between extraordinary life and routinized existence (Weber, 1968: 789–90, 818–28, 1111–57; 1948 [1915]: 328; 1948 [1919a]: 155).

While writers such as Eliade and James tend to offer us a unitary, religious picture of sacred experience, however, Durkheim and Weber usefully examine how the sacred can be manifest in different, religious and secular, forms or, as we refer to them, modalities; modalities that serve to structure and pattern societies as well as the experiences of individuals within them. In this context, there are three particular aspects of their writings that have not been developed fully within contemporary debates on secularization, yet form a cornerstone of our approach. The first key feature is that, under certain circumstances and within particular limits, manifestations of the sacred can *steer* social life through the impact they have on people's embodied thoughts as well as feelings and habits. For Durkheim, manifestations of the extraordinary during collective assemblies arouse in participants 'passionate energies' that restructure individuals' feelings and thoughts in line with their symbolism, serving to internalize social facts in the bodies of the social group (Durkheim, 1952: 57; 1973: 159–63; 1995: 138, 212). For Weber, extraordinary phenomena direct society by influencing the practical techniques through which bodies are trained, adjusting the '*psycho-physical apparatus*' (the feelings and thoughts) of humans (Weber, 1968: 1156; 1975: 149; Maley, 2004: 75–9).

The second feature of Durkheim's and Weber's works core to our concerns is their recognition that, in assuming various forms, manifestations and experiences of sacred phenomena can possess strong but also weak/non-existent other-worldly dimensions possessed of variable relationships to religious and secular forces. Weber (1991) saw in Protestantism, for example, a distinctive religious ethic that promoted the extraordinary secular forces of rationalization and bureaucratization. These forces were bereft of other-worldly orientations, but nevertheless became consecrated as sacred within modern law and governance. Similarly, while Durkheim (1995) viewed *Gemeinschaft* societies as permeated by the sacred in the sense that there was a pervasive interpenetration of worldly and other-worldly elements, he identified the dynamic division of labour of modernity as fracturing and secularizing experiences of sacred phenomena, which henceforth have a more worldly character (Durkheim, 1952, 1984). This sense that the experience of the sacred can possess a this-worldly character has been explored more widely (Hammond, 1985, 2000; Hervieu-Léger, 2000: 106). Maffesoli's (1996) analysis of the 'return of the sacred' as an emotionally constituted tribalism, for example, identifies the power of extraordinary experiences to shield people from modern disenchantment *without* this effervescence being linked to institutional religion (see also Demerath, 2000, 2007; Asad, 2002; Masuzawa, 2005; Scott and Hirschkind, 2006).

Third, if there are elements of convergence between Durkheim and Weber, an important difference between their theories enables us to identify variable constraints upon distinct forms of sacred experience relative to patterns of differentiation and de-differentiation. Weber's (1991) engagement with the impact of Protestantism upon the emergence of modern capitalism suggests a proliferation of life-spheres wherein each is subject to what can be seen as the de-differentiating impact of rationalization and bureaucracy. In recent years, this has been manifest by the increasingly extraordinary forces of bio-political governance operating across *all* sections of the 'iron cage' of capitalism, resulting in progressively uniform modes of control (Agamben, 1998). In contrast, Durkheim (1952, 1984) insists modernity brought with it increasingly complex levels of social differentiation, alongside a growing division of labour. These circumstances stimulated an increase in secularism, alongside the death of 'old gods', even if certain forms of sacred persist on the basis of personal preferences operating within segmented societies that prize 'the cult of the individual' (Durkheim, 1984: 122).

These features of Durkheim's and Weber's work have important implications not only for the conceptualization of distinct forms of sacred experience, but also for the potential of these experiences to contribute towards and culminate in the formation of religious forms of habitus. This issue, concerned with the development of general orientations and dispositions towards religion, has been marginalized within contemporary secularization debates, yet is recognized as important more generally within sociological studies of religion. There have been a number of valuable empirically-oriented studies that draw upon this notion of the religious habitus, moreover, with its view of embodiment as 'the principle generating and unifying all practices' (Bourdieu, 1977: 124). Prominent among these is Csordas's (1994) insightful analysis of the embodied character of Catholic charismatic healing. Yet the notion's importance for the sociology of religion goes beyond specific studies.

In a globalized world characterized by the increased interaction between religious and secular modalities of the sacred, we shall suggest that exploring the challenges facing the creation of a religious habitus enables us to identify the embodied bases upon which processes of secularization or the revitalization of religion are enacted. There is no guarantee that forms of religious habitus will endure or be reproduced in successive generations, and secular forces can shape people's embodied experiences in ways that challenge the viability of religious orientations. These dispositions and orientations towards religion cannot be considered apart from the structural position and authority of religious institutions in differentiated societies. Nevertheless, if a religion is to secure a firm basis for its reproduction amongst subsequent generations, the capacity of embodied experience to provide a route to the establishment of appropriate forms of religious habitus becomes a crucial issue.

## Chapter Outlines

Chapter 2 explicates the foundations of those religious and secular modalities of the sacred, and the engagements with sacrifice through which they are sustained, that we regard as central to debates about secularization and the revitalization of religion. These modalities possess an ideal typical character. Nevertheless, they offer a useful framework for assessing questions about the correlation between modernization and secularization, processes of social differentiation and de-differentiation, issues of worldly and other-worldly influence and authority, and the role of embodiment in these processes. Assessments of secularization today have at their centre unanswered questions about the degree to which religious attempts to enframe human experience are successful or not, relative to non-religious modalities, and it is the interrogation of this question that occupies the following chapters. Here, via an examination of certain 'bridging experiences', we intend to cast fresh light on the operationalization of the sacred today and the conditions in which it remains possible for forms of religious habitus to be constructed.

This focus is important as questions concerning the incorporation of individuals into religious and non-religious modalities of the sacred direct attention to the embodied conditions of their co-habitation. These conditions are recognized in Taylor's (2007: 14) discussion of modernity's 'immanent frame'. He questions whether it is now possible for experience to be enframed in religious ways. What he does not do is examine specific types of experience sociologically, in relation to the practical, everyday encounters, negotiations and impacts of social life, exploring whether these can still constitute a bridge towards distinctively religious forms of life (Turner, 2010a: 659). In the classical sociological theories of Durkheim and Weber, however, and in contemporary developments of them, we can identify the basis for just such an examination.

We undertake these explorations within chapters that focus upon bridging experiences emergent from the work of Durkheim and Weber, though our analyses of them extend far beyond these figures and illustrate their significance by drawing on examples mostly from Pentecostal Christianity and Islam, two of the most resilient and globally 'vital' contemporary forms of religion (Cox, 2001; Martin, 2002, 2005; Westerlund, 2009; Thomas, 2010). The first of these, examined in Chapter 3, concerns *intoxication*, which – particularly in the work of Durkheim and his followers – is an embodied process through which religious experience occurs. In global modernity, however, intoxication has a more ambivalent relationship to society than implied in Durkheim's writings on the effervescent intoxication of traditional religious forms. It is also subject to a range of regulative and reflexive engagements that acknowledge its capacities for generating extraordinary experiences, yet seek to strip it of its religious potentialities.

Chapter 4 builds on another experience central to Durkheim's work – though it is also key to Weber's account of theodicy – by exploring how *pain* is productive of culture. Focusing on religious asceticism, we analyse how specific cultures engage with pain in distinctive ways (Durkheim, 1995: 316–7). The experience of pain has historically been a key means through which individuals develop religious identities. Contemporary Western culture, however, is characterized by a general aversion to pain, and a view of it as an unproductive threat to cultures and identities. In observing the cultural marginalization of Christian explorations of pain, and Western distaste for current Islamic engagements with pain, such phenomena can clearly be located within a narrative of secularization, but not a simple one.

In a discussion that builds on Weber's understanding of the other-worldly-oriented 'psycho-physical apparatus' of humans, Chapter 5 explores how *charisma* has historically constituted a route to religious experience. In contrast to Weber's analysis of the inevitable diminution of charisma, within his vision of modernity as an era of 'disenchantment' and relentless rationalization, we focus on the persistence of charisma in such secular contexts as consumer culture and business leadership. Distinguishing the pedagogic charisma associated with early Christian teaching communities, Weber's conception of the charismatic personality, and our own conception of a material and manufactured aesthetic charisma, we identify how these invocations of the extraordinary can be associated with distinct patterns of authority and contrasting experiences, including the bio-economic sacralization of the brand.

Chapter 6 examines *eroticism* as a bridging experience. While Weber and also Bataille identified eroticism as possessing religious potential, it has become a site of contestation between competing modalities of the sacred. On the one hand, the circulation of erotic experiences and identities within a bio-economic market of lifestyle choices is complemented by increasingly global bio-political dominance over matters of reproduction and fertility. On the other hand, however, Bataille's suggestion that images, icons, texts and other material phenomena possess the capacity to be fetishized provides continuing opportunities for institutions and individuals to harness eroticism to the promotion of religious experiences and identities. In confronting the challenge of retaining the extraordinary status and affectual charge of their own images, icons and objects, moreover, religious movements have engaged in processes of 'enhanced sacralization'; something most evident in cases of religious conflict and violence.

Chapters 3 to 6 investigate whether *particular* experiences still possess religious potentialities. Chapter 7, in contrast, moves away from analysing specifics to asking whether the contemporary enframing of experience *in general* remains conducive to the construction and maintenance of forms of religious habitus. Contrary to Bourdieu's (1987, 1991) use of this term, which reduces the habitus to a legitimating reflection of social inequalities, we understand the religious habitus as an active crafting of particular embodied subjectivities that can reshape social life in significant ways during an age in which reflexive knowledge of alternate beliefs, practices, and modalities of the sacred is greater than ever before. In so doing, we identify the existence of grounds on which it remains possible to *instaur* religious forms of habitus, from modes of experience that have become increasingly deliberative, yet also highlight the contingency of these forms in relation to their location within bio-economic and bio-political contexts.

Finally, Chapter 8 discusses more broadly the implications of our analysis of the secularization of the sacred. Here, we conclude that it is possible to acknowledge the value of a 'strong', albeit contextually variable, model of secularization, while also accounting for the contemporary vitality of certain forms of religion and, more broadly, the resurgent significance of specific constructions of the sacred.

## Notes

1.  It has been noted that notions of the 'post-secular', which have been steadily proliferating in recent years, not only have a highly heterogeneous character, but also tend to trade on simplistic notions of the secular limited attentiveness to history, and to flatten out 'all the intricacies, contradictions, and problems of what counts as religion': indeed, frequently possessed of a literary, theological or philosophical character, it has been suggested that such notions imply an inherent antipathy to the social scientific study of religion (Beckford, 2012: 16–17). This antipathy is expressed in the association of the sociology of religion with the modern rationalism and secularism now understood to have been swept away by the 'return of the sacred' (Carruthers and Tate, 2010; D'Costa, 2010), rendering reflection on secularization processes outmoded and irrelevant. In what follows, however, we shall demonstrate that it is simply not possible to understand key manifestations of the sacred today unless we engage constructively, and afresh, with patterns of increasing secularization.

2.  Ensuring that we do not 'write off' experience as either entirely 'socially' or 'biologically' constructed, this approach also allows us to explore the consequences for thought and feeling of religious and secular educational, disciplinary and training regimes referred to variously as 'techniques of the body' (Mauss, 1973a), 'technologies of the self' (Foucault, 1986) and 'body pedagogics' (Shilling and Mellor, 2007; Mellor and Shilling, 2010a). Despite their references to the body, each of these approaches is concerned with the structuring of both flesh and thought. Indeed, Mauss's conception of religious and other body techniques possesses strong parallels with our conception of experience in its recognition of biological, cultural and psychological components to the manner in which people's capacities and orientations to life are formed. Recognizing the importance of these various components of experience also allows us to explore changes in their relative importance over time. Elias's (2000) historical study of 'civilizing processes', for example, suggests that long-term developments in the interdependent formation of society and personality have significantly *increased* the role of reflexivity in the formation of experience and reduced those occasions on which stimuli and feeling are translated into individual action irrespective of deliberation. This is something that we return to in our analysis of contemporary forms of religious habitus.

3.  The relative simplicity and flexibility of this approach also, importantly, clears the way for us to concentrate on the relationship between religious and secular modalities of the sacred and embodied experience, without having to engage in the prolonged and unproductive *philosophical* discussions that have come to dominate contemporary debates on 'the body'. Our main concern is to utilize the approach outlined here in order to interrogate more adequately various issues involved in the secularization/revitalization of religion debate, not to become fixated upon the issue of embodied experience in relation to abstract issues unrelated to our theoretical and substantive investigations. Having said that, it is important to note that the multidimensional nature of this approach to experience enables us to avoid the analytical conflations evident in both neurological and culturalist theories that reduce religious and other feelings to either evolutionarily processes concerned with natural selection (e.g. Pyysiäinen, 2003; see Franks, 2010), or to volumes and intensities of affect that circulate beneath consciousness (e.g. Massumi, 2002; see Leys, 2011).

# 2

## Modalities of the Sacred

### Introduction

Debates about secularization and the revitalization of religion have become more sophisticated over the years – acknowledging distinctions between macro- and meso-levels of analysis that facilitate the identification of contrasting religious trajectories within societies – yet still gain inspiration from the two classical figures most important to the sociology of religion. Weber's (1991) analysis of the diminishing social role of religion under the impact of modern rationalism, a key theoretical support for the secularization thesis, continues to be mined for value by those concerned with the weakening of religious forms within structurally differentiated societies. Those interested in the revitalization of religion, in contrast, tend to reject Weber's focus on the secular consequences of modernity, drawing instead on Durkheim's (1995) emphasis on the foundational and enduring social significance of religious processes.

Framing discussions of secularization and de-secularization through a polarization of Durkheim's and Weber's writings may be common, but it is also problematic. This is because both theorists understand religion, and also the issue of people's engagements with the sacred, in *related*, if distinct, ways; a factor that renders questionable juxtapositions of them as opposites. In addition to these limited convergences, moreover, the distinctions between, and variations within, their writings highlight, or at least point towards, the emergence of *competing* religious and secular modalities of the sacred; modalities that possess contrasting implications for the enframing of embodied experiences.

Dealing with these convergences, distinctions and variations in turn, the notion that there exist modalities of the sacred builds on commonalities between Durkheim and Weber. Both writers define manifestations of the sacred as extraordinary phenomena able to influence social action through the manner in which they transform embodied experience. While Durkheim (1952: 57; 1973: 159–63; 1984; 1995: 138, 212) and Weber (1968: 1156; 1975: 149; 1991) agree that manifestations of the sacred can impart directionality to societies, however, they differ regarding the fate of these forces. Weber (1968) associates a loss of socially emboldening sacred (if not regulatory) forces in modernity with the individualizing habits of Protestantism. This development is reinforced by the problematization of any community based on non-rational factors in the 'iron cage' of mechanical capitalism characterized by the differentiation of life-spheres (Weber, 1991). Durkheim (1995), in contrast, suggests that every society contains conceptions of the sacred and is underpinned by elementary religious processes; an analysis that imparts a common, de-differentiating moral basis to even complex modern societies.

Rather than concluding that Durkheim's and Weber's writings provide us with stark either/or models of sacralization and de-sacralization, secularization and de-secularization, variations *within* their analyses can be used to identify contrasting conceptions of what is meant by the sacred and of the consequences of these extraordinary phenomena for embodied experiences. These modalities of the sacred can be summarized here in terms of their *socio-religious, bio-economic, transcendent,* and *bio-political* forms.

It is Durkheim (1995) who provides us with an analysis of the *socio-religious* modality of the sacred; a modality constructed and maintained through an other-worldly cosmology and practices that sanctify *society* as religious. This is elaborated in his account of the universal significance of religion and the sacred in *The Elementary Forms of Religious Life*. Centred on tribal groups, but also concerned with the basic processes informing *all* societies, Durkheim reveals a pervasive intermingling of religious and social phenomena. Social life is permeated by strong other-worldly elements (other-worldly in that they transport individuals from natural organic existence to a *supernatural* social and moral existence); elements that impart a de-differentiating quality to any society (Durkheim, 1973).

In other parts of his work, however, Durkheim (1952, 1984) provides grounds for developing a conception of the *bio-economic sacred*. This modality is evident in modern societies possessed of a developed economy and an advanced division of labour in which *anything*, including worldly phenomena, can be 'set apart' from and emotionally responded to as 'special' in relation to mundane life (Durkheim, 1984). It is facilitated by the decline of religious rites that previously structured embodied identities; a situation in which individuals' physical, biological properties become available to be attracted to, or stimulated and manipulated by, commercial products and processes. Secularism increases in these circumstances, alongside the death of 'old gods'; yet forms of the sacred persist, even if they have a more worldly character and develop on the basis of personal preferences operating within segmented societies that prize 'the cult of the individual' (Durkheim, 1984: 122). This is something quite distinct from the socio-religious sacred, and is suggestive of the *consumerization* of religious *and* non-religious forms of the sacred within a market of lifestyle options that appeal directly to the biologically grounded, yet commercially shaped, emotions of individuals.

It is to Weber (1991) that we must turn for an account of the *transcendent sacred*, a central explanatory device in his bleak view of the relationship between the Protestant ethic, secularization and disenchantment. Here, extraordinary forces are located *above* and *outside* society. In further contrast to Durkheim's account of the social influence of the sacred and religion in *The Elementary Forms*, Weber's (1991) analysis of the transcendent sacred recognizes that this modality of the extraordinary *co-exists* with a secular sphere. Specifically, Weber's depiction of Protestantism accepts that there exists a worldly existence distinct from religious forms, even though it seeks to steer the former via other-worldly directed norms and disciplines.

Having provided us with the basis for exploring a transcendent modality of the sacred bonded to a major axial religion, Weber was nonetheless insistent that the forces of rationalization and bureaucratization embedded within modern law and governance were bereft of religious, other-worldly orientations. These forces not only eroded religion, but also extended subsequently into the realm of bio-politics, stretching across the varied sectors of society and affecting a de-differentiating impact upon them. Weber himself did not see such phenomena as sacred, but his focus on the *extraordinary scope* and *power* of the technological domination of science in the management of life provides space for the recognition that the sacred has been reduced to what Agamben (1998) refers to as 'bare life'. This minimalist *bio-political modality of the sacred* is consistent with a system of this-worldly governmentality that seeks to both reduce and extend the extraordinary, in a de-differentiating manner, to the productive possibilities inherent within mere existence.

Instead of identifying Durkheim and Weber as opposites in debates on secularization, then, we argue that they enable us to identify four modalities of the sacred. The socio-religious and transcendental involve a bonding with religious forms, in that they are characterized by other-worldly orientations towards worldly activity. The bio-economic and

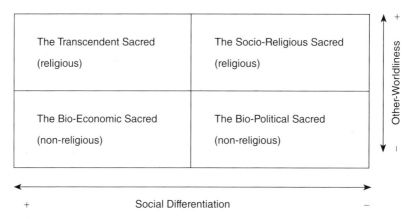

**Figure 2.1**  Modalities of the sacred

the bio-political, in contrast, are associated with secular, non-religious developments, possessing weak or non-existent other-worldly aspects. It is the transcendent and bio-economic modalities that share an acceptance of, or accommodation to, social differentiation, however, with the socio-religious and bio-political possessing a de-differentiating orientation. These can be presented diagrammatically as shown in Figure 2.1.

Having summarized these modalities, it is now necessary to explicate them if we are to demonstrate their analytical utility for illuminating contemporary religious developments.

## The Socio-Religious Sacred

Durkheim (1995) is best known for his view that society can ultimately be equated with religion; a bonding he views as reinforced by the intimate relationship these phenomena have with the sacred. This analysis is centred around a conception of the *socio-religious sacred*, wherein that which is extraordinary reflects and enables individuals to experience as religious 'the society of which they are members and the obscure yet intimate relations they have with it' (Durkheim, 1995: 227). The socio-religious sacred is created and consolidated, moreover, via a thoroughly embodied process in which individuals gather together in the context of totemic representations that symbolize their social group, and are 'swept up' by a collectively generated effervescence that attaches them to these social symbols. Transformed into social beings, re-energized in their commitment to moral norms shared by and depicted in these group gatherings, it is ultimately *the society of which they are part that is represented as sacred and worshipped as religious.*

Durkheim (1995) analysed the socio-religious sacred in relation to its elementary forms in 'primitive' Aboriginal clans, but insisted that the processes whereby its distinctive parts were bound together possessed universal relevance for the constitution of societies and religions. Furthermore, while his conception of the socio-religious sacred traces the cause and consequence of religious forms and extraordinary forces to society, this origin does not make it less potent as a force operating on humans and their relationships. The socio-religious sacred enframes experiences of the natural and social world within emergent religious forms experienced as other-worldly to the extent they become confrontations with the sacred or with profaning threats to the sacred. This situation is exemplified by Durkheim's analysis of the French Revolution, a period character-ized by a collective effervescence that propelled people into acts of 'superhuman heroism and bloody barbarism', and by the develop-ment of dogma, symbols, altars and feast days that marked as reli-gious those seismic changes brought about in the reorganization of society. An extraordinary event, the French Revolution became – ironically, given its self-consciously secular aspects – an extraordinarily religious experience.

This capacity of the socio-religious sacred to overwhelm phenom-ena that might otherwise be experienced as secular is thus also apparent in the manner it is *naturalized*, via the incorporation of collective symbols and mythologies, within the human body. The sense across a range of religious forms that human blood and hair, for example, possess holy qualities is evidence for Durkheim (1995: 228–9) of a 'diffusion' of the sacred into the very substance of bod-ies, making them 'naturally' available to being incorporated into religious forms.

This naturalization of the sacred provides an organic, ontological basis for the recurrent pattern of collective rituals that control and shape human experience through the moral force of the sacred (Lienhardt, 1961). It is also evident in the religious enframing of other recurrent aspects of human embodiment, such as the experi-ence of pain. Such enframings signal that this operationalization of the sacred is enacted through the transubstantiation of collective energies that would otherwise have volatile consequences into rela-tively stable and recurrent religious experiences (Durkheim, 1995: 351; see also Van Gennep, 1960; Turner, 1969). In addition, this instantiation of the sacred in the organic matter of human bodies is complemented by the predominance of other *material* emblems of community, such as a totem or a flag, that help reinforce this anchorage of religion in the *tangible* products of community (Durkheim, 1995: 60, 222–3, 386).

The socio-religious sacred is able to impart this overwhelming character to society and people's embodied being because it is effected via a particularly strong *polarization* of the sacred and profane. Representations of the sacred incorporate the *moral force* of society as a whole, while taboos separating the sacred from the profane arouse a combination of fascination and terror in that the prospect of their transgression appears to threaten society (Durkheim, 1995: 36). The strength of this polarity is also reflected in the fact that 'religion' is for Durkheim not *one* cult but a *system* of cults – including positive and negative cults that structure and forbid specific interactions with the sacred – working together to transform individuals' experiences of themselves and the world around them (Durkheim, 1995: 41; Ruel, 1998: 113). Imprinted onto embodied experience, this polarity works to integrate individuals into 'organic' communities via a ritual, mythical and symbolic experience of society as religious (Durkheim, 1995: 438).

One of the major manifestations of this strong polarity characteristic of the socio-religious sacred, and the transformations it can effect on people, is evident in the significance Durkheim attributes to *law* as a socially solidifying regulator of human action (Cotterrell, 1999). In societies sanctified and experienced as religious, crime is an offence not simply against other humans, but against the otherworldly *divine*, which is why punishments for crime under religious law tend to be harsher than under secular penal systems (Tiryakian, 1964). The religious force of society is also signalled by the collective violence that can be provoked when transgression of a taboo has taken place (Durkheim, 1995: 213–6).

Durkheim's account of how society is made religious through the operationalization of the socio-religious sacred has profound implications for debates regarding secularization predicated on the assumption that structural differentiation has inevitably limited the influence of religion at the macro-level of society. His analysis not only indicates how a sacralization of apparently secular phenomena can occur, as in the French Revolution, but problematizes a macro-level differentiation of society into religious and secular spheres: the socio-religious sacred underpins, animates and regulates the *whole* of social and embodied life. Its presence marks the existence of viable collective institutions. Its absence initiates the disintegration of social phenomena. In this regard, *insofar as* operationalizations of the socio-religious sacred are evident today, this modality presents a particular challenge to, and exists in a state of potential conflict with, highly differentiated societies.

Durkheim's conception of the socio-religious sacred is one modality of the sacred. It cannot account for the diverse and complex traditions of belief and practice, manifest across a range of global and local contexts, characteristic of the world's major religions. Nonetheless, we can identify significant elements of the socio-religious sacred in some contemporary forms of Islam, and thereby utilize it to help account for those anxieties about the incorporation of Islam into Western culture and politics evident in debates today (Turner, 2010a: 655). These are manifest in the 'Danish cartoons' and 'Innocence of Muslims' film controversies, for example, where the significance of positive and negative cults in 'setting apart' and 'forbidding' pictorial representations of Muhammad sparked global condemnation and violence (Bleich, 2006). The potency of Islamic symbols of the sacred was also clear in the similarly tumultuous response to stories of US soldiers in Afghanistan burning copies of the Qur'an, which is not only Islam's holy text, but a *material* emblem of the sacred (D'Souza, 2012). To dismiss this violence as irrational is to misunderstand that it is a response not to symbolic sleight, but to an infringement of the sacred perceived to threaten the profanation and destabilization of Islamic societies and religion as a whole.

Insofar as some Islamic forms exhibit a commitment to a 'total' socio-religious society (making social realities conform to the will of Allah), they are expressive not only of the moral force Islam can exercise over those who constitute the community of the *umma*, but also of the ways in which this modality of the sacred challenges differentiated conceptions of social life (Black, 1993: 59; see also Bonner, 1992, 1996). Islam's very strong focus on the primacy of bonds with other Muslims above local particularities, cultures and institutional variables is, for example, embodied in the enactment of the obligations to other followers through *salat* (Henkel, 2005: 489; McGinty, 2006: 103).

This challenge to differentiation is also evident in the fact that the key functionaries of *sharia* – fundamental to Islamic practice as a 'timeless manifestation of the will of God, subject neither to history nor circumstance' – are not priests but interpreters of law, thus revealing the close link between legal regulation and social solidarity Durkheim identifies within the socio-religious sacred (Ruthven, 1997: 73; see Volpi and Turner, 2007). The relative severity of many punishments encoded into this law, in comparison to secular systems, also supports Durkheim's arguments here. The fact that the penalty for apostasy is death is of particular note (Rahman, 2006), since, from a Durkheimian view, this is not only the ultimate offence against the divine, but also a challenge to the naturalization of the sacred through the construction of a 'Muslim body'. This importance placed on the naturalization of the sacred is also evident in anxieties amongst many Islamic communities about the permissibility of organ transplants between Muslim and non-Muslim bodies and the possibility that post-mortem examinations might profane Muslim bodies (Gatrad, 1994; Sheikh, 1998; Hayward and Madill, 2003).

Recognition of the centrality of law to Islam, and the anxieties about the potential conflict with macro-level and meso-level differentiation it implies, is reflected in Bruce's (2003: 234) provocative suggestion that whenever Muslims are found in significant numbers, they 'always want to either take over the state or secede from it – the goal being the imposition of shariah'. Taken together with other key features of the socio-religious sacred, such examples indicate how this modality offers a potent means for imparting a particular directionality to social life, one that can exist in a relationship of tension and conflict with other cultural values and, as we now explore, contrasting modalities of the sacred.

### The Transcendent Sacred

The transcendent modality is centred upon a strong polarization of the sacred and profane, as is the socio-religious sacred, but this polarity is mapped onto a vertical tension between the other-worldly and this-worldly that embraces a distinction between the 'spiritual' realm of the Church and the 'temporal' realm of politics, economics and society. This distinction effectively accepts, and can indeed be seen as contributing to, the existence of a secular sphere that the socio-religious sacred is so opposed to. Relatedly, the transcendent sacred is operationalized through a 'lifting' of people and their experiences *out of* existing immanent (and secular) social identities and bonds, rather than by categorizing all social life and experience as an engagement with the sacred or with that which threatens to profane the sacred and undermine society.

The embodied experiences and expressions associated with the transcendent sacred are, furthermore, predicated upon an emergent individualism in which ultimate religious meaning is found above and beyond the 'immanent' ethnic or cultural loyalties of social communities, and in opposition to the socio-religious sacred 'diffusion' of collective symbols and mythologies into the bodies of *all* (Eisenstadt, 1989: 205). This reflects a religiosity involving what Simmel (1971a) identifies as 'reaching beyond' the boundaries and limitations of the secular; a reaching that is not intended to negate the secular, however, but to reframe individuals' experiences within it in the light of an other-worldly source of truth. When this happens, experiences no longer appear random, contingent or chaotic, but meaningful in relation to 'God's will' (Simmel, 1997: 32). Weber's (1948 [1915]: 347) interest in eroticism provides an example of how individuals can invest immanent experience with a unique, transcendent meaning that lifts them out of society.

This 'reaching beyond' is the key to how the transcendent sacred imparts directionality to society. As Luhmann (2000: 77) argues, the contribution of religion informed by this modality of the sacred to the development of complex social systems rests on its capacity to 'call out' individuals from their immanent lives, and to provide them from the standpoint of an infinite, transcendent order with the space to critically judge society. This orientation exists in clear tension with the socio-religious sacred, in which rites rather than reflexivity traditionally steered people's engagements with society. It is also opposed to those secularist belief systems which espouse 'unbelief' and reject any notion of religious transcendence (although secularist belief systems tend to share with the transcendent sacred acceptance of structural differentiation) (Dawkins, 2006; Harris, 2006).

This modality of the transcendent sacred can illuminate important features of a number of religions. Martin (2011), for example, notes the significance of polarizations of notions of the 'transcendent' and the 'immanent' in a range of axial religions, while Taylor (2007) utilizes them in relation to Buddhism, Taoism and Hinduism (Taylor, 2007: 15, 18–19, 676; Martin, 2011: 43). Both, however, note their particular significance in Christianity, though others have gone further and questioned the legitimacy of utilizing them outside this context on the basis that they imply an interiorized, mystical and implicitly Protestant polarization of the spiritual and the material (Orsi, 1999: 6; Vásquez, 2011: 1). As in the case of Islam, Christianity's diverse history and theology embraces more than one modality of the sacred, but it is indeed with regard to Christianity, and its Protestant forms in particular, that this transcendent sacred is most significant.

In elaborating upon this point, Martin (2011), Taylor (2007) and others have identified a variable but nonetheless clear pattern within Christian history in which a growing distinction between the transcendent and immanent developed alongside a determination to eradicate or radically re-conceive socio-religious forms of the sacred by promoting secular views of this-worldly relationships. Here, we have a prioritization of Christian conceptions of the sacred as existing *beyond* this world, over alternative conceptions of this world as suffused with sacred properties: the transcendent-sacred does not bring about the enchantment of immanent realities in the manner of the socio-religious, but promotes *disenchantment*. Thus, while enchantment may be essential to many religious forms, both Catholicism and Protestantism have 'been built on its partial or total denial' (Taylor, 2007: 553). In this regard, Taylor (2007: 427–8, 437), amongst others, criticizes secularization theories that *conflate* notions of the decline of religion with processes of disenchantment, suggesting instead that those histories of secularizing and de-secularizing 'zigzags and reversals' in Christian societies are intimately related to the development of its own transcendent sacred polarity (Casanova, 2011: 441–2; Martin, 2011: 19). This Christian approach towards disenchantment, and its antagonism to the socio-religious sacred, is most apparent in the religious individualism associated with Calvinism. It is also evident, however, in the individualization of the notion of moral force evident in Christianity's rejection of religious *law*, and the contrasting emphasis it places on individual conscience in adjudicating moral action (albeit often in conjunction with the guidance of the Church) (Weber, 1991).

In actively facilitating the disenchantment and secularization of social realities relative to the socio-religious sacred, of course, Christianity's orientation towards the transcendent sacred risks undermining its own potential to steer worldly realities in other-worldly directions. Berger's (1967) account of secularization is able to depict Christianity as 'its own gravedigger' precisely because the emergence of the realm of the secular that eventually undermines its status follows a distinctly Christian trajectory. As Weber (1991) argues, this involves an orientation towards disenchantment, the shrinkage of the scope of the sacred and the ethicization of religion, and was interrupted only temporarily and partially by the re-enchantment of the world in medieval Catholicism. Gauchet's (1997: 4) notion of Christianity as the religion that produces 'the exit from religion' is a more recent articulation of this idea.

If the transcendent sacred has historically been associated with the disenchantment of society, however, it remains the case that studies of the charismatic, Pentecostal and evangelical forms of Christianity across the world today suggest it possesses continuing vitality. Biblicism and conversionism are key characteristics of these forms (Bebbington, 1989), reflecting the New Testament emphasis on the idea that Christians are *called out* of the world (John, 15:19) and that this involves *changing their bodies* so that they walk, talk, desire, think and feel in a manner entirely at odds with their previous existence yet reframed in transcendent terms (Ephesians, 4: 22, 5: 1; Philippians, 3: 21; Martin, 1990: 163; Robbins, 2004: 128).

The vitality of the transcendent sacred is also evident in the continued Christian opposition to the socio-religious sacred: the evangelical emphasis on the individual freedom to respond to the call of God encourages an 'opting out' of social 'sacred canopies' and promotes reflexive engagements with social and political pluralism (Freston, 2007: 224). This opting out also sometimes involves 'leaping above' local communities, in contrast to the socio-religious sacred which involves the religious enframing of the collectivity, especially in the case of ethnic-minority Christians linking themselves to 'evangelicalism as an expression of transnational modernity' (Martin, 2005: 277). Indeed, it has been suggested that conversion in this context is 'not only a conversion to modern forms of these religions, but also to religious forms of modernity' (Van der Veer, 1996; Adogame, 2010). This is because conversion to a religion that incorporates within it a transcendent sacred facilitates assimilation, on religious grounds, into contexts marked by modern patterns of differentiation, and modern valuations of mobility and voluntarism (Freston, 2007: 209).

## The Bio-Political Sacred

Weber's writings had at their centre not only a concern with the world-transforming effects of the transcendent sacred, associated most directly with Protestantism, but also a vision of the bleak spectre that followed the extension of rationality facilitated by this modality. The disenchanting impetus of rationalized culture reaches a stage in Weber's work where it controls and defines the secular realm so completely that society is removed from *any* link to religion. These circumstances provoke a radical weakening of the sacred/profane polarity insofar as there is no longer any outside to the 'iron cage' in which people exist, no contact with any sense of the transcendent, and nothing considered ultimate apart from the power and reach of this instrumentalist mode of governance and activity.

Far from resulting in a complete disappearance of the sacred, however, the implications of Weber's (1968: 24–5, 1156; 1991) analyses can be interpreted as identifying the extension of technological culture itself as an exceptionally powerful and prized incarnation of the extraordinary. This culture is not segmented within any single institutional sphere, moreover, but imparts a rationalizing and domineering approach to politics and to the management of biological life itself, reflecting a process of de-differentiation in which its reach underpins every aspect of social life and human existence. In clarifying the nature and scope of this technologically informed bio-political modality of the sacred, Agamben has done most to explore and extend the implications of Weber's analysis.

Agamben (1998) emphasizes that the operationalization of bio-politics possesses major differences from transcendent and socio-religious modalities of the sacred. Contrary to their legitimations of worldly activity and being with reference to other-worldly authorities, Agamben traces the meaning and existence of bio-political management to the etymological and juridico-political contexts relevant to what he views as the sacred's origins. This takes him back to Ancient Greece and archaic Roman law, and also to the manner in which the sacred was subsequently transformed by and incorporated within modern systems of governance (Agamben, 1998: 1, 3–12, 80).

In revealing what is at stake in the modern sacralization of the bio-political, Agamben (1998: 1) begins by demonstrating how this conception of the extraordinary inverts the priorities associated with the Ancient Greek distinction between the valued 'way of living proper to an individual or a group', and mere or *bare life* ('the simple fact of living common to all living beings'). While the former possessed noble associations, reflecting politically forged creations of 'the good life' within the polis, the latter resided outside the realm of governance within the domestic sphere of reproduction. In illustrating how the bio-political sacred reversed this exclusion, Agamben (1998) refers to Foucault's analyses of the incorporation of bio-politics into 'the mechanisms and calculations of State power'. Politics is here transformed into bio-politics and 'the species and the individual as a simple living body become what is at stake in society's political strategies' (Agamben, 1998: 3).

This transformation means that while bare life was once the negative reference of noble life validated by the polis, it has become consecrated as the focus of state activity. Disciplinary control is here exercised and extended through new forms of bio-power in which technologies are directed towards the creation of productive but 'docile bodies'; a process Arendt (1998) associated with 'the transformation and decadence of the political realm in modern societies' (Agamben, 1998: 3, 4).

The idea that this focus on the control of bare life reflects an extension rather than a diminution of that which is considered sacred may appear counter-intuitive, but in detailing how the bio-political is constituted as extraordinary, and what follows from its operation, Agamben turns to the ambiguous figure of *homo sacer* within archaic law. Homo sacer, or 'sacred man', is exceptional and ambiguous not because of the potentially volatile energies Durkheim associated with effervescent gatherings of the collective, but because of 'his' relationship to the *law*. Acquiring this status once legally condemned to exile, homo sacer is august *and* accursed: he is august as expulsion excludes him from the possibility of being sacrificed in accordance with divine law, yet is accursed as a consequence of being excluded from the safeguards guaranteed by human law (he can be *killed*, with impunity) (Agamben, 1998: 8, 73). Homo sacer thus becomes sacred by being placed in an exceptional space in which removal from the auspices of both state authority and divine power reduces this figure to the extraordinary status of bare life.

In contrast to Foucault's exclusive association of bio-politics with the modern era, then, Agamben traces the sacralization of bare life back to those exceptional acts that occurred during the institution of political sovereignty; acts that signalled an early phase of secularization insofar as the sacred was cut adrift from religion and became a juridico-political category expressive of sovereign power over individual bodies. What is different about modernity, however, is that rather than being an *exception*, this sovereign power over bodies has become the *norm*. We are all *homines sacri* now, with the sacred being foundational to the modern age through the state's 'totalizing' power to manage embodied individuals on the basis of life and death (Agamben, 1998: 111).

Evidence for the apparent pervasiveness of the bio-political sacred in contemporary society can be seen in various areas. In legal debates about euthanasia, the notion of a 'life unworthy of being lived' reminds us of the state's power over 'bare' ('sacred') life, while technological interventions into the bodies of coma patients have facilitated new legal definitions of life, death or liminal states between these (Agamben, 1998: 139, 186). Bare life has also been extended to research and policy initiatives ranging from the pursuit of control over the building blocks of human life via the human genome project, to the management of the unborn foetus (having reached a stage in the United States where pregnant women classified as having 'at risk' lifestyles can be incarcerated in order to safeguard future life) (see also Rose, 2007). These and related initiatives involve weakening the boundaries between humans, machines and rationalities of control that complement Heidegger's (1993) account of the *technological* 'enframing' of humans. For Heidegger (1993), humans become positioned as a 'standing reserve' for technologically driven demands for efficiency within the 'immanent frame', vacated by the transcendent sacred, and forced to yield their properties and potential to any efficiency-based demand placed upon them (Bell and Kennedy, 2000; Virilio, 2000; Taylor, 2007).

Heidegger's argument is that the instrumentalization of embodied individuals, core to the bio-political sacred, involves 'enframing' nature, calling upon the physical and the environment to be 'immediately on hand' as a 'standing reserve'. In this context, insofar as they endure, religious attempts to enframe nature, society and humanity in moral and metaphysical forms are challenged by the technologically determined bio-political routines of everyday life, wherein the 'psycho-physical apparatus of man is completely adjusted to the demands of … the tools, the machines' (Weber, 1948 [1919a]: 149; 1968: 1156; Maley, 2004: 75, 79). This is why, for Weber, secularization is not simply about the critical scrutiny applied to religious *doctrines*, but also the promotion of a *technologically enframed experience* that renders religion marginal to social and cultural life. If these processes of technological enframing disenchant social life, though, they are not associated with a *neglect* of the body, but with a new *prioritization* and indeed sacralization of it, since it becomes the key site for the intervention, regulation and control of technological culture (Agamben, 1998: 186–7).

For Agamben, the ultimate expression, or *nomos*, associated with the bio-political intervention into bodies and the technological enframing of experience is, contrary to the socio-religious sacralization of society or the transcendent realm of otherness, to be found within the death camps of Nazi Germany, since these reveal the final reduction of humanity to bare life. That these camps continued to operate on the basis of *homo sacer*, moreover, is evident in one of the few rules to which the Nazis adhered during the 'Final Solution': Jews could be sent to the camps 'only after they had been fully denationalized (stripped even of the residual citizenship left to them after the Nuremberg laws)' and thus placed into the category of those who could be killed with impunity and without danger of them becoming sacrifices productive of martyrdom (Agamben, 1998: 132, 166).

In this regard, we can note how very different the bio-political sacred is from other modalities of the extraordinary, but also identify points of intersection. In constituting a sacralization of what is secular, it undercuts strong polarizations of the sacred/profane, thus making it difficult for this-worldly matters to be experienced or expressed on the basis of other-worldly, religious perspectives. Nevertheless, we have already suggested that insofar as the bio-political sacred represents an extension of Weber's (1991) analysis of the rationalization of the body in Puritanism, it retains a relationship with the transcendent sacred. This is because the differentiation of the religious from the realm of the political, alongside the differentiation of the religious from the bodily evident in what Taylor (2007: 554) refers to as the *excarnational* impetus of modern Christianity, leaves embodied experience vulnerable to the exercise of bio-political sovereignty.

## The Bio-Economic Sacred

Durkheim is best known for analysing the socio-religious sacred, in which he highlights how religious rites and meanings enframe societies. Nevertheless, his writings, like those of Weber, also allow us to identify a secular modality of the sacred wherein that deemed extraordinary is dislocated from any conception of society as religious and any notion that it is connected to a transcendent realm. This fourth modality of the sacred emerges from Durkheim's analysis of the advancing division of labour, a development that he suggests results in an increase in secularism. We are witnessing the death of 'old gods', and while forms of the sacred persist, they have a more worldly character and develop on the basis of personal preferences and emotional responses of biologically and economically 'liberated' subjects operating within segmented and commercialized societies that prize 'the cult of the individual' (Durkheim, 1984: 122).

Valuing as it does the autonomy of embodied subjects to consecrate what they find to be extraordinary on the basis of their choices and feelings (preferences often based on socially shaped instinctual bodily reactions or stimuli that can signal as sacred a huge variety of phenomena), this *bio-economic* modality of the sacred is not involved in the degree of control of people's actions associated with socio-religious or bio-political modalities. Neither does it suggest the wholesale transformations of modern societies allied to processes of disenchantment inherent within bio-politics, or the confinement of the extraordinary to the other-worldly characteristic of the transcendental sacred. Instead, this bio-economic modality is grounded in the consumerization of the sacred in which there exists a proliferation of re-enchantment options available to individuals and groups within a broad, socially differentiated market.[1]

Whether this proliferation of options, and the potentially transient embodied excitements or attractions with which they are associated, constitute anything more than a 'hollowed out' form of the sacred that cannot be bonded to religious forms is questionable. This is not least because it is difficult to see how these attractions, alongside the marginalization of the cognitive and structural dimensions of religion, might lead to the constitution of experiences that have religious consequences. The character of this modality has, however, been explored further in two developments of Durkheim's work.

The first of these, Maffesoli's (1996) *The Time of the Tribes*, engages with the emotional aspects of this modality in heralding as benevolent the return of the sacred. Maffesoli associates this return with the emergence of a widespread, emotionally constituted tribalism that counters the existential bleakness brought about by modern rationalism and individualism. Here, people's 'free-floating' emotions receive temporary stimulation and collective validation in fleeting gatherings based around commercial locales such as cafés, shopping centres and sports arenas that enable them to 'keep warm' against the 'cold winds' of modernity (Maffesoli, 1996: 9, 32–3). The contemporary appearances of 'flash mobs' can be seen as another example of this phenomenon. Yet Maffesoli detects no manipulations of the effervescent energies he focuses on, only a spontaneous bubbling up of sacred experiences. He thereby ties together sacralization with emotional, biologically grounded stimulation, while leaving aside questions regarding the economic exploitation of affect. Yet it is notable that in many of the examples he cites there is an association of emotional currents and commercial enterprises unrelated to religious institutions.

The possibility that commercial enterprises might exploit emotions regarded as special brings us to the second appropriation of Durkheim's interest in the fate of the sacred within societies characterized by advanced divisions of labour. Here, Meštrović's (1997) *Postemotional Society* reinterprets the developments analysed by Maffesoli and others as evidence of an instrumentally rational manipulation of 'sacred' emotions for economic (as well as political) ends. Human feelings become post-emotional through being enframed by commercial and other 'deceptive' and 'illusory' world-views that harness intimations of the extraordinary to a modality of the sacred that joins together human biology and economic instrumentalism.

Meštrović's concern with the relationship between the commercial exploitation of extraordinary emotions has been complemented by other explorations of how 'affective energy' is utilized in, as well as outside, consumer culture (e.g. Thrift, 2004). Holloway's (2006: 185) study of the séance, for example, explores how sacred energy is produced by experiencing and feeling bodies through relational, sensuous affects such as awe, joy, sobbing and convulsive quivering; energies that have historically been utilized for the generation of profit (Massumi, 2002; Dewsbury, 2003). Other analysts support the idea that there has in particular been a secular, commercial exploitation of emotions stimulated by religious symbols (Gauchet, 2002: 344–5; 1997; 2005; Braeckman, 2009: 291). For Turner (2010a) this highlights how the contemporary sacred has indeed become 'hollowed out' via its incorporation into markets promoting multiple 'spiritualities' in books, the internet, TV and various other contexts (Sutcliffe and Bowman, 2000: 7–8; Utriainen et al., 2012: 196).

Drawing upon Marx's (1976, 1978) depiction of capitalism's 'fetishism of commodities', Vásquez (2011) develops this argument about the commercial potentialities of the sacred by drawing attention to the *material* aspects of its incorporation into the cycle of production, circulation and consumption of cultural goods (see Kalra and Hutnyk, 1998). This is not the materialization of the socio-religious sacred outlined by Durkheim, but aestheticization for gain. In this context, consumer products such as Coca-Cola and McDonalds become invested with 'transcendence, omnipotence and omnipresence'. Even capitalism itself is sacralized as 'a this-worldly eschatology in which endless consumption is the mark of grace' (Comaroff and Comaroff, 2000; Chidester, 2005: 34).

As the secular becomes sacralized, and it becomes clear that *anything* can be identified and experienced as sacred, multinational corporations spend increasing resources on market research seeking to identify and control the mechanisms implicated in people's affectual responses to signs and images of 'extraordinary' products in consumer culture. To the extent that governmental and market pressures are able to 'reach down' to control the physiological responses, feelings and reflections of embodied subjects, there is here a *dissemination* of the sacred into the bodies of individual subjects very different from the naturalization of the sacred analysed by Durkheim.

This analysis of the bio-economic sacred has particular implications for those 'holistic' or 'New Age' forms of 'spirituality' that self-consciously mark themselves out from contemporary capitalism in pursuing what they perceive to be truths antithetical to it (Heelas, 1996; Sutcliffe and Bowman, 2000). For Fenn (1978: 70–71), holistic spiritualities have such weak other-worldly referents that they operate entirely harmoniously with the secular, differentiated imperatives of modern societies: 'Policeman can be Satanists and bookkeepers can become spiritualists' without interfering with their 'normal occupational duties'. Recent writings reinforce the sense that these spiritualities are more part of, than set aside from, commercialism in highlighting how they 'ransack the world storehouse', enabling individuals to consume, in whatever mix suits them, cultural phenomena able to transform the boundaries of their experience (Bell, 1976: 13–14; Turner, 2011; Utriainen et al., 2012: 196).

Taken together, New Age spiritualism's acceptance of differentiation and consumerism exemplifies what Hammond (2000) has called the 'extravasation' of the sacred though, contrary to his focus on this as a multi-directional process, it frequently involves rechanneling the sacred in the direction of the economy (Gauchet, 1997; 2002: 344–5; 2005; Carrette and King, 2004). Here, religious traditions can be ransacked selectively and there is no expectation that they will, *as cosmological and practice-oriented wholes*, shape individuals' experiences (Wood and Bunn, 2009: 290–9). Instead, New Age fashions reinforce the sense that there exists a bio-economic modality of the sacred in which commercial interests stimulate a 'combination of somatic effects' in searching for economic advantage (Bennett, 2001: 4–5; Holloway, 2006: 186).

Such developments highlight the continuing relevance of MacIntyre's (2007: 23) suggestion that forms of *emotivism* are indicative of the increasingly manipulative social strategies inherent to economic and social life, despite their putative claims to 'authenticity'. Here, questions about the status of the sacred vis-à-vis the secular, and, more broadly, the moral and evaluative elements of socio-religious or transcendent modalities of the sacred, dissipate into questions about individual feeling. This results in the 'obliteration' of any genuine criteria that would allow us to adjudicate between 'manipulative and non-manipulative social relations' (MacIntyre, 2007: 11–12). In this light, emotivism, certain forms of the 'return of the sacred' and an economy of lifestyle options are closely interlinked. Furthermore, while theorists such as Taylor (2007: 516–18) suggest there may be positive opportunities for religion following its 'unhooking' from established institutions and communities (see also Beckford, 1989, 2003; Hervieu-Léger, 2000), it seems difficult to deny that such developments are strongly suggestive of secularization rather than de-secularization.

## Modalities and Conflation

The four modalities identified in this chapter enable us to highlight how sacred forces can both reinforce and also, in different circumstances, undermine religion. The bio-economic modality, for example, suggests that commercial engagements with and constructions of the sacred marginalize religious forms. This clarification of secular as well as religious encounters with extraordinary phenomena is, however, obscured within undifferentiated accounts of the sacred; a problem evident in the emerging 'anthropology of secularism'. This anthropology suggests that secularism is neither incompatible with religious forms of the sacred nor a structural state that promotes 'unbelief'. Instead, its exponents argue that the emotions, symbols and rituals associated with secularism are analysed more adequately as *competing forms of religion*, albeit in secular guise (see Asad, 2002; Navaro-Yashin, 2002; Özyürek, 2006). This approach allows the secular sacred to be distinguished from institutionalized religion, but still identifies all manner of sacralized forms (ranging from healthcare practices and the dress codes of airline flight attendants, to topics such as child abuse and 'mediatized' constructions of 'humanitarianism') as operating in broadly 'religious' ways (Knott, 2005; Knott and Franks, 2007; Wilson, 2011; Lynch, 2012).

One of the problems of this approach, however, is that it fails to distinguish analytically between *other-worldly* claims to authority inherent within specifically religious modalities of the sacred and *this-worldly* forms of influence central to secular modalities of the sacred. Relatedly, it glosses questions regarding the relative integrative capacities of those sacred forms harnessed to religions in comparison with those incorporated within secular developments (Wickström and Illman, 2012). In these cases, it is worth recalling Durkheim's (1995: 40) distinction between religion and 'magic': for him, the latter suggests a *clientele* rather than a church, characterized by transient, shallow and typically anonymous sets of mutual relations. These relations may still be characterized by enchantment, but in a way that recalls the original English meaning of 'enchant' as 'bewitch', rather than a collective transformation embracing all social life.

An additional example of the problems caused by failing to disentangle religious and secular modalities of the sacred is evident in those enormously popular rational choice models centred on a denial of secularization. These models first came to general prominence within the sociology of religion as part of a 'new paradigm' challenging the notion of secularization (Warner, 1993). Around the same time, 'new paradigm' evangelical Christian churches, that embraced growth-oriented business models looking to deliver a standardized but personally rewarding experience to religious consumers, also rose to prominence (Watson and Scalen, 2012). Eschewing *transcendence* for a focus on self-improvement (Watson and Scalen, 2012: 20), such churches arguably mark a transition from the transcendent modality of the sacred to a bio-economic one, and can thus be seen as possessing an affinity with the commercialization of the sacred (see Chidester, 1996). The nature and import of such transitions eludes economistic models of analysis in the sociology of religion, however, because these models share similar assumptions about consumption, markets and preferences to those held by new paradigm churches, purveyors of New Age spiritualities or those actively engaged in the fetishization of preferences for financial gain.

The emphasis we place on maintaining sensitivity to differences between the religious and secular modalities of the sacred does not mean that these modalities are without points of cross-over or convergence. Just as the bio-political sacred retains a relationship with the transcendent sacred (via the latter's embrace of the differentiation of the religious from the realm of the political that opens the body to the exercise of bio-political sovereignty), so too is it possible to identify a particular link between the transcendent and the bio-economic sacred. Campbell's (2005) re-reading of Weber's work to identify the origins of secular consumerism in the 'other' Protestant ethic of Pietism (wherein emotional connections to God were emphasized above Puritan asceticism) suggests just such a link. Nonetheless, recognizing the distinctions between these modalities places us in a much better position to identify and assess the particular characteristics and challenges pertinent to religious and secular attempts to impart particular directionalities to social and cultural life.

## Modalities of the Sacred and Forms of Sacrifice

The importance of recognizing the distinctiveness of the four modalities we have explored can be demonstrated further by reflecting on how each engages with *sacrifice*. This is an important issue as, while there have been criticisms of the deployment of expansive and vague notions of 'the sacred' (Bruce, 2002: 199–203; Beckford, 2003: 204), little attention has been directed to questions about how the sacred is *made*.

Hubert and Mauss (1964) provide a general theory of sacrifice as a phenomenon involving a setting apart from, *and* giving up of, something by which that something is made sacred (Halbwachs, 1930: 475–7; Strenski, 2003: 8). In contrast to Hubert and Mauss (1964), however, we suggest it is not just making sacrifices, but *engaging* with sacrifice (via promoting particular forms as valid, prohibiting others as invalid, or even seeking to create a society without sacrifice) that results in the crafting of phenomena considered extraordinary. Exploring the various ways in which engagement with sacrifice makes things sacred can help us understand why certain phenomena rather than others become sacred, and how societies come to be steered in particular directions rather than others. Relatedly, it helps us explain how individuals are stimulated to become certain types of social subjects, via the enframing of experiences in particular ways, rather than others.

In relation to the socio-religious sacred, sacrifice can be seen as a 'total social fact', that is, something that is simultaneously individual but also religious, juridical, moral and economic, cutting across 'different institutions, values and actions' and 'penetrat[ing] every aspect' of the 'social system' (Mauss, 1969b: 3–4, 102; Gofman, 1998: 67). Durkheim's (1973) conception of *homo duplex* explores how this operates within individuals, with social existence itself enforcing a 'giving up' of egoistic appetites in the face of the overwhelming religious force of the collectivity. Bataille's (1988: 55–56) neo-Durkheimian account of sacrifice as a recurrent expenditure of collective energies, serving to restore the sacred to the heart of society, also demonstrates the violence that can accompany sacrifice in its socio-religious modality (see also Caillois, 1950). Here, collectively experienced threats of profanation are responded to via a violent reassertion of the other-worldly priority of the sacred over all aspects of mundane life. In *potlatch*, for example, the worldly utility of goods is destroyed when exchanged as 'gifts', though their sacrifice binds individuals into sacred social obligations (Bataille, 1988: 65). Bataille (1988: 89) also identifies violent sacrifice in the case of Islam, arguing that it was 'open from the start to an apparently unlimited increase of power' through its virulent opposition to 'the infidel enemy'. More recently, the use of 'suicide bombing' in religious conflict has also evidenced this reassertion of the other-worldly priority of the sacred, binding individuals eternally and through their dissolution into a social and religious totality that exists in opposition to the 'infidel enemy'. Relatedly, Girard's (1977, 2001) focus on the key role of sacrifice in the operationalization of the socio-religious sacred explores the idea that violence can unify society. In the face of potential threats to a social fabric experienced as sacred, the sacrifice of a surrogate 'scapegoat', onto whom is projected the source of intra-group rivalries that threaten the separation of the sacred and profane, can restore harmony and order (Girard, 1977: 4–5; 1987: 26).

The engagement with sacrifice within the transcendent sacred modality can, however, be very different. Bataille (1988: 127, 133–6) suggests that Christianity in general and Protestantism in particular, for example, have been radically opposed to such destructive forms of sacrifice. So too does Girard (2001: 56), for whom New Testament writings reveal Jesus as disrupting this (socio-religious) sacrificial pattern, such as when he prevents the stoning to death of the woman taken in adultery. In contrast, Girard associates Christianity with its own model of sacrifice centred on voluntary *renunciation* of one's own desires – and even life – in this world, in order to experience transcendent existence in the next. Sacrifice is not for the socio-religious collectivity, but for the transcendent sphere of future existence. This model is exemplified by Christ's preparedness to offer his life in order to absolve the sins of others. Simmel's conception of sacrifice as a pattern of 'transcendent exchange' is also relevant here, involving individuals 'giving up' something of themselves in a way that 'goes beyond' immanent social realities yet invests them with meaning in pursuit of an integrated personality guided by an authenticity that exists above and beyond specific objects or satisfactions (Simmel, 1971a: 353; 1971b: 48; 1990: 85).

This explication of divergences in the two religious forms of sacrifice should not be interpreted as a value judgement on them. Socio-religious forms tend towards violence, but might be more effective at stimulating commitment among individuals, and producing a more resilient modality of the sacred than is the case with transcendent forms. In this context, we can note Girard's (1995: 31) suggestion that opportunities for sacrificial violence show no sign of abating, and threaten to overcome the Christian influences and associated judicial systems that seek to constrain them.[2] What this comparison between forms of sacrifice can do, however, is illuminate what is at stake when people talk of the 'return of the sacred' as if this is *one* thing, rather than a number of heterogeneous things. If we are indeed witnessing a resurgence of various modalities of the sacred, they are likely to have very different characters, and very different social consequences. This can be illustrated further with regard to the two non-religious modalities of the sacred we have identified.

Despite their differences, what unites the forms of sacrifice evident above is their religious referent. Things are given up and made sacred on the basis of engagements with religion, with the former involving sacrifices *within* a religious milieu and the latter practising sacrifice *in relation to* a transcendent religious milieu. The bio-political and bio-economic engagements with sacrifice, however, are secular. The bio-political involves a giving up of sacrifice itself; a rejection that makes everyone sacred by appropriating to the state control over bare life. This rejection of sacrifice is, indeed, a defining feature of the bio-political sacred; a modality operationalized through total control of a sphere possessed of no 'outer' existence (religious or other) in relation to which a sacrifice can be operationalized.

The bio-economic sacred is also underpinned by a secular engagement with sacrifice. To the extent that this modality of making things sacred involves sacrifice, it is not a matter of punishing those who appear to threaten profanation of a society considered sacred, in acts viewed by Girard and Bataille respectively as scapegoating or as sacralizing. Nor does it involve self-sacrifice in a manner that valorizes one's orientation to the transcendent over and above the religiously and temporally limited sphere of the immanent. Instead, it simply involves individuals incurring 'opportunity costs' by engaging in transactions that benefit their variable, often transient, preference schedules for goods to which they attach value. Individuals are here attached to economic flows and orders not through the painful 'giving up' of egoistic desires central to Durkheim's model of *homo duplex*, but as a consequence of attractive, exciting, pleasurable and commercially oriented stimuli. The broader context for this involves the liberation of goods from social relationships in order that exchange can proceed on the basis of individual-affective preferences (preferences sometimes reduced to the level of neuro-scientific structure of brain chemistry; Camerer, 2007), rather than as gifts embedded within collective moral forces in systems of law, taboo and positive and negative cults possessed of far greater integrative potential (Coleman, 1990; Iannaccone, 1997; Demian, 2004). The bio-economic sacred, in short, is fully compatible with structural differentiation and the secularization of religion at both macro- and meso-levels of society.

The secularizing affinities that exist between bio-political and bio-economic modalities are, therefore, evident in similarities that exist in their approaches to *sacrifice*. As Gauchet (1997, 2005) argues, the historical trajectory of the sacred has from this perspective culminated in an *increasing unwillingness to sacrifice*, a sentiment developed in Žižek's (2002) critique of contemporary forms of 'spirituality' as entailing no sacrifices from their adherents, a circumstance likely to consolidate rather than challenge the operation of globalized capitalism (Hunt, 2005; Turner, 2010a: 651). While the bio-political forbidding of sacrifice has a de-differentiating character, the bio-economic engagement with sacrifice as exchange can be associated with a privatizing or segmenting pattern of sacralization that tends to reinforce social differentiation, albeit within a broader marketization of social and cultural phenomena.

## Conclusion

This chapter has explicated distinct modalities that offer contrasting frameworks for assessing what the sacred is, and how expressions and experiences of it might be socially and religiously significant today. Each modality possesses significant implications for debates about the relationship between secularization, differentiation and religious authority, and for questions regarding the enframing of embodied experience with which they are associated. This latter issue in particular is key for analysing the potential that still exists for forms of religious habitus to be created and sustained.

In terms of the relationship between secularization and religious authority, the *socio-religious sacred* is opposed to any secularization insofar as this would interfere with its religious consecration of society into phenomena that are either sacred or that threaten profanation of the sacred. To admit a non-religious, secular sphere would be to open a plane of existence in which experiences are cosmologically meaningless. The *transcendent sacred* is also opposed to wholesale secularization. Its equation of society with an immanent, this-worldly sphere that contrasts with an other-worldly realm, however, presupposes and even valorizes at least a degree of secularization in which secular influence is accepted alongside religious authority. Both socio-religious and transcendent modalities of the sacred, though, are associated closely with cosmologies and practices that consecrate society, or a realm that exists outside of society, as religious. *Bio-political* and *bio-economic* modalities, in contrast, involve a weakening or collapse of the sacred/profane polarity and its links to institutional religion, and a displacement of other-worldly legitimations of authority in favour of this-worldly political or economic foci. It follows that they are both linked with secularizing processes; processes manifest as either a technologically driven bio-political materialization of the sacred as 'bare life', or a bio-economic identity-based emotivism within consumer society.

In terms of their specific relationship with structural differentiation, the existence of transcendent and bio-economic modalities provides evidence for those who identify an institutional segmentation of religion at the macro-level of society. Socio-religious and bio-political modalities, however, exist in considerable tension with this view. Thus, the *socio-religious* sacred is completely opposed to any limitation of the significance of religion throughout society, and to the extent it exists as a tendency in contemporary religious movements is likely to challenge the on-going structural differentiation of societies. The *bio-political* sacred, in contrast, though divorced from formal relationships with religion, can also be seen as exerting a de-differentiating impact on modern societies, albeit one that extends a rationality and control of bare life across all sectors of society.

Most generally, three of these four modalities can be viewed as *promoting* secularization, albeit to very different degrees, problematizing classification of them on the basis of static polarizations of the secular and the sacred. In validating a secular sphere, the *transcendent sacred* can and has been viewed by Weber and others as preparing the conditions for religion's decline. Both *bio-political* and *bio-economic modalities*, moreover, create space for the elevation of this-worldly over other-worldly forces (with the logic of the former disallowing the acknowledgement of any other-worldly sphere, and the latter eroding religion through commercialization). It is only the socio-religious sacred that is wholly incompatible with the secular, as reflected in Asad's (1993) comments on the difficulties Muslims face in participating in the public sphere in the West; a sphere predicated on the Christian acceptance of a distinction between the (private) religious and the secular.

It is important to reiterate that these modalities of the sacred are ideal-types. Nevertheless, as this chapter has shown, important elements of them are manifest in the modern world. The major global religions have exhibited elements of more than one of them across history, while globalization further encourages such intermingling. Immigrants into the US from Latin America, Asia and Africa, for example, bring with them various religious forms that have been 'affected by capitalism, modernization, and globalization in uneven and contradictory ways', encouraging them to combine 'official' and 'grassroots' experiences of the sacred in novel combinations (Vásquez, 2011; see also McDannell, 1995; Appadurai, 1996; Orsi, 1999).

We have suggested that Islam has many features suggestive of the socio-religious sacred, including the fact it allows no space for a differentiated sphere of the secular. This would indicate a marked antipathy to the secular modalities of the sacred considered in this chapter, which is certainly a common theme in contemporary assessments of Islam. Ahmed (1991: 230), for example, addressing what we have called the bio-economic modality of the sacred from an Islamic perspective, suggests there is here more than a clash of cultures and more of a 'straight fight' between secular materialism and the other-worldly asceticism of the Islamic faith (see also Gellner, 1992; Turner, 1994). Godazgar's (2007: 391, 407) study of consumerism in Iran, however, finds the market to be deeply embedded there: even while Islamic authorities unequivocally condemn it and seek to eradicate it, global trends towards consumerism reinforced through the internet and (illegal) satellite television increasingly make Islam one part of a differentiated existence. Similarly, we can note how Gökariksel's (2009: 665) exploration of Muslim women's adoption of the veil in Turkey can be said to suggest a strong, socio-religious challenge to the bio-economic sacred in modernity, but it is also notable that these women may take advantage of the specialist fashion outlets catering for the veiling market, introducing choice and consumer culture into their decisions.

Despite this intermingling, however, these modalities of the sacred indicate analytically distinct ways of enframing embodied experiences. While we explore in detail the degree to which religion is still able to shape and steer embodied experience in the rest of this book, it is important to emphasize that we are dealing here with the extent to which there still exist conditions conducive to the construction and maintenance of religious forms of habitus. This is a complex issue. While bio-political and bio-economic modalities may be increasingly efficacious in the contemporary era, they have not achieved complete domination over the framing of human experience and have to contend with the violence characteristic of certain types of the socio-religious sacred. For Girard (2008), for example, the Islamist violence of September 11, 2001 and bombings in London and Madrid, as well as the wars in Afghanistan and Iraq and an increasing range of terrorist activities across US and European contexts, signal what a resurgence of strong forms of the socio-religious sacred might look like.

Further to this, the following chapters explore the extent to which conditions still exist for the construction of religious forms of habitus with reference to a number of key bridging experiences that, so far, we have mentioned only briefly. While Durkheim and Weber, as well as a range of other theorists, address questions concerning the religious enframing of experiences with reference to a wide range of examples, they identify experiences relating to *intoxication, pain, charisma* and *eroticism* as centrally significant means for this enframing. The first two of these are identified within the work of Durkheim, though their religious dimensions are now challenged by the bio-political modality of the sacred in particular. Charisma and eroticism, in contrast, which have significant roles in the writings of Weber, are increasingly subject to bio-economic enframings of experience. This does not mean that religious forms of habitus have disappeared, but our analysis does suggest that the means and mechanisms through which these are constructed have changed. Traditionally, forms of religious habitus could be constructed in milieu characterized by the overwhelming dominance of a particular religious modality of the sacred. In the contemporary era of global modernity, however, characterized by unprecedented degrees of knowledge about and experience of competing religious and secular forces, individuals and groups are placed increasingly in a position where they have to reflexively piece together and maintain constant vigilance over their religious dispositions and orientations.

## Notes

1.  This highlights an irony in Durkheim's work, as well as in Weber's. For Weber, the immense social significance of the transcendent sacred in the emergence of the spirit of capitalism prefigures its undermining by the bio-political reduction of humans to bare life. In contrast, Durkheim's analysis of the sacred, within the context of his antipathy to notions of *homo economicus*, exists alongside his suggestion that modernity is associated with a marginalization of the socio-religious sacred as a result of the extraordinary importance placed on the actions and preferences of 'economic man'.

2.  The removal of law from the sacred, which follows from Christianity, facilitates the emergence of modern legal systems that divorce punishment from the self-reinforcing cycles of violence central to scapegoating (Girard, 1995: 31, 307; Juergensmeyer, 2003; Abufarha, 2009).

# 3

# Other-Worldly and This-Worldly Intoxication

## Introduction

Intoxicating other-worldly experiences have long been associated with the development of religious sensibilities and practices, but their analysis has not always featured in sociological theory. Weber was suspicious of that mysticism which persisted amidst the advance of rationalization in the modern West, for example, while Marx dismissed intimations of the extraordinary as either a primitive defensive response to spectacular natural events or a later consequence of ideological mystification associated with commodity fetishism. Durkheim's writings constitute an exception to this tendency, however, and we can discover at their core a theory of embodied intoxication as both a bridge to religious experiences and a key feature of otherwise diverse societies.

This theory of embodied intoxication was developed most extensively in Durkheim's (1995) *The Elementary Forms of Religious Life*, in which he associated Aboriginal totemism with socially affirming religious experiences and identities. Totemism effected these outcomes because of processes whereby tribal members were i) enthused or intoxicated sufficiently to sacrifice their egoistic appetites and inhabit their physical being on the basis of religious and social priorities, while also being ii) physically marked with totemically related insignia and customs associated with collective matters of extraordinary importance that facilitated normative patterns of recognition, action and interaction.

Reflecting the operation of the socio-religious modality of the sacred, this embodied marking and intoxication consecrated as religious the tribal societies in which it occurred. Revolving around the totemic images that stood as sacred counterparts to profane life, such processes directed as well as reflected the rituals and effervescences governing collective existence. As Durkheim (1995: 141, 151) argued, the totem offered to the clan 'a conception of the universe' while all things constitutive of the tribal group – people, plants, inanimate objects – were 'modalities' of this cosmic 'being' and attained significance because of their existence in relation to it. In this context, a totem consisted not only of a surface image and representation, but also possessed a religious depth that mirrored to the collectivity a morally informed vision of itself that could predispose people towards particular sentiments and actions. These predispositions were linked with the totemic capacity to elicit in clan members an 'inward transformation' (involving complementary stimuli, feelings and thoughts) of 'the society of which they are members and the obscure yet intimate relations they have with it'; relations that include a sense that the tribe is itself divinely inspired and steered (Durkheim, 1995: 213–22, 226–9).

Durkheim's analysis remains important for exploring whether intoxication still constitutes a bridge to religious experiences and identities in the current era. His belief that ethnographic data could allow him to identify the elementary (socio-religious) forms of *all* religions and societies, including those of considerably greater complexity, may have been mistaken. Nonetheless, his account of intoxication offers a valuable basis from which to examine both the divergent ways in which such experiences are enframed within religious and secular modalities of the sacred, and the implications of these interactions for the significance of religion today.

In what follows we explore Durkheim's account further, before illustrating its utility via two contemporary examples of intoxication. The overwhelming emotional communions with the Holy Spirit associated with forms of Pentecostalism, and the strong excitements that continue to inhere within an increasingly commercial and instrumental sphere of sport, illustrate the divergent priorities to which intoxicating experiences can be harnessed. We then focus on how the commercial exploitation of intoxication, and the bio-political regulation of such experience through chemical means, can limit the capacity of this experience to result in religious outcomes while also threatening an increase in 'abnormal' forms of intoxication.

## The Socio-Religious Ritualization of Embodied Intoxication

The Warramunga totemic black snake ritual is one of many examples Durkheim offers to demonstrate how socio-religious collectivities stimulate and regulate experiences of intoxication. In detailing its operation, he identifies three significant processes evident across such contexts. The first is a pre-requisite for the existence of totemic collectivities, involving individuals being communally stimulated and emotionally energized to occupy and develop the social dimensions of their bodies at the expense of egoistic appetites. This is manifest among the Warramunga in the form of intense activity, a violent trembling and shaking, and a renewed vitalism among clan members that Durkheim (1995: 233–4) refers to as collective intoxication. It is this contagious experience of hyper-excitement that leads people 'instinctively' to copy the symbols, customs, affective foundations and consciousness central to the totemic rituals of effervescent assemblies.

To be intoxicated, for Durkheim, is to be open to surpassing the individual characteristics of one's embodied self. Stimulated by the collective experience of congregating amidst totemic representations of ultimate importance, participants are 'pulled away from… ordinary occupations and preoccupations', and moved to the point of delirium involving 'the religious state' (Durkheim, 1995: 386; Ramp, 1998: 141). In exciting individuals about, and propelling them to invest in, the collective aspects of their embodiment, such stimuli and feeling exceed the self, sensitizing the body to others, and encouraging the pursuit of impersonal and religious 'rules of conduct' (Durkheim, 1973; 1995: 213).

The second key process involves inscribing totemically-related *markings* on and in the bodies of tribal members, as evident in the black snake designs on the backs of the Warramunga. As Durkheim (1995: 138, 233) argues, individuals 'imprint' totemic images of collectivity 'in their flesh, and it becomes part of them'. Such actions 'affirm the communion of individuals in a shared moral whole', revealing that the body is not simply an 'individual possession' but that it possesses 'sacred potential' which 'erupts onto the surface' as a result of 'cutting, scarification, tattooing, [and] painting', identifying it as a location for the symbolization of religion and society. This corporeal imprinting of tribal members is for Durkheim 'the most important' mode of representation within and beyond totemic societies, though he emphasizes that bodies are marked by collectivities in ways that exceed the surface flesh. This is clear in his analysis of rites that facilitate individual contact with the totem.

In the analogous case of the Arunta, for example, participants *mimic* jumping kangaroos, flying ants or crying eagles; a mimicry that alters feelings and appearances, and shapes dispositions (Durkheim, 1982: 39, 52–3; 1995: 357). Such internalizations of external social facts illustrate, for Mauss (1973a), how body techniques are developed, revealing how seemingly natural actions are *learned* through collectively structured apprenticeships (a process key to the continuation of religions and societies). When transmitted and incorporated successfully, such techniques facilitate a biological, psychological and cultural connection of the subject to the collectivity, informing how individuals engage with the social group and wider cosmos of which they are a part. It is also important to note that totemic markings are not confined to the flesh, being inscribed 'on the outside of houses and canoes, on weapons, instruments and tombs' in identifications that associate the environment with what is religious (Durkheim, 1995: 114). Durkheim reminds us, then, that being identified with a collectivity is accomplished through marks of membership.

These collective rituals, involving effervescent intoxications and bodily markings, are effective because people experience them as enacted *social* and *religious force* (Rawls, 1996). This leaves them with an awareness of inhabiting a body that is stronger because it is marked, 'possessed' and 'regenerated' by an 'external power' represented by the masks, decorations and physical 'inscriptions' that occur within or are re-focused upon by the ritual assembly (Durkheim, 1995: 218, 229, 353). Contemporary theorists such as Deleuze and Guattari (1972) utilize various terms, including 'Body without Organs', to express the openness of embodied subjects to external linkages, but Durkheim anticipated this insight while also demonstrating how individuals assume this expansionary existence through an intoxicating inhabiting of the collectively marked body. In focusing upon intoxication, moreover, Durkheim anticipated biological, neurological and psychological arguments that reinforce the significance he attributes to this process (Franks, 2010). These hold that intoxication involves neural pathways responsible for the pleasure we derive from social activities (including sex and social interaction) crucial to our evolutionary survival, and mirrors those strong feelings involved in the formation of human bonds (Tyler, 1988; Smith, 1992). Such arguments suggest that intoxicating experiences are key to stimulating involvement within collectivities. Intoxication is a 'ground form' of the social condition (Smith, 1992: 249), having operated alongside collective body markings/shapings in forming culture since before classical Graeco-Roman times (Wale, 2001: 2; Boothroyd, 2006: 10).

If the first two characteristics permeating the Warramunga and other socio-religiously effervescent assemblies involve stimulating and marking bodies in ritual gatherings, the third concerns the *directionality* of these processes. The term 'directionality' is associated with Weber's comparative interest in the particular expectations associated with specific religions (Roth, 1987). It is also akin to the function Parsons (1978) ascribes to cultural values in steering actions towards social norms (values that Parsons traced in the case of American 'institutionalized individualism' back to Christianity). Durkheim's concern with the trajectory initiated by totemically informed marking and intoxication, however, places as much importance on the direction of stimuli and feelings as on cognitive symbolism.

It is the totemic symbols and rites through which tribal gatherings are organized that mediate the directionality of those effervescent assemblies analysed by Durkheim. In the case of the Warramunga, this trajectory is governed by the need to appease the black snake prior to becoming immersed in an energetic remembrance of the ancestral creation of the tribe (Durkheim, 1995: 375–6, 379–82). More generally, the importance of directionality is evident in Durkheim's distinction between 'positive' and 'negative' systems of rituals or cults. The former focuses on the potentially sacrilegious encounter with what a collectivity holds to be sacred (e.g. the hallucinogenically-inspired meetings of tribal members with totemic animals in American Aboriginal religions, or the Christian Eucharist where God is eaten symbolically/sacramentally) (Reichel-Dolmatoff, 1990 [1972]). The latter maintains a separation between sacred and profane through – amongst other things – taboos. Historically, these have often excluded 'unclean' menstruating women from places of worship, for example, but also commonly maintain individuals as 'pure' by forbidding certain foods and practices on holy days.

Both positive and negative cults can increase the social and 'religious zest of individuals', whether proceeding via '[a]nointings, purifications and blessings' or through the personal sacrifices involved in 'fasts and vigils … retreats and silence' (Durkheim, 1995: 314). Neither affects a simple *quantitative* increase in stimulation, however, as both mark and prepare embodied subjects to act *in certain ways*: participants are imparted with a directionality in relation to the totemic priorities of the collectivity (ibid.). Hyper-excitement occurs *in relation to* the norms of the socio-religious sacred, organizing individual bodily markings and motivations in a manner that emboldens the collectivity.

The directionality informing embodied intoxication steers the whole tribal group, and also directs intra-group role transitions. Here, individuals often approach the threshold of status-passages through a period of liminal embodied-reconstruction-in-progress during which they are energized to inhabit newly marked bodies as they move through societal structures (Turner, 1969). Durkheim's (1995) account of the positive rites of Native American males, for example, highlights a series of exercises through which the young male works himself into a state of 'intense super-excitement', provoking 'hallucinatory' mental representations (Durkheim, 1995: 163–4). Drawing on Heckewelder's work, Durkheim (1995: 164) describes how preparation for this period involves fasting and intoxicating concoctions, resulting in 'visions' and 'extraordinary dreams to which the entire exercise' leads. In combination with the influence of dominant cultural symbols, this experience results in initiates encountering 'patron' animals to guide them in their new lives.

This mention of 'intoxicating concoctions' signals Durkheim's (1995: 228, 387) recognition that the directionality of totemic assemblies is often affected by *additional* stimulants that extend and shape further the delirium associated with collective gatherings. Poole's (1985, 1998) analysis of the Bimin-Kuskusmin of Papua New Guinea also recognizes that additional intoxication facilitates a 'journey inebriation' (Escohotado, 1999) in which the senses are 'spectacularly empowered' to facilitate contact with the divine. The core features of Bimin-Kuskusmin lore are transmitted via male initiation rituals demarcated through 12 stages of cultural hierarchy, physical conditioning and increasingly potent intoxicants. They culminate with ecstatic trances in which the individual 'remains in the body whilst the "social person" spirit travels out of the body, visiting the ancestral underworld to learn the secrets of esoteric knowledge' (Rudgley, 1993: 83–5). Schultes (1990 [1972]: 46) reveals another dimension to the directional potential of intoxicants in his study of the Algonkian Indians of eastern North America. Male initiates were administered *wysoccan*, that induced in them 'violent madness' and occasioned a loss of memory, enabling them to start adulthood by 'forgetting that they ever had been children'. Such assemblies of 'possession inebriation' (Escohotado, 1999) remove critical consciousness as a means of redirecting individuals into different roles via powerful culturally shaped stimuli and feeling (Rawls, 1996: 448).

Durkheim's analysis of totemically directed embodied intoxication was developed in relation to ethnographic materials on Aboriginal tribes, though he did not limit it to such contexts. Suggesting that collective body markings were associated with the origins of the world's major religions, he followed Procopius in noting that the first Christians had the name of Christ or the sign of the cross imprinted on their skin, for example, while early pilgrims tattooed their arms when visiting holy places 'with designs representing the cross or the monogram of Christ'. In more recent contexts, he identifies as significant collective markings among 'soldiers of the same camp, sailors on the same ship, and prisoners in the same house of detention', noting that such signs are not confined to 'mechanical solidarities' but exist within societies that celebrate individuality. Markings associated with particular styles or traditions have, indeed, flourished in Western milieu associated with 'the cult of the individual' (Durkheim, 1995: 234; Shilling, 2005b).

Some critics view Durkheim's theory as a Western anthropology of 'primitivism' that depicts traditional societies as inferior to 'the modern' (Kuper, 1988). In addressing such concerns, it should be noted that Durkheim was aware of the inadequacies of rigid histori-cal dichotomies, and emphasized the diversity of non-European peoples. He also studied non-Western cultures as a means of *criti-quing* Western cultural developments for their individualism, their reduction of humans to *homo economicus*, and their marginalization of collective religiosity (Mauss, 1969a; Durkheim, 1984; Kurasawa, 2003). Understood in this context, Durkheim's work on embodied intoxication remains relevant to the modern age, though we suggest it requires extending in relation to his other studies, and to contrast-ing modalities of the sacred, if we are to appreciate its utility and limitations.

## Intoxication and Social Differentiation

Durkheim's analysis of totemic tribes demonstrates how embodied intoxication and marking can constitute a bridge to socially consoli-dating religious experiences. Nonetheless, this analysis is appropriate to a *socio-religious* sacred context. Despite Durkheim's claims for its universal applicability, moreover, his writings on education and nationalism, professional ethics, the division of labour, and suicide, raise doubts about the scope and efficacy of intoxication in modern contexts. In particular, we can note Durkheim's concern about the growing differentiation of societies wherein religion becomes one social sphere amongst many, raising questions about whether socially consolidating experiences of intoxication can still impart directionality to *whole* societies, rather than to segmented groups within them.

This is the context in which we can appreciate the importance of Durkheim's distinction between religious and secular modalities of the sacred, each seeking to enframe experiences of intoxication in specific ways. Such a distinction is apparent in Durkheim's (1952: 158–9) analysis of the post-Reformation spread of Protestantism, and the subsequent emergence of an individualizing 'spirit of free inquiry', resulting in a fragmentation of collectively enframed experiences of the socio-religious sacred. This fragmentation increased risks of alienation and anomie in economies unfettered by moral foundations, and also fostered the differentiation of the religious and the secular that became the focus of Weber's analysis of the transcendent sacred. It is against such trends that Durkheim (1961, 1984, 1992) emphasized the importance of generating currents of enthusiasm in a secular sacred mode, in contexts such as education, reflecting his hope that modern individual experience could be enframed in ways that fostered broader patterns of social cohesion than those reflective of a now differentiated sphere of religion.

Durkheim may have been concerned to suggest how the generation and collective enframing of intoxicating experiences associated with religious and secular modalities of the sacred could constrain the deleterious effects of a 'market economy', but it is perhaps more realistic to utilize his interest in intoxication to explore how its contemporary manifestations are informed by radically opposed trajectories. This can be illustrated by focusing on 'prosperity Pentecostalism' as a form of mostly transcendently-oriented religious intoxication, before reflecting on the significance of sporting intoxication as a secular alternative harnessed to bio-economic and bio-political priorities.

## Other-worldly intoxication

It has been suggested that the huge growth of Pentecostalist Christianity during the latter decades of the twentieth century contains strong affinities with the international spread of capitalism – a relationship particularly evident in the case of 'prosperity Pentecostalism' (Martin, 2002; Poloma, 2003: 17; Meyer, 2004; Robbins, 2004). This 'health and wealth gospel' was not part of early twentieth century Pentecostalism, but by mid-century the idea that recipients of God's grace could receive financial and other blessings became prominent (Hollinger, 1991; Coleman, 2000). Centred on the message that it is God's will for believers to be 'rich, healthy, and successful', this religious form is centred upon an intense, individualized experience of religious intoxication. Involving personal encounters with the Holy Spirit, conversion and worship typically involve followers 'opening up' their bodies and minds to divine presence. Manifest through dramatic instances of the supernatural possession of embodied subjects – including speaking in tongues and fainting from the bliss of His presence in the mortal body – this intoxication has an other-worldly source and is frequently felt as 'a time of both great interiority and divine connection' (Miller, 1997: 91; Albrecht, 1999: 28–9; Poloma, 2003: 2, 21, 41).

Despite its differences from the Puritanism analysed by Weber as an exemplar of the transcendent sacred, Pentecostalism can be seen as recapitulating the Calvinist distinction between the religious and the secular. The intoxicating effervescence central to it has an extra-societal, religious source, while the worldly values it promotes appear to recognize and provide space for success within a secular, capitalist sphere. One of the defining features of prosperity Pentecostalism, indeed, is the extent to which it validates secular economic activity outside, as well as inside, major global centres of affluence. Maxwell's (1998) analysis of the Zimbabwe Assemblies of God, for example, demonstrates how the intoxicating presence of the Holy Spirit reinforces the Church's focus on habits of righteousness – involving charity, literacy and marital fidelity, and avoiding debt, smoking, drinking and secular entertainment – resulting in social mobility for some, while providing for others 'a code of conduct' which safeguards against 'poverty and destitution' (Maxwell, 1998: 351). Similarly, Chesnut (1997) associates the attractions of Pentecostalism in Brazil with its ability to provide individuals with an experientially emboldening spiritual power conducive to freedom from material deprivation. Founded in 1977, The Universal Church devotes two days a week to 'preaching the virtues of entrepreneurship' and, after gaining over a million members by the 1990s, even opened temples in the United States (Chesnut, 1997; Coleman, 2000: 37).

More broadly, the capacity of this religious form to adapt to, and thrive in, cultures as disparate as those in the United States, Sweden, Brazil and Zimbabwe suggests that the experiences and beliefs it promotes allow individuals to establish a productive connection to the economics of modern global capitalism (Comaroff and Comaroff, 1999, 2000; Coleman, 2000; Haynes, 2012). It is perhaps hard to think of a contemporary form of religion (associated with an intoxicating power seen as external to this world and individualized in its effects) that could be further removed from the totemism of which the black snake ritual of the Warramunga was part (discussed earlier as an example of what Durkheim identified as the intoxicating force of the socio-religious sacred). We might be tempted to suggest, in fact, that the forms of embodied marking and stimulation associated with the transcendent orientation of Pentecostalism provide an ideal counterpart for the consolidation and *expansion* of an economically dynamic secular sphere. For Berger (2006) and others, indeed, this religious form is responsible for the promotion of a 'revised protestant ethic' suited ideally to this outcome (de Boeck, 2004: 198; Wiegele, 2005; Haynes, 2012: 124).

Before making that conclusion, however, it is worth noting that Haynes (2012: 10), amongst others, rejects such interpretations (Brouwer et al., 1996; Maxwell, 1998; Meyer, 1998; de Boeck, 2004: 108; Gifford, 2004: 105ff.). Focusing on Pentecostalism and the morality of money on the Zambabwian Copperbelt, Haynes finds not rampant individualism but an enhancement of religious sociality and social cohesion among residents and Pentecostal churches in Nsofu. Inequalities were accepted and conspicuous consumption valued as a sign of grace, but consumption possessed social dimensions, signalling to others in the community those who might provide financial assistance in exchange for labour. As Haynes (2012) concludes, 'the bonds formed by such exchanges' are central to Copperbelt life.

Prosperity Pentecostalism and associated forms of charismatic worship do indeed build upon long standing 'seeds of individualism' evident in Christianity (Louth, 1997: 126–7). They also provide a transcendentally-oriented form of religion in which the primary focus of intoxicating encounters with divine force remains that of preparing people for an *other-worldly* community to be realized fully only *in the future*. Nevertheless, while Pentecostalism recognizes a differentiated secular sphere, it is concerned with transforming people's experiences of that sphere. Attempting to embody the Word of Christ – via such techniques as developing personal accounts of conversion, and seeking to externalize the Word as a guide to their daily action (Coleman, 2000) – the 'spirit-filled believer' ideally comes to see 'God at work in, with, through, above, and beyond all events' (Johns, 1999: 75; Poloma, 2003: 23). In this respect, following prominent themes within New Testament teaching, believers are *called out* of the world (John, 15: 19). In being 'called out', however, they are stimulated to *change their embodiment in this world* so they feel, think and act in a manner at odds with their previous existence (Philippians, 3: 21; Ephesians, 4: 22, 5: 1; see Martin, 1990: 163; Robbins, 2004: 128).

These transformations suggest that the aim of this religion is to reconfigure the individual's habitus so that it can at least partially effect an other-worldly steering of secular economic relationships. This is comparable to Poloma's (2003) study of the epicentre of the charismatic Christian revival, the Toronto Blessing. Worshippers were marked and emboldened in their relation to God as individuals (experiencing presences of God's love by laughing hysterically, weeping uncontrollably, or succumbing to the 'sacred swoon'). Nevertheless, they also returned with renewed enthusiasm to their workaday lives; revivified with a powerful sense that the commercial activities in which they were involved should be assimilated into their concern with belonging to a religious community (Poloma, 1996, 1998; Miller, 1997: 91).

The Pentecostal emphasis on this-worldly religious community may not be as strong as the socio-religious example used by Durkheim (1995), but it is evident even in the most unlikely of settings. Marti's (2008: 3) study of the neo-Pentecostalist Oasis Christian Centre in Hollywood (possessed of one of the largest multi-racial congregations in the country), for example, reveals how an experiential focus on the Holy Spirit was combined with a practical emphasis on 'financial well-being'. Yet far from religiously justifying unbridled economic individualism, Marti suggests that the Oasis Centre constitutes a religious community based on con-servative moral values that effect 'changes in self-perception'. Individuals saw themselves as, and became part of a team under, a spiritual authority that resulted in many turning down lucrative jobs in the entertainment industry on the basis of transcendent criteria (Marti, 2008: 172).

In summary, while the transcendent orientation of Pentecostalism does not display the inextricable bonding of the this-worldly and other-worldly characteristic of socio-religious modalities, it does have implications for earthly collectivities (Poloma, 2003: 30–2, 89–91, 95; see also Csordas, 1988). While Weber placed a secular-izing logic at the heart of his conception of the transcendental sacred, and while Pentecostalism certainly exhibits an elective affinity with global capitalism that may in future result in it becoming structured increasingly by economic considerations, this religious form can for now be seen as stimulating a resur-gence of religious feeling at the meso-level of people's private lives *and* in their attitudes towards the differentiated sphere of the workplace.

### Worldly intoxication

If prosperity Pentecostalism is illustrative of an other-worldly form of religious intoxication, commentators have associated an increasing range of apparently secular phenomena with overwhelming experi-ences that can substitute for religion in exerting socially cohesive effects on their participants (Featherstone, 1991; Tiryakian, 1995; Maffesoli, 1996; Malbon, 1999; Geraci, 2010). These phenomena range from rock concerts and rave/clubbing environments to politi-cal movements, shopping centres and virtual life on the internet. It is the sphere of *sport*, however, that has probably been assessed most frequently as fulfilling this purpose through its capacity to stimulate a heightened sense of excitement that binds people together within shared symbolic universes of meaning.

Taking inspiration from Durkheim's (1995) *The Elementary Forms*, the quasi-religious, intoxicating nature of sport is signalled variously with reference to its 'tribal' nature, with teams possessing totemic signs, and fans' bodies marked with replica shirts, scarves and sometimes tattoos. It is reinforced through observations that such inscriptions are 're-charged' while individuals gather together in arenas that function as sacred sites for effervescent, ritualistic and symbolic celebrations of collective identities (e.g. Goodger and Goodger, 1989; Miller-McLemore, 2001; Magdalinski and Chandler, 2002: 1).

While studies of sport often fail to distinguish between sport experienced as sacred and sport conceptualized as religion, it has become common to examine the collective rituals and celebrations of sports such as gridiron and NASCAR as manifestations of the socio-religiously embedded nation-state (Hoffman, 1992; Newman and Giardina, 2011). Explored more closely, however, the history of the relationship between sport and religion in the West has often involved more significant differentiation than such socio-religious approaches suggest. The Olympic Games originally honoured the gods and the state (Novak, 1992: 35), but sport has long been viewed as occupying a secular sphere, even if it has at times been thought of as possessing potential to steer individuals towards other-worldly goals.

Sport's association with a secular sphere goes back at least to St. Paul. Building on Aristotle's view that a healthy body could contribute to a balanced person, Paul utilized athletic images in his letters (Kerrigan, 1992: 253), but reminded Christians that 'worldly victories were fleeting and laurel leaves withered' (Flake, 1992: 175). Hoffman (1992: 111–2, 116–7) has articulated a contemporary manifestation of this tension by highlighting the dilemmas faced by evangelical athletes who seek to 'ritualise their performances as acts of worship' while not being sure that sport's 'win at all costs' social dynamic is worthy of 'sacred offering'. The key issue here is the *contingent* utility of sporting excitement for other-worldly ends. Examples of where this contingency has proved positive for religion include the role of 'Muscular Christianity' in shaping the upper classes in Victorian Britain (Mangan and Walvin, 1987), the evangelical aims of the Fellowship of Christian Athletes (founded 1954) in America, and Chandler's (2002) analysis of how the playing styles of Catholic and Protestant rugby teams in England were connected to divergent other-worldly orientations and patterns of Christian identification.

Viewed from the context of such religious forms, sport gains a level of 'moral seriousness' significantly different from that relating to individual sacrifices in the pursuit of 'limit performances' (Virilio, 2000). Its continued location within the secular sphere, however, becomes clear when sport is confronted with catastrophes. As Edge's (2007: 162) reflections on following Liverpool football club conclude, while 'the communion shared with' one's team can become essential to life, external realities 'compel even the most diehard fan' to reach beyond the differentiated sphere of sport to grapple with larger matters. These may not be irrelevant to sport, as the deaths of 96 Liverpool fans at Hillsborough in 1989 reveal, but are irreducible to them and evidence of a clear distinction between sport and religion. As Hervieu-Léger (2000: 105–6) argues, the treatment of Anfield as a shrine in which victims were remembered did not mean that there existed a 'religion of football', but that religious sentiments found expression in sporting milieu. Sport may be an activity treated as sacred by many of its participants, but this does not itself make it religious.

Moving away from Christian contexts that evidence distinction between the religious and sporting spheres, however, sport has elsewhere assumed strong elements of the socio-religious. In Japan, rituals associated with sumo wrestling – directed towards acknowledging and stimulating the intermingling of other-worldly forces with this-worldly practices – have been managed by successive ruling orders in order that they become an expression of Shintoism. In the case of Islam, Nauright and Magdalinski (2002) have demonstrated how the development of Muslim rugby teams in twentieth-century South Africa was harnessed to the goal of enabling individuals to cultivate assertive religious identities through the effervescent experiences associated with competition. Sport is here subjugated to *sharia* law – so that it constitutes an expression of the religious injunction to maintain the body's health, purity and modesty (Nauright and Magdalinski, 2002; Walseth and Fasting, 2003) – while it is intoxicating precisely because it is saturated with religious significance. A related example of this is that the *hijab* serves for many (not all) Muslim women as a means of demonstrating religion's importance to sport, as in other areas of social life.

Predicated upon weak levels of social differentiation and a strong sense that society is layered by other-worldly considerations, this socio-religious valuation of sport has been associated with conflict when competing modalities co-exist within a societal space or when it confronts other approaches towards sport. This is evident in Silverstein's (2002) analysis of sport and Islam in France; in the conflicts over religious dress in sport (Harkness and Islam, 2011); in the controversy caused by team names in a Californian Muslim football league (e.g. 'Soldiers of Islam' and 'Mujahideen'); and in analyses suggesting that sport in the West 'correlates unevenly with Islamic beliefs and codes of behaviour', excluding those who would utilize it as an extension of Islamic faith (Baker, 2007: 218; Burdsey, 2010). These examples highlight the importance of Magdalinski and Chandler's (2002: 5) warning that analyses of sport need to be attentive to how the combination of religious and secular influence in the field can constitute 'a divisive mechanism'.

If the intoxicating experiences associated with sport have been incorporated into both transcendent and socio-religious modalities, constituting a bridge to the consolidation of religious forms, the extraordinary economic valuation of competitive sport has in recent decades been highlighted by its global spread and commercialization. This commodification, coupled with the heightened instrumentalism and rationalism directed towards participants and spectators, suggests that the intoxicating experience of sport has been colonized increasingly by bio-economic and bio-political forces (Slack, 2005).

Economically, there is more at stake in many sports than ever before, with the benefits of winning and costs of losing adding heightened intensity to experiences of participation and spectatorship. Nevertheless, when children are signed up to represent sportswear companies, when wealthy competitors strike for higher wages (Mathisen, 2001), when television companies determine football schedules, and when players are fined more for wearing company logos that breach sponsorship deals than for racist behaviour on the pitch, the idea that sport exerts a 'religious' influence on the immanent frame of this-worldly activities seems increasingly far-fetched. Instead, it seems more plausible to suggest that sport is invested with extraordinary importance through being located within a market economy of lifestyle choices and options, profits and losses. In 2005, Americans alone spent over $89 billion on sports goods, for example, while over 7.6 billion admission tickets were sold to sports events (Hoffman, 2007: 2–3). Sports fans must expend considerable financial resources if they are to follow their team in person and/or via pay-per-view or subscription-television.

This does not prevent us from recognizing that competitors pray before, or wear symbols of their religious affiliation during, sporting events. It is also the case that some view as sacred 'peak' athletic experiences (James, 1983; Cooper, 1998; Csikzentmihalyi, 2008). Nevertheless, the degree of marketization and commercialization to which sport has become subject makes it difficult to associate it with what Durkheim sees as the integrative possibilities within socio-religious modalities of religious intoxication. Olympic games, world championships and cup finals may prompt excitement, but their usual location outside any significant other-worldly cosmology means there is less possibility for people to be united by conceptions of what is sacred to a group *as a whole* and with any *enduring* impact on social solidarity (Wickström and Illman, 2012). In discussing sports 'mega-events', for example, Horne and Manzenreiter (2006) and Giulianotti and Robertson (2012) recognize celebratory aspects of these occasions, but provide no grounds to suggest that any 'imagined' national or global community they evoke exerts enduring effects on the collective conscience. Indeed, in contrast to Durkheim's suggestion that the socio-religious sacred operates via the embodiment of *collectively mediated* religious phenomena, it is worth remembering that the construction of the bio-economic sacred depends on potentially transient *personal preferences*. As such, the influence of economic considerations in sport can be seen as exacerbating rather than lessening Durkheim's concerns about how socially consolidating experiences of intoxication might continue to impart directionality to society as a whole, rather than to socially segmented groups within it.

If sport has become linked increasingly to the economically directed stimulation and exploitation of experience, de-differentiating bio-political influences raise further questions about its capacity to constitute a bridge to religious forms. Of central importance to these influences is that sport has become an exemplar of the governmental regulation of bodies (Turner, 1984), with the hosting of major events enabling states to implement extraordinary security measures in relation to diverse populations (Haggerty and Boyle, 2012: 256; see also Atkinson and Young, 2008; Giulianotti and Klauser, 2012). Relatedly, the history of sports reveals a disciplining of bodies via a regimented organization of space in which performance is prioritized over creativity (Eichberg, 1998). Anxieties over performance-enhancing drugs highlight an additional element of bio-political governance via a concern with the molecular and genetic components of the body. This anxiety and regulation has taken place amidst the growing pharmaceuticalization of society in general (Bloor et al., 1988; Williams et al., 2011; Dumit, 2012). However, the existence of highly trained athletic bodies provides an ideological basis on which the general rationalization of the body can be naturalized as the fulfilment of human destiny rather than as a technologically directed imposition. As we shall now discuss, bio-political attempts to regulate intoxication in society *as a whole* also challenge Durkheim's account of intoxication as a bridging experience to a religious habitus.

## Intoxication and Bio-Political Regulation

Having illustrated how intoxicating emotional experiences can be harnessed to contrasting modalities of the sacred, we turn to Durkheim's (1984) concern that modernity was vulnerable to *abnormal forms* that failed to attach embodied subjects to religion or society. Durkheim's apprehension was associated with his view that the *quantity* and *quality* of embodied intoxication were crucial to determining whether the marking and effervescent motivating of body subjects would strengthen religious and social collectivities. While the former concerns the *amounts* of stimulation required to join individuals to something greater than themselves, the latter is concerned with directional issues regarding whether particular rituals and specific intoxicants actually attach individuals to the collectively shaped aspects of their embodied being (rather than, for example, to objects, 'highs' or obsessions undermining of these collective dimensions of physical being). In these terms, insofar as they do not attach individuals to societies *as a whole* but only to groups within differentiated social spheres, both the religious and the secular illustrations of *modern* intoxication we have considered so far can be considered 'abnormal'.

Durkheim's use of 'abnormal' arguably reflects nostalgia for societies shaped by a socio-religious modality of the sacred, since it implies that a totalizing social order shaped by surplus intoxication leading to a highly integrated cultural directionality is *the* baseline for analysis rather than one model amongst others. This nostalgia is also evident in his picture of modernity as a 'dispersed state', wherein life becomes 'monotonous, slack and humdrum', and people lack incentives to energetically occupy the body markings or habits through which they recognize themselves and others as members of an overarching collectivity (Durkheim, 1995: 217).

Despite such caveats, Durkheim's arguments can help clarify the distinctiveness of a modern context where the dominant approach to intoxication is characterized by bio-political and economic considerations, rather than being acknowledged as an experiential medium through which individuals become social beings (Durkheim, 1984: 291–328). Contemporary societies remain dependent on degrees of carefully regulated intoxication in order to produce the 'energized body/productive self' fit for capitalism, but increasingly legislate *against* the dangers of 'excessive' intoxication. This governance and stimulation of embodied subjects possesses a de-differentiating effect, moreover, in that it cuts across distinctive social spheres. It also ordinarily represents an engagement with *chemical* rather than collectively effervescent modes of intoxication. In this context, while Durkheim's primary interest in intoxication rested on that effervescence understood to be intrinsic to collective gatherings, his discussions of the use of plant-based stimulants to achieve complementary experiences help clarify the bio-political trajectory regarding intoxication in modernity (Durkheim, 1995: 228, 386–8).

In the socio-religious contexts examined by Durkheim, these stimulants were often viewed as possessing divine origins, and enabled those who consumed them to experience altered states of consciousness that illuminated the significance of mundane life (Schultes, 1990 [1972]: 14). Even in such contexts, however, stimulants were highly regulated: Fernandez (1990 [1972]: 250) shows how tribal cult leaders prevented the substantial ingestion of drugs outside initiation ceremonies in order not to confuse 'the flow of ritual action and the imitation of heavenly activity'. The regulation of intoxication is not new, then, but its transition from religious modalities to a non-religious modality of the sacred, centred on 'the government of people as biological beings by means of the administration of their bodies', signals the transfer of the *pastoral* powers of religious elites to the *bio-power* of the sovereign state (Foucault, 1983: 213–4; 1997; 2004a; 2004b; Segato, 2008: 204–5).

This transition involved cross-national and cross-religious struggles over legitimate intoxicants (propelled by colonial violence and intra-societal regulation and repression). The condemnation of alcohol within Islam, for example, was associated initially with its capacity to result in transgressions of social order, and with later attempts to discredit branches of Sufi mysticism, while the Catholic Church brought before the Inquisition Spaniards who returned with tobacco from America (smoking was perceived as satanic) (Escohotado, 1999: 56). Indeed, during the seventeenth century, the trafficking and consumption of tobacco attracted the death sentence in China, Persia and parts of Germany, as well as excommunication from the Catholic Church because of its supposedly deleterious effects on a range of religious and social priorities (Escohotado, 1999).

Despite the historical variety of these attempted regulations, how-ever, there emerged with Western colonialism the associated influ-ence of Christian notions of individualism and its recognition of a secular sphere; the rising importance attributed to rational imperial governance and economic productivity; and a global direction to intoxication's authorized ends. This was most evident in relation to industrialization. As Winkleman and Bletzer (2004: 347) note, sugar was readily accepted in Europe and its consumption encouraged by colonial administrations as a source of energy for labour, while cocaine was initially supplied to African-American dock and ware-house workers in the early industrial United States as an energizing means of raising productivity. Alcohol also had its place as a prophy-lactic against the demands of work, being seen temporarily in Britain and beyond in the seventeenth century as an anaesthetic against the strains of modern life, often included as part of the pay of labourers (Szasz, 2003: 45).

Views regarding the productive benefits of particular drugs were not uniform or static. Following a period of nineteenth-century lib-eral experimentation, Western states legislated against intoxicants associated with the dissolution of ego boundaries and the promotion of sociability (Jay, 2000). Alcohol was banned from workplaces (and for periods in the early twentieth century prohibited from parts of Europe and in America), while governments criminalized other intoxicants, such as marijuana, viewed as inimical to instrumentalism and possessive individualism (McKenna, 1992: 154, 160; Roberts, 1992; Bancroft, 2009: 30). In America, impetus for banning opiates came after the US invasion of the Philippines in 1898. Protestant missionaries reported 'socially debilitating' levels of addiction among Filipinos, initiating a sustained anti-drug campaign at home that led to the Harrison Act of 1914 (Winkleman and Bletzer, 2004).

The increased dominance of Western colonial powers – coupled with the tendency in Islamic societies to ban alcohol – resulted in a trend for acceptable forms of intoxication to become fewer and weaker. Tobacco was used previously in mind-altering strengths in its countries of origin, for example, in order to open individuals to intox-icating experiences of the socio-religious sacred. However, after its early denigration as a drug possessed of satanic connotations, it was used in the modern West in mild forms suited to palliative relief from the routines of instrumental life, yet ill-suited to reinforcing the delirium associated with effervescent assemblies (Lenson, 1995: 37; Hughes, 2003: 6). As tobacco became regulated, following concerns regarding its effects on health and productivity (Jackson, 1995), one of the most widely used stimulants became an intoxicant of legitimate choice. Of all modern intoxicants, given the resurgent demonizing of tobacco that emerged towards the end of the twentieth century, *caffeine* sits at the centre of attempts to enframe experiences of intoxication in secular terms, notably the bio-political regulation of bodies in the interests of productivity and the bio-economic commercialization of intoxicating products.

Possessed of a history in the West related to the development of commerce, insurance and bourgeois respectability (McKenna, 1992; Smith, 1995: 154–6), coffee was consumed ritually in commercial sites associated with 'honesty, reliability and moderation', helping to energize business dealings (Smith, 1995: 154–5). As Klein (2008) notes, coffee became a 'performance enhancer', a 'wakeful' drink, its popularity reflected in the 3,000 coffee houses that existed in London by 1700. These rivalled the popularity of taverns, and accelerated social change (ibid.: 96). While alcohol 'dulled the senses', coffee increased mental acuity, 'thereby promoting better business', and has become *the* liquid drunk by individuals needing to wake up for, and obtain a boost during, work (Gusfield, 1996: 69).

If the 'early morning caffeine fix has in the present day become so acculturated as to be hardly recognized as the chemical stimulus that it is' (Klein, 2008: 92), 'energy drinks' and a new generation of 'lifestyle drugs' such as Adderall and anti-anxiety medications have added further to those enhancements of productivity derived from chemical stimuli enabling people to feel alert and focused for extended periods (Miller, 2008; Dumit, 2012). These are balanced by other drugs, including anti-depressants, dispensed in large quantities in order to help people cope with the pressures of life within contemporary capitalism (Bancroft, 2009). The potential capacities of 'smart drugs' to raise productivity and performance to new levels, indeed, has provoked calls from scientists and ethicists for a public debate about such 'enhancements' (Jha, 2012).

Whereas traditional intoxication helped merge individuals into religious and social wholes, authorized drugs in the industrial era provided workers with the energy and attention necessary for a bio-political intensification of labour (Herlinghaus, 2010). While drugs that did not complement the norms of productivity and Christian sobriety were, under certain circumstances, placed within the control of medical authorities (Escohotado, 1999: 74–7), non-medicinal use was stigmatized and classified as immoral and illegal. Nor was this approach towards modernization confined to America, or the West. As Szasz (2003: 50) points out, Tehran prohibited opium in

1955 in an attempt to speed development at a time when use of the drug 'was considered a shameful hangover of a dark Oriental past'.

Thus, while authorized intoxication has not been obliterated within modernity, the prescriptive approach adopted by legislatures – manifest in the case of intoxicants labelled 'illegal drugs', but also evident in legislation controlling marches, meetings and worship – is suggestive of a context at odds with Durkheim's focus on the quantities and directional qualities of other-worldly attachments secured by the bodily stimulations of distinctively religious forms. Of concern here, in Durkheim's (1995: 218–9) terms, is whether 'the first phase' of low intensity 'monotonous, slack and humdrum' life has overwhelmed second phase assemblies in which frenzied body markings and intoxicating experiences reinvigorate society.

One of the problems associated with such 'overwhelming', if it has occurred, is that it can expose people to the dangers of pursuing 'egoistic' forms of intoxication in which desire to escape from devitalized life is pursued *as an end in itself*. This is arguably the case in modern drug addiction. A recurring theme in sociological studies of drug use classified and experienced as highly addictive, for example, is how the search for supply dominates users' lives (Bourgois and Schonberg, 2009). *What we have here is a meeting of insufficient intoxication at the societal level, and excessive intoxication at the individual level*: at each level, there is an absence of *collective* regulation (as opposed to legislative prescription). Addictive drug use still involves rituals, but these are highly localized and also result frequently in ill-health, disease and anti-social behaviour (Bourgois and Schonberg, 2009).

The danger of such egoistic tendencies is that they leave individuals exposed not only to the socially corrosive excesses of, for example, 'illicit' drug use, but also to the intoxicating appeal of sectarian groupings centred on centripetal nationalism, ethnic revivalism and terrorism (Meštrović, 1994; Scheff, 1994; Hervieu-Léger, 2000). Durkheim witnessed this in the anti-Semitism that characterized the Dreyfus Affair, and the virulent nationalist sentiment that contributed to the First World War. His concerns anticipated the rise of a fascism characterized by leaders seen as 'saviours', and associated with an iconography, dress and body techniques predicated upon drawing firm distinctions between insiders and outsiders (Durkheim, 1961: 77). In all these cases, *the vacuum of an insufficiently stimulating society provides the context in which individuals engage in practices damaging to themselves and/or overarching moral order*.

One major issue that leads us to the final substantive section of this chapter concerns the ambiguity that characterizes the relationship between religion and bio-political governmentality. We have noted that various religious forms have been actively supportive of governmental attempts to regulate intoxication, such as in the Christian and Islamic antipathies to alcohol. The vast, financially lucrative range of Protestant Christian dieting and fitness regimens in the US, furthermore, can be seen as confluence of religious and secular bio-political interests (Sack, 2000; Griffith, 2004).

Conflicts between the religious and secular are also centred increasingly on bio-political grounds; a fact reflective of the persistence of religions with a strong sense of their own other-worldly authority to exercise pastoral care and regulation over the body. This authority is, moreover, exercised typically in relation to matters of life and death increasingly enframed within the bio-political modality of the sacred. Such conflicts are often reduced to the *ethics* of bio-political interventions into bodies in relation to issues such as sexuality, conception and the family (Turina, 2013). Nevertheless, both transcendent and socio-religious modalities of the sacred also continue to exhibit emotionally *intoxicating* potentialities that not only challenge secular bio-politics generally, but also manifest violent reassertions of religious force in 'hyper-intoxicating' forms.

## Resurgent Religious Hyper-Intoxication

Durkheim (1995: 218, 313) suggested that religious collectivities can stimulate a hyper-intoxication so intense that resultant wild passions 'can be satisfied only by violent and extreme acts' even if these remain ultimately directed towards the reinforcement of collective orders. Thus, the brutal aggression of the Crusades and the French Revolution, and the delirium evident in tribal funeral rites and orgiastic feasts, are all identified as religious processes in which collective life is strengthened through an intoxication that threatens to overwhelm it, but that gets bequeathed to subsequent generations via symbolic and affectual 'chains' of memory that tie people to their legacy (Halbwachs, 1980; Durkheim, 1995: 213, 218, 397–403; Ramp, 1998; Hervieu-Léger, 2000). Mauss's (1969a: 11–12, 37) analysis of excessive intoxication within the *potlatch*, and Bataille's (1988) evaluation of the 'primitive feast', support further Durkheim's (1995: 209) emphasis on the importance of excessive as well as more mundane exchanges of intoxicating energies in overriding tendencies towards individualism and utilitarian calculation that might otherwise dominate social interaction.

With reference to modernity, however, there is ambivalence in Durkheim's writings concerning whether such hyper-intoxication remains conceivable. On the one hand, his analyses of suicide and the division of labour note the dangers, and growth, of inadequate social integration. Here, people's passions are left overregulated or unformed by collective relations and deprived of sufficient opportunities to be expressed in, and moulded through, socially authorized occasions (Durkheim, 1952: 258; 1984: 306). This can result in them developing 'unregulated temperament[s]', and searching for 'new sensations' disassociated from the consolidation of the collectivity. Such outcomes are damaging not only for social cohesion, but also for those individuals who fall victim to the 'infinity of desires', lost in a destructive inner search for a referent firm enough to impart sense to the experience of intoxication, and ultimately only feeling 'intoxicating' the prospect of death (Durkheim, 1952: 288, 281). On the other hand, however, Durkheim was convinced that religious intoxication is a basic human need and that new religious forces, new collectivities shaped by hyper-intoxicating effervescence, would emerge in the future (Pickering, 2009).

The first of these possibilities may be taken to suggest that the energizing, coping and lifestyle drugs characteristic of modernity constitute evidence that intoxication has been directed, rather inefficiently, towards regulating bare life. The second possibility, however, suggests that strong forms of intoxicating effervescence may become attractive to individuals, disrupting this bio-political orientation. The most spectacular manner in which this has occurred in recent decades involves the socio-religious resurgence of *sacrificial killing*.

Violent attacks involving sacrifice of self or others as a means of defending sacred rites and their associated forms of effervescence include the 'Jewish zealots' from the first century AD, the 'Hindu thugs' in India from the time of Herodotus, and the Muslim Ismaili 'Assassins' of the twelfth century (Bloom, 2007: 4). In recent decades, following its use in Lebanese conflict from the 1970s, so-called 'suicide bombing' has become a favoured technique of certain Muslim groups wanting to engage in 'psychological warfare' that can affect a large public audience. This situation was exemplified most tellingly in the terrorism of 9/11. Motivations for engaging in such 'suicide' attacks vary, but analysts point frequently to the significance of overwhelming, intoxicating emotions and the narrative linking of these to discourses of and reflections on injustice and humiliation. Esposito (2002), for example, cites the 'litany of deeply felt Muslim grievances against the West' – including the Crusades, European colonialism and the creation of Israel – 'superimposed upon current events' in such areas as Palestine, the Gulf and Chechnya. Coupled with the re-appropriation and reinterpretation of the Islamic notion of *Jjahiliyyah* (a damning condition of ignorance and unbelief associated with unbridled materialism, avarice and corruption) and the importance in the Qur'an of *jihad* together with its valorization of martyrdom, there emerges at times an intoxicating rage that helps motivate attacks involving the sacrifice of self and/or others (Anderson, 1983; Bloom, 2007: 86).

The assertively *religious* nature of such other-worldly legitimations of violent sacrifice operate in conflict with a wider societal/international context experienced as antagonistic to that religion's normative expressions of effervescence and associated conceptions of ultimate importance. Recognition of this is central to Strenski's (2003: 19, 26) discussion of Palestinian 'suicide bombers' who challenge the modern social order, in Israel, through violent expenditure of human life (see also Abufarha, 2009). For Strenski (2003: 19, 26), however, 'sacrifice' rather than 'suicide' best captures the actions of these bombers: they 'become holy' within their community through the effervescent sacrifice of themselves and their victims (sacrifices that reveal subordination to greater socio-religious imperatives), while their actions approximate to what Mauss refers to as 'total social facts', rather than strategic acts, in spilling over and influencing all areas of life. This is evident in the sacralization of the sites of their violence, the circulation of heroic stories about their lives, the offerings given to their bereaved families, the commemoration of them in prayer, and the revitalization of their communities in the face of conflict.

If modern secular forms of intoxication are typically segmented and limited in the sacrifices they require and the religious potentialities they contain, these virulent religious forms provide us with a reminder of what effects can be wrought by intoxication underpinned by forms of sacrifice characteristic of the socio-religious sacred. Such sacrifice is not the giving up of life on the basis of purely transcendent criteria, but involves a violent reassertion of the other-worldly significance of this-worldly threats of profanation; a violence that binds individuals into a socio-religious totality in opposition to the 'infidel enemy'.

## Conclusion

The continued vitality of Pentecostal worship and the growth of sacrificial bombings suggests that embodied intoxication may still constitute a bridge to religious experiences and identities despite the differentiated, segmented character of modern societies. The sacrificial killings practised and valorized in some Islamic groups do not only assert the sovereignty of God over matters of life and death with regard to the voluntary embrace of death by the 'suicide bombers', but also with regard to all others sacrificed as a result of the bombers' actions. In utilizing modern technological means of destruction, however, Islamic sacrificial bombings can be interpreted as an attempted reassertion of the other-worldly authority *in a bio-political form*. Similarly, prosperity Pentecostalism's attempted transcendence of a purely bio-economic modality nonetheless exhibits *adaptation* to its prevailing ethos via a focus on earthly success, thrift and other industrious habits.

Durkheim conceptualized such patterns of constraint, adaptation and marginalization relative to the determining features of modern societies as an 'abnormal' state of affairs, in that religions could not fulfil their 'normal' role of integrating individuals into a whole society. In the present, however, the development of social differentiation in terms of identities and lifestyle options alongside a de-differentiating bio-political regulation of bodies has been regularized. Our next chapter concerns the importance of *pain*. While religious enframings of intoxication continue to exert a significant social influence despite the constraints imposed by secular modalities of the sacred, the extraordinary power of the bio-political enframing of pain offers a less ambiguous example of the secularization of key areas of life in global modernity.

# 4

## The Bio-Medicalization of Pain

### Introduction

Debates about secularization often revolve around matters such as church attendance and expressed commitments to particular belief systems (Stark and Bainbridge, 1985; Casanova, 1994; Voas and Crockett, 2005; Bruce, 2011). It has long been recognized, however, that issues involving the biological constitution of human beings (particularly where these suggest *ontological frailty* in terms of disease, aging, pain and death) might be more fundamental in accounting for the continuing attraction of religious forms (Berger, 1967; Luckmann, 1967; Giddens, 1991; Turner, 1991; Turner and Rojek, 2001). Such recognitions typically invoke the power of *theodicy* (i.e. systems of thought that render unpleasant or threatening experiences meaningful) as a way of explaining religion's capacity to survive within modernity. Yet both religious and secular modalities of the sacred have historically sought to enframe and shape not just meanings, but also the general *embodied experiences* associated with human frailty (Mellor and Shilling, 2010b).

Having suggested in Chapter 3 that intoxication is contextualized increasingly within patterns of bio-economic and bio-political secularization, we now argue that experiences of *pain* offer a persuasive example of the diminishing power of religion in the wake of the increasing authority of the bio-political sacred. In making this argument, we demonstrate that while religious modalities of the sacred traditionally possessed power over ultimate matters of life and death, these have in many ways been reframed as a *secular* management of the 'sanctity of life' within modern bio-medicine at both macro-institutional and also more private, personal levels of society (Bataille, 1993; Benjamin, 2004). Surgeons and physicians, rather than religious elites, are now the authorized 'technicians of pain relief', achieving this status alongside the invention of anaesthetics, the growth of pharmaceuticals, and the incorporation of pain as a variable in the 'sick role' (Parsons, 1991). The accelerated pace of contemporary work and leisure, coupled with the sedentary nature of many jobs and pastimes, may have resulted in a proliferation of health complaints that echo late nineteenth-century suggestions that modernity promotes stress-related 'neurasthenia' among its urban populations. Nevertheless, the only legitimate 'answer' to these problems, across differentiated sectors of society, is increasingly found in medicine rather than religion (McTavish, 2004; O'Malley, 2005).

This bio-medical dominance contrasts with what might be referred to as the *bio-religious* manner in which pain was dealt with in earlier ages. Here, religious theodicies justified the existence and distribution of pain (Bowker, 2007), philosophies promoted approaches to pain incorporating 'the form or way of living proper to an individual or group' (Agamben, 1998), and collectivities engaged with pain as a moral issue. Plato believed pain could restore order to the soul (Glucklich, 2001: 18), for example, while Durkheim (1995) viewed as 'techniques of morality' the self-harm central to Australian Aboriginal piacular rites. Individuals' experiences of pain were linked to the symbols and moral orders of society and the cosmos, acting as a potential bridge to a religious habitus.

Modern bio-medicine, in contrast, has restricted the meaning of pain to a technical problem within the confined space of the individual organism. Scientific and medical developments over the last two centuries even suggest that research into the molecular levels and micro-mechanisms of pain, alongside recent pharmacological advances, could result in its wholesale eradication (Coakley and Shelemay, 2007). Pain itself, however, has been less than fully cooperative in this project; an obstinacy recognized by neuroscientists. As Fields (2007) argues, the gap between the physical trauma and stimuli that cause pain and people's widely differing felt experiences of and reflections on pain shows the importance of both neural pathways *and* the power of culture, social relationships and religious commitments in shaping subjective experiences of pain.

Another reason that pain refuses to become a technical issue is that religious and cultural norms still shape people's views of the *value* of pain. Pain, in some contexts at least, is viewed positively, and the authority of bio-medicine has been contested. In August 2008, for example, Syed Mustafa Zaidi, a 44-year-old man from Manchester, was convicted of child abuse for pressurising two boys, aged 13 and 15, to engage in self-flagellation with a five-bladed whip (*zangir-zani*) as part of a traditional Shi'a Muslim Muharram ceremony commemorating the death of Hussein (the grandson of the Prophet Muhammad). The reaction to his trial throughout the British media was almost uniformly hostile to, and uncomprehending of, the socio-religious justification offered for Zaidi's actions (Kazmi, 2008). In Shi'a parts of the Muslim world, however, such practices are admirable, since they are associated with grieving the martyrdom of Hussein while also signifying, through indifference to pain, a purity and willingness to undergo any ordeal for their religion. Amongst Shi'as in Pakistan, for example, self-flagellation in Muharram begins early, with boys as young as five participating, watched proudly by their mothers in admiration of their 'manly courage' (Hegland, 1998: 248).

The prosecution of Zaidi raises questions about the extent to which pain might still be a bridge to religious experience (rather than an issue of cruelty and abuse or, alternatively, a symptom of illness), and this chapter addresses the potential of pain in three stages. First, we account for the incredulity displayed towards the religious practice of individuals such as Zaidi by exploring how the contemporary sensitivity to pain developed in Western modernity. The invention of anaesthetics and the dominance of bio-medicine were important, but so too were far wider changes in governance, penal reform, and the influence of Christian as well as secular ethics that validated the pursuit of pleasure. These factors contributed to a gradual hiding away of violence and pain behind the scenes of social life that stimulated changes in the affectual make-up of individuals (Elias, 2000). It was in this context that the religious impositions of pain came to appear primitive and dangerous.

Second, after noting how sociological analyses reflect this aversion to pain, but also reveal the existence of a zone of indeterminacy in which religion can validly help individuals deal with its effects, we focus on the constructive potentialities of pain. Mauss's analysis of 'body techniques' demonstrates that the physiological stimuli associated with pain, people's subjective feelings of pain, and their classifications of and reflections on pain have been, and still are, combined in various ways. Durkheim (1995: 403) takes this analysis further by suggesting that pain is foundational to the construction of *any* culture or social identity. Viewed in this context, the bio-medical conception of pain appears as but one of several approaches evident across distinct modalities of the sacred.

Third, we develop these analyses of Mauss and Durkheim through a comparative account of socio-religious Shi'a Muslim encounters with pain and those transcendental orientations characteristic of early and medieval Christianity, demonstrating that people's orientations and reactions to pain need to be understood in the context of variable patterns of religious and secular authorization. These patterns have ranged even within the West from the self-in-pain as a normative Christian identity involving self-sacrifice, to the pain-free self as a model of contemporary productivity.

In conclusion, we recognize that bio-medical authority central to the extraordinary power of bio-political governance has reduced the capacity of pain to act as a bridge to religious experiences and identities, but suggest that the relationship of this authority to Christianity is complex. The medicalized belief that the world can be saved *from* pain contrasts with Christian beliefs that the world could bear pain, could be cured from pain, but could also be saved *through* pain, and rejects the view of pain as a vehicle of self-sacrifice. Nevertheless, both bio-medicine and Christianity express a *heightened sensitivity* to feelings of pain. This differs from the Shi'a *indifference* to pain, raising the possibility that Christianity itself helped reduce the capacity of pain to constitute a bridge to religion in the West. As Parsons (1978) suggests, if Christ helped save the world from pain, have not these values become institutionalized through bio-medical authority in the West?

## Saving the World From Pain

The bio-medical approach, and its opposition to the infliction of pain for non-medical purposes, is associated with the re-classification of pain as localized and manageable. This approach gained ground during the nineteenth century, supported by the invention of anaesthetics in the 1840s, a development that enabled pain to be seen as 'strictly a medical problem and a matter that pertains to the body rather than the entire person' (Glucklich, 2001: 179). This new outlook was allied to the development of physiology as an experimental science and took inspiration from the Greek physician Galen's writings on the subject and Descartes' idea of a pain system carrying messages from skin receptors to the brain centre. Pain became a *natural* symptom, removed from associations with other-worldly matters, and a readable inscription of physiological problems amenable to surveillance, control and treatment (Melzack and Wall, 1988; Armstrong, 1995; Lupton, 1997; Conrad, 2007; Hankinson, 2008).

Two things followed this subsuming of pain within medical science. First, individuals in pain were transformed into *patients*, subject to the medical gaze, and charged with entrusting a physician with their 'problem' (Glucklich, 2001: 7, 179). Pain could only be validated in this way: if a doctor associated pain with a recognized cause it was real, but patients who refused to seek such recognition or who found themselves possessed of medically unexplained pain were left to struggle with an illegitimate 'condition' (Nettleton, 2004). Second, it became difficult to approach the experience of pain outside the parameters of aversion and avoidance. Pain, at most, was to be borne temporarily as a side-effect of treatments designed to restore health: it was not a vehicle of self-sacrifice, and neither was it to be visited on others as a sacrificial offering (Morris, 1993: 22–3; Pincikowski, 2001; Norris, 2009: 23). Withstanding *unavoidable* pain remained a mark of character, and often a badge of masculinity (Mangan, 1986; Seidler, 1998). While it was recognized that the rigors of industrial society could provoke painful disorders in women and intellectuals (Mullan, 1988), the *wilful* infliction of pain on the self was usually perceived as a marker of mental 'illness'.

This bio-medical approach revolutionized pain's significance – altering its experiential meaning and reducing radically the social and cosmic space it inhabited – but it was not the only factor to effect these changes. Elias (2000) has argued convincingly that shifting approaches to pain developed alongside the growth of state monopolies of violence, and a division of labour that multiplied the social interdependencies individuals had to negotiate in order to survive and prosper. These circumstances necessitated that people took more note of how they inflicted and responded to pain (unplanned outbursts could result in punishment and spoilt identities), resulting in a gradual moderation of people's 'affect structures'. As physical violence came increasingly to be 'stored behind the scenes of everyday life', and impression management became more important, there was a growth in barriers and sensitivities associated with the imposition and experience of pain (Elias, 2000: 372–3).

There is no absolute start point to the processes identified by Elias, but the arguments he makes about increasing sensitivity towards pain, a sensitivity that facilitated the dominance of medicalization, can be illustrated with reference to two related developments. These involve the rise of secular utilitarian ethics, which followed their Christian counterparts in identifying pain as a negative value, and associated penal reforms that altered fundamentally the roles of pain and violence in systems of discipline.

The first of these, the rise of secular utilitarian ethics, occurred after the collapse of Absolutism and associated notions of Divine Order following the sixteenth-century religious wars in France and the seventeenth-century English Civil War. Rulers and philosophers across Europe faced anew the task of identifying a firm basis on which social life could be organized in order to avoid a Hobbesian 'war of all against all'. In Britain, this quest sought to discover in human sentiments and passions 'the very currency of sociability' (Mullan, 1988: 24), and assumed religious and secular manifestations. Gay (1939 [1731]), for example, invoked a benevolent God to justify the pursuit of happiness as a moral and religious good, while Bentham (1789) developed a far more influential variant of utilitarian philosophy. Building on the writings of Hume (1739–40), Bentham suggested that the promotion of pleasure and avoidance of pain provided firm secular principles for morally righteous action. Actions, irrespective of whether they were religiously significant, could be classified as good if they increased happiness and pleasure for the greater number, and discreditable if resulting in a net increase in pain.

This growing identification of pain as a negative value was reflected further by the efforts of Bentham and others in penal reform. These reforms constituted a radical break from early and medieval European systems of justice that placed pain at their centre. Past forms of punishment included 'trial by ordeal', and judicial torture in which finely graded degrees of pain were applied to the body in order to elicit confession from the guilty. Most spectacularly, the infliction of pain was central to sovereign displays of public punishment wherein the monarch's power was imprinted on the offender's body in a ripping asunder of flesh and bones. This continued well into the eighteenth century, as evidenced by Foucault's (1979) powerful description of the 1757 execution in France of Damiens, the regicide. Reformers during the late eighteenth and nineteenth centuries, in contrast, shifted punishment away from bodily pain, towards control and correction. This was exemplified by Bentham's proposal for the Panopticon, a prison in which constant visibility and surveillance encouraged inmates to monitor and reconstruct their *own* behaviour. As Foucault (1979: 11) notes, '[f]rom being an art of unbearable sensations', reformers sought to transform punishment into 'an economy of suspended rights' in which the body was controlled 'only to reach something other than the body itself': the mind or soul of the prisoner (ibid.).

Penal reform was motivated by various factors, but rising sensitivity to the imposition of pain and its social consequences was certainly one of them. Focusing on the brutality of public executions, middle-class reformers in Britain became concerned about the 'hardened indifference' of spectators, and the disincentive such spectacles exerted on the development of fellow feeling which could promote social solidarity between individuals from different social backgrounds (McGowen, 1986: 315, 322). Reformers such as Wilberforce favoured gentler justice that could restore society to the offender (ibid.: 327), more in keeping with broader social reforms and medical advances: the development of anaesthesia was significant not only for making surgery bearable, but also because it contributed to a commitment in Victorian Britain to a general alleviation of pain (Snow, 2008).

These attempts to minimize pain in society were accompanied by a more general regulatory regime in which labour was viewed as an effective moral 'tutor'. Hard work was identified by governments, by Puritans, and by Counter-Reformation Catholics as a pedagogic means of developing moral values, and increased importance was placed on society's productive capacity (Garland, 1990: 98). Pain was here a negative disruptor of moral 'education' and economic efficiency, and attempts to contain its 'contaminating' consequences grew during the nineteenth century before culminating in the twentieth century with the institutionalized 'sick role' (Parsons, 1991). Mediating the patient–doctor relationship in a manner congruent with society's moral values and productive capacity, the sick role refuses to ascribe pain with positive meaning outside of specifically authorized exceptions associated with this-worldly instrumental goals (Morris, 1991, 1993; Rey, 1995; Pincikowski, 2001).

If medicalization developed in a context that narrowed the normative meanings of pain, and the social space in which it is legitimized, it is no surprise that religious practices involving its wilful imposition should be viewed with suspicion. In centuries past, pain could be validated as 'visionary', providing means for individuals to glimpse the Divine in this world, while both European and Eastern ideas about purifying the self from sin involved voluntarily imposed painful ordeals (Morris, 1991: 131; Glucklich, 2001: 28). The bio-medical paradigm had, by the twentieth century, however, equated pain with this-worldly issues of sensation, location and control (Kleinman, 1988). It was no longer governed by religious considerations (Conrad and Schneider, 1992; Morris, 1993: 195).

The modern West may display unprecedented sensitivity to pain, but exceptions exist to this general picture. Elite athletic training involves pushing the body to its limits, for example, while retired competitors frequently suffer from arthritis, and the term 'battered child athlete' has become commonplace in describing the effects of overtraining for young children (Hargreaves, 1994). Coping with pain and 'playing hurt' features in many sporting cultures, while the ability to withstand and inflict pain has long been characteristic of masculine success in contact sports (Curry, 1993; Howe, 2004;

Atkinson, 2008). Pain is here authorized in relation to the instrumental goal of winning, with personal sacrifice validated if it helps the team/nation overcome opposition. Occupations other than sport also socialize members into accepting pain. Labouring as an army cadet or ballerina may seem to involve diametrically opposed gendered roles, but both cultivate the ability to distinguish pain from injury, and the capacity to cope with high levels of pain (Kotarba, 1983; Aalton, 2007; Lande, 2007). Pain is used in these and cognate professions as a means of objectifying the body in order to produce individuals inured to the hurts that could otherwise disrupt their performances.

Contemporary body modification shares this 'no pain, no gain' philosophy, as evidenced by the deprivations associated with dieting regimes (Monaghan, 2007), working out (Sassatelli, 2000), and cosmetic surgery dedicated to building the 'body beautiful' (Pincikowski, 2001). Increasing numbers of people are prepared to endure risk and pain in order to approximate more closely to ideals of physical beauty (Davis, 2003; Gimlin, 2012). Sexual subcultures centred on sadomasochism, tattooing, piercing and scarification embrace pain even more willingly, though do so in a constrained way: the primary emphasis of sadomasochism centres on issues of consent and sensitivity to others' feelings, involving carefully circumscribed engagements with pain (Beckmann, 2001: 102). Similarly, while the 'neo-primitive' movement associated with Fakir Musafa seeks to construct identity through painful ritual techniques drawn from traditional cultures, it is the modification of the body, rather than the desire to embrace pain, that underpins them (Farvazza, 1996: xviii; Klesse, 2000: 16). Furthermore, participation in such sub-cultural forms remains voluntary and individualist, rather than obligatory and communal (Torgovnick, 1995; Klesse, 2000; Turner, 2000), suggesting that they do not constitute those widely *culturally authorized* body techniques possessed of general social efficacy analysed by Mauss.

These engagements with the body are diverse. Nevertheless, while their 'no pain, no gain' philosophies transgress bio-medical norms, they possess characteristics that imply that their deviation from this model is not as great as might first appear. First, while they indicate acceptance of a limited degree of self-sacrifice, they are exceptions made in pursuit of *instrumentally rational, this-worldly* ends. Second, such instances of acceptable pain remain subject to surveillance by the medical profession (e.g. the British Medical Association's opposition to boxing). In other words, they do not operate completely outside the medical/scientific gaze and, as in the case of controversies surrounding cosmetic surgery, are vulnerable to contestation because of this gaze (Liao and Creighton, 2007).

If we wish to explore whether pain might still be enframed in ways that escape these shared characteristics, potentially offering a bridge to a religious experience, we face a problem. Recent writings in sociology are of limited help: critical of the bio-medical approach to health and illness, they nevertheless tend to reinforce its conception of pain as negative. Despite this limitation, however, they usefully identify a 'zone of exceptionality' in which bio-medical norms do not apply; a zone that prompts us to view pain in alternative ways.

### The sociology of pain and the pedagogic techniques of pain

Sociologists have analysed patient attempts to have their pain validated (Priel et al., 1991; Nettleton, 2004); cultural and gendered variations in feelings of and reflections on pain (Zborowski, 1952; Zola, 1966; Bendelow and Williams, 1998); the damage chronic pain inflicts on self-identities (Charmaz, 1983); pain relief in child-birth and dentistry (Arney and Neill, 1982; Nettleton, 1989); and pain as a challenge to mind–body dualism (Bendelow and Williams, 1995). Pain has also been explored within analyses of 'the problem of sociodicy' (Morgan and Wilkinson, 2001), and is central to Turner's (2006: 9) theory of human rights. Nevertheless, while exploring pain as a phenomenon that *threatens* identities and cultures, such studies have yet to explore fully how it can be *embraced collectively* as *positively constitutive* of culture. Illich (1977) recognizes that pain was made tolerable historically by its integration into meaningful settings. Kotarba (1983) explores how pain is managed in occupations such as heavy manual work, and Carmichael (1988) analyses how people put pain to creative social use. Frank (1997) and Kleinman (2007) supplement these analyses in exploring how illness and crises can result in creative insights into life. Contributions focusing on culturally normative flights into pain are rarer, however, suggesting that sociology equates pain with *disruption*; a disruption which remains difficult to communicate as meaningful outside of medical parameters (Smith, 2008).

While sociology is often critical of medical norms, then, its dominant approach towards pain displays a similarly instrumental orientation. Pain is negative because it interrupts our intentional activity: the social and material world recedes from view and we become reduced to our organic being. Pain is 'the very concretization of the unpleasant', placing on recipients 'an affective call' that summons attention to its 'gnawing, distasteful quality' (Leder, 1990: 73), yet at the same time is meaningless (Morgan, 2002a: 79; 2002b). This can result not only in the recession of meaning, but also, as Scarry (1995) argues in the case of torture, the *obliteration* of the cultural and of the individual self. Pain *unmakes* selves and worlds.

More usefully, sociology has revealed a zone of exceptionality that emerges when inexplicable pain and terminal illness defeats bio-medicine and in which religion is drawn upon by individuals in a manner no longer viewed as unacceptable (Berger, 1967; Frank, 1997; Morgan and Wilkinson, 2001). Norris's (2009) account of people using religion to cope with terminal cancer and other painful life-struggles provides an excellent exploration of this zone. Her study reveals that attempts to draw upon notions of Christ's sacrificial suffering as redemptive in the face of mortal illness often occur after the failure of medicine, but are sanctioned normatively only in the context of palliative pain relief as individuals progress towards death (Norris, 2009: 30).

Another important issue raised by Norris's (2009: 30) study is the importance of early religious training in shaping engagements with pain. For Norris (2009: 30), particular forms of religious training in childhood shape orientations towards pain amongst the terminally ill, even if they had consciously rejected the religious faith of their childhood in later life. In the face of crises, for example, and despite the adoption of alternative religious identifications (e.g. becoming a Buddhist), those raised as Catholic Christians eventually returned to their faith, such as the woman 'brought back to Catholicism by her cancer' (Norris, 2009: 30). Confronting pain untamed by medicine, early habits of prayer, confession and worship resurfaced as resources enabling it to become meaningful in the event of medicine's failure and death's inevitability.

These observations highlight again the importance of the development of body techniques for the construction of a religious habitus. We know from the writings of Mauss (1973a, 1973b) that the seemingly most natural or unnatural actions of embodied subjects are learned through apprenticeship in culturally specific contexts. It is these body techniques that constitute the biological, psychological and cultural phenomena through which societies reproduce themselves. Thus, the ways in which individuals feel and express pain, and the broader cultural classifications and reflections associated with these feelings and actions, are subject to a learning process. In the contemporary West, children learn from a young age how to express their pain (McGrath, 1990; Moules and Ramsay, 2007). Patients learn how to articulate pain during medical encounters, and soldiers, amongst others, learn to ignore pain under certain circumstances or appreciate its significance as a signal of life under others (Morris, 1991; Pincikowski, 2001: 5).

Mauss's analysis also recalls Durkheim's (1982: 39, 52–3) emphasis on social facts becoming evident in the experiences, habits and appearances of individuals as much as in social institutions (Durkheim, 1982: 39, 52–3), while Norris (2009) highlights the importance of these writings. Her study reveals not only how early forms of learning can resurface in acutely distressing situations, but also implies that while the acquisition of body techniques associated with Christianity may result in the resurfacing of religion, the dominance of other religious techniques may be associated with a *far larger presence of religious engagements with pain*. This is the context within which we now consider how body techniques different from those dominant in the contemporary West are associated with distinctive alignments of pain's physiological, feeling and reflexive dimensions.

## Saving the World Through Pain

Norris's (2009) research on pain and the limits of medicine suggests that there exists a space for religion that begins when bio-medicine fails, in which religious hope and action become an understandable refuge of last resort for those dealing with incurable pain and terminal illness. In contrast to the idea that pain occupies a residual space in social and personal life, however, Durkheim provides us with a contrasting perspective that makes the human engagement with pain *central* to the constitution of *any* society or social subject. In this context, Mauss's suggestion that body techniques structure how individuals interact with pain becomes central to our understanding not only of how people engage with pain when medicine fails, but also as an ongoing aspect of sustaining society and their social existence within it.

Durkheim (1973: 152–3) explicates this view in his analysis of the *homo duplex* nature of humans; an analysis that enables us to assess voluntarily embraced pain as socially normative rather than deviant. For Durkheim, the collective character of shared morals and practices inevitably clashes with the egoistic desires of individuals; desires which must be sacrificed for individuals to enjoy the fruits of cultural existence (Pickering and Rosati, 2008). Society, indeed, 'cannot be formed or maintained' without us making 'perpetual and costly sacrifices' involving 'painful tensions' and 'violence to certain of our strongest inclinations' (Durkheim, 1973: 163). While pain is in one sense constitutive of culture in general (Durkheim, 1995: 316–7; Rosati, 2008: 50), specific modalities of the sacred engage with and build upon pain in distinctive ways.

This is most evident for Durkheim (1995: 403) in socio-religious contexts wherein pain is systematically nurtured through rituals of asceticism and mortification, affirming and intensifying commitment to a society saturated in every respect with religious significance. Nevertheless, different religious forms have utilized pain in contrasting ways. The iconographies of Buddhism and Christianity, for example, where the serene detachment of Buddha contrasts with the agonized body of Christ nailed to a cross, signal very different things about pain and suffering (Mellor, 1993). However, while Buddhist *detachment* from pain can be contrasted to the Christian *embrace* of it, in what follows we seek to illuminate further the case raised in the introduction to this chapter by exploring what is at stake in a comparison of the latter with traditional socio-religious Shi'a ritual practices, which seek to nurture *indifference* to pain.

### The Christian embrace of pain

Two defining features of Christianity have been the belief that Jesus was God *incarnate* as a human being, and the attempt to make sense of the fact that he died, following torture and crucifixion, in agony. This is made still more poignant for Christians by the fact that Christ was especially sensitive to pain (to that inflicted on others, but also to pain inflicted upon him) and that the cause of pain was associated with original sin. These characteristics connected pain with truth in Christian theology, promoting an associated interest in the religious potentialities of the human body (Von Balthasar, 1982; Asad, 1983; Bynum, 1987, 1989; Cohen, 1995; Beckwith, 1996). As early as the second century, Christianity developed a view of the human self as a body in pain that facilitated religious explorations of how believers could not just bear pain, or be cured of pain, but be *saved through* pain (Perkins, 1995). Such orientations gave rise to distinctive and sometimes overlapping Christian traditions towards pain that included, from the thirteenth to the fifteenth century, extreme sensitivity to the pain Christ endured for the sake of humanity, combined with fascination for how pain might be experienced and expressed in ways that offered a route towards religious illumination and salvation (Cohen, 2000; Trembinski, 2008). The relationship between pain and the transcendent sacred was here investigated in various ways, using diverse means.

Exploring the first part of this history, from the second century, Perkins (1995) contrasts the Christian valuation of pain and suffering with the vision of a self ultimately untouched by these experiences, evident in different cultural sources such as Greek romance narratives and Stoic texts. Building on other cultural innovations, including developments in Greco-Roman medicine in the early Empire, early Christian writings envisaged the world as full of decay and death, and portrayed the religious body as 'universally lacerated and harassed … scraped with claws, pierced with knives, roasted, whipped, strangled and mauled by beasts' (Perkins, 1995: 142, 15). Instead of representing such pain as defeat, dishonour or irrelevant to virtue, however, reports of martyr acts shared between Christian communities, and the so-called *Apocryphal Acts of the Apostles* (texts relating the lives and deaths of John, Peter, Paul, Andrew and Thomas), depict pain, suffering and self-sacrificial martyrdom as *means to* Christian fulfilment and salvation. As Andrew argued, martyrdom was not reserved for the apostles, but was reward for *all* who placed faith in God (Perkins, 1995: 27). This was reflected by the subsequent popularity of hagiographies that began to appear in the middle of the fourth century containing an unprecedented focus on pain and suffering.

These varied accounts expressed distinct orientations towards pain. As Perkins (1995) notes, written reports of martyr acts evoked the righteousness of, impassivity to and endurance of pain and torture, while also portraying Christians as impervious to punishments inflicted upon them. These would sometimes follow the *Apocryphal Acts* in highlighting the superior curative powers of Christianity, but also attribute to suffering divine affirmation. God sometimes visits punishment on humans 'not necessarily for chastisement, but because suffering is best' (Perkins, 1995: 130). Nonetheless, these accounts are united by a vision that considers issues pertaining to pain and death in the context of a victory of transcendent faith against corrupt social orders (Brown, 1988; Barton, 1994). In contrast to its contemporary bio-medicalization, Christianity did not view pain in relation to its implications for the accomplishment of this-worldly health and functioning, but in the context of *other-worldly* interventions and commitments.

Christian explorations of pain assumed greater expressivity during the late medieval era. The fact that all major discourses on the subject – in theology, medicine and law – viewed physical pain as a function of the soul made its experience and expression of huge transcendental significance (Cohen, 2000: 44). Martyrdom was rarer during this period, but the religious potential of pain meant that the thirst for it 'was ever present' while much of the devotional life of holy figures during this period revolved around (often self-inflicted) pain (ibid.: 61–3). Emphasizing the enthusiasm with which bodily practices including self-flagellation, whipping, cutting and crucifixion were associated, Bynum identifies evident *delight* in feeling pain, since suffering bodies brought the faithful closer to God (Bynum, 1987: 246–50; 1989: 163–70). The body in pain was a privileged route towards redemption signalled by the tortured, suffering body of Christ nailed to the cross (Bynum, 1989: 170).

These themes are developed in Beckwith's (1996: 62–3) discussion of 'crucifixion piety' during this period, a phenomenon characterized by prayers to Christ's limbs, and by the popularity of poems focused on pain's productive religious consequences. *The Prickynge of Love*, for example, articulates the widespread 'cult of the five wounds' in which the worshipper expresses a desire to 'merge' with the nails piercing Christ's body, and with the cross on which he hangs, while the wounds themselves are 'wombs' or 'breasts to be sucked' (Beckwith, 1996: 58). The desire to *imitate* Christ's suffering is a particularly strong feature of this religiosity, reflecting the transcendent sacred capacity to enframe this-worldly experience in other-worldly meanings. Discussing the English saint Margery Kempe, for example, Beckwith (1996: 81–2) talks of an 'apprenticeship in suffering enjoined by her imitation of Christ', a willing assumption of pain so visceral Kempe imagines herself *becoming* Christ.

Christian body techniques involving self-inflicted pain were deployed publicly as well as privately. Self-flagellation, in particular, was sometimes a private act, but processions of self-flagellators exhibited patterns of ritual scourging that were brutal and bloody, yet carefully staged public events (Largier, 2006: 89; Kreuder, 2008). Here, the aspiration was 'not merely to have faith', but 'literally' to embody an image of Christ during the performance of flagellation (Kreuder, 2008: 181). As public acts, and in a context where contemplation on, and imitation of, the physical suffering of Christ was immensely important to lay devotion (Trembinski, 2008), such flagellations had a profound emotional effect upon spectators (Kreuder, 2008: 183).

It is important not to over-generalize about these practices (Cohen, 2000). During the Black Death, for example, flagellants were more common in Germany and Hungary than elsewhere in Europe and, when engaged in militant pilgrimages, were condemned as heretical by the Catholic Church. This reminds us that even though Christian engagements with pain possessed other-worldly considerations, they also often indicated a specific directional orientation towards the human societies in which they occurred. Elias's writings on pain in the medieval era recognize this: self-inflicted flights into pain were indicative of circumstances conducive to the existence of a relatively volatile affect structure, but also constituted ways of identifying with, and engaging in, certain relationships, and exhibiting distance from others (Elias, 2000). They were both constructive of new, and critical of existing, cultural formations.

These religious engagements with pain clearly go beyond the issue of 'theodicy' as a *philosophical* attempt to 'solve' the problem of human suffering, and the practical use of Christianity as a resource with which to *cope with* terminal illness in contemporary Western culture. The centrality of pain to Christianity, however, is not completely absent from the modern Church. This is illustrated by Pope John Paul II's observation that, as Christianity was founded upon the redemption that comes through a crucified God, pain and suffering occupy a central place in salvation (Von Balthasar, 1982: 339; Glucklich, 2001: 4). Whether this offers theological warrant for *self-inflicted* suffering is debatable. Nevertheless, it is clear that the immersion within an identity that takes seriously the idea of a 'path to God through the Cross' can not only help individuals find religious meaning in afflictions, including terminal illness, but can also open the way for broader religious engagements with pain. In contrast to the medicalized reduction of pain to stimuli, what we have here are experiences of pain made meaningful and also, crucially, socially and culturally productive. This occurs through a religious cosmology and practices that prompt a very specific alignment and co-constitution of the stimuli and feelings of pain, and the classifications/reflections about pain.

### The Shi'a indifference to pain

These Christian engagements with pain help us to re-contextualize the outrage to Shi'a flagellation mentioned earlier: self-inflicted pain has long been validated by the major religious tradition of Western culture. These engagements also provide us with examples of how pain has helped constitute religious cultural meanings and identities. Such practices should not, however, be interpreted as evidence of an *identity* between transcendental Christian and the socio-religious Shi'a approaches to pain.

Shi'a flagellation is similar to past Christian flagellation in its embodied imitation and emulation of a religious model, and in involving self-inflicted violence. Shi'a Muharram ceremonies encompass a range of practices to demonstrate and stimulate *matam* or mourning. The most dramatic feature processions of flagellants beating themselves with chain-and-knife scourges that produce a bloody spectacle of intense religious devotion (women also perform *matam*, usually indoors or in courtyards, but while these gendered practices may include dramatic wailing they do not normally involve blood loss (Wolf, 2007). Here, however, the scourging is in honour of Hussein, whom Shi'a Muslims view as the rightful heir to leadership of Islam after Muhammad, and who was martyred in a battle for supremacy within Islam in AD 630. Martyrdom achieved in battle has long appealed to Muslims, since it embodies – and dramatizes – jihad as the struggle to conform to the Will of Allah (Heck, 2004: 100–1), but identification with Hussein's cause is perhaps the major distinguishing feature of Shi'a religiosity.

There is another key reason why these body techniques are associated with a different type of religious habitus, reflecting a different alignment of the various dimensions of pain. Rather than enacting Christian humiliation in a manner commensurate with a transcendent model of self-sacrifice, Shi'a flagellants use bloody self-mortification to signal *indifference* to pain and the defiance of this socio-religious collectivity to profaning threats. As Wolf (2007: 344) argues, 'The very piety that Shi'ahs demonstrate by willingly inflicting wounds upon their bodies is said to be that which prevents them from being hurt by these wounds'. Such phenomena are not alien to Christian history: the story of St George, who was so impervious to pain he could be stabbed, whipped, stoned, drowned, hacked into pieces and killed *four times* before finally dying, is notable here (Pincikowski, 2001: 15). Nonetheless, in Christianity this notion of the 'impassibility' of, or indifference to, pain gradually gave way, in the Middle Ages, to the 'philopassianism', or the creative exploration of pain, associated with the imitation of Christ (Cohen, 1995), in contrast to its *continued centrality* to Shi'a Muharram ceremonies.

This centrality is evident in Hegland's account of these Shi'a ceremonies in Peshwar. Hegland (1998: 245) notes that the 'flagellants were not supposed to show any discomfort; in fact, one girl told me, they do not feel pain', while their spectators are not moved to tears, but become proud of, and impressed by, their courage. As Hegland (1998: 249) suggests, the flagellants 'are sending messages, written on their very flesh, to Imam Hussein about their loyalty and reverence, to other Shi'a about their credentials and adherence, and to enemies about their courage and conviction', while Wolf (2007: 347) adds that they are also communicating with themselves through the 'experience and contemplation of pain in a manner central to their religious experience'. Bloodshed, the visual impact of which is intensified by the white tunics worn by the flagellants, signifies 'readiness for martyrdom', but is also the product of body techniques that maximize blood flow while minimizing permanent injury (Hegland, 1998: 248–9; Wolf, 2007: 343). The fact that public Shi'a flagellation excludes women, in contrast to the historically widespread and enthusiastic participation of women as well as men in Christian engagements with pain (Bynum, 1987, 1989), appears to be related to their orientation towards exhibiting 'manly courage' in the face of potential martyrdom (Hegland, 1998: 245–6). A common feature of both types of flagellation ceremony, nonetheless, is the use of pain to produce experiences that reinvigorate religious commitment (Glucklich, 2001: 6).

This approach directly challenges the prevailing psychiatric consensus that individuals who violently mutilate themselves (for religious or other purposes) invariably suffer from personality disorders (Farvazza, 1996: 27). While the actions of disordered personalities are often involuntary, the adoption of techniques centred on honouring Hussein, or identifying with the suffering body of Christ, depends on a learning process involving the structuring of stimuli and feelings of pain as well as reflection on its meaning. It is in this context that pain can be experienced as liberating and transformative, however shocking its self-infliction might appear. The stage-management of flagellation processions, with their religious symbols and synchronized bodily movements, also indicate a performativity that is creative in the symbolism it enacts and the relationships it forges rather than being pathologically compulsive (Beckwith, 1996: 61; Largier, 2006: 89). Sociologically, it is important to step back from the bio-medicalized approach if we are not to conflate how the transcendent, socio-religious and bio-political modalities with which we are mostly concerned in this chapter can promote different engagements with pain.

## Conclusion

This chapter has addressed the capacity of pain to constitute a bridge to religious experiences and identities by exploring its culturally constructive, as well as its corrosive, potential. After examining the dominance of the bio-medical approach to pain as negative, we drew on Mauss's analysis of body techniques as means through which cultural norms are internalized, and Durkheim's suggestion that pain is sometimes nurtured through rituals of asceticism and mortification. These writers allowed us to explore how divergent engagements with the distinctive dimensions of pain have been evident through time and across different religious contexts. In concluding, we make four points that emphasize how this comparison highlights the specificity and power of the dominant Western approach to pain in the contemporary era, and address the extent to which pain can still constitute a route to forms of religious habitus.

First, viewed in light of Christian and Shi'a traditions, the modern bio-medical approach has encouraged an intense sensitivity to pain. This modern approach highlights the deconstructive cultural consequences of pain (a potential reinforced by the numbers of torture victims who find they cannot re-build meaningful lives after surviving their ordeal; Scarry, 1995). From the increased consumption of 'pain-killers' for minor discomforts to the promotion of euthanasia, sensitivity combines with aversion in what appears to be a comprehensive cultural flight from pain (McTavish, 2004). Here, it is hardly surprising that the public response to the case of Shi'a self-flagellation described earlier should be one of appalled incomprehension. This sensitivity to pain is even and perhaps especially evidenced by the secrecy and controversy associated with the use of torture by America in the 'War on Terror' – as practised in Abu Ghraib, Guantanamo, Afghanistan and Iraq – and the simultaneous condemnation of violence whenever employed by others.

Second, this flight from pain appears tied to the historical marginalization of religion in modern societies. Today, religious approaches to pain that retain credibility exist in a zone of exceptionality in which they *complement* medicalized approaches, especially at the point that medicine fails in the fight against death. This strictly limited role of religion stands in contrast to those medieval Christian, Shi'a or other groups that explore issues of ultimate meaning and seek to embrace religious modalities of the sacred through a physical and doctrinal *embrace* of pain. Rather than seeking to 'resolve' the problem of suffering, these tend to *create* and *intensify* the human engagement with pain among their followers.

This assessment is complicated, however, when we remember that certain Christian orientations towards pain sought to rescue people from suffering. The *Acts of Peter*, for example, affirmed the superior healing power of Christianity, as well as recognizing suffering as profitable (Perkins, 1995: 125), while Parsons (1978) highlighted the importance of Christian traditions of healing for the contemporary medical focus on pain relief. These traditions cannot account for the degree of instrumentalization within modern orientations to pain, given their transcendent dimensions, but display an elective affinity with them.

Third, while it is useful to contrast Christian and Shi'a religious cultural flights into pain with the contemporary Western aversion and sensitivity to pain, these transcendent and socio-religious approaches are not identical. The Shi'a ceremonies we explored are associated with different religious identities and a different approach to sacrifice. While Shi'a flagellation is just as violent, using similar tools to cut participants' bodies, and has a similarly imitative and collective character, Muslim flagellants use their bloody self-mortification to signal indifference to pain and incorporation into the religious community. To the extent this involves sacrifice, *it is the sacrifice of any individual feelings in order to signify the strength of the socio-religious collectivity*. Indeed, they claim *not* to experience pain, and thereby to resist the infliction of suffering upon them. This possesses limited similarities with the indifference to pain exhibited by early Christian martyrs, but contrasts with the embracing of pain as a means of experiencing a sacrifice that would lift them towards the transcendental realm evident in the actions of these Christians or in those of their late medieval successors. As Weber (1993) argued, there are directionalities to the types of habitus promoted by different religious groups, and it would be wrong to conflate them.

Fourth, given these differences, the rational orientation towards pain avoidance in the modern West may not be unrelated to its specific religious history. The centrality of suffering in late medieval Christianity suggests an intense sensitivity to pain nurtured by a habitus centred on the crucified Christ as mimetic model (Girard, 2000, 2004). Today, while the ability to engage positively with pain experientially, publicly and meaningfully in the West may have been lost, it is possible to argue that the sensitivity to it that Christianity systematically nurtured still endures, albeit in secularized form. This is manifest through a commitment to *pain relief* that marks not only medical interventions into body and mind, but also those social attempts to ameliorate the injustices, violence and oppression that characterize the 'brutal realities of social existence' (Morgan and Wilkinson, 2001: 209). If, as Morgan and Wilkinson (2001: 200) have suggested, 'the lived experience of adversity and suffering has seldom been the explicit focus of sociological analysis and research', it is not, perhaps, because of an indifference to such things, but a heightened sensitivity which, locating no inherent meaning or value in them, consolidates a desire for their eradication.

In short, Western culture has moved from the belief that the world could be saved *through* pain, as represented by certain early Christian and by late medieval Christian orientations, to one possessed of a strong affinity with the Christian belief that the world can be saved *from* pain. For Thomas Aquinas, 'the blessed in heaven possessed every human sensibility except pain' (Cohen, 1995: 50; Pincikowski, 2001: 15): this Christian vision of heaven has now been translated into a secular bio-political programme for the alleviation of pain and suffering on Earth. This is the context in which those who actively seek pain out appear 'deviant', 'barbaric' or, simply, 'mentally ill' (Farvazza, 1996), while those who dare pressurize others into activities involving self-inflicted pain risk prosecution for cruelty. Relatedly, it is also the context in which the scope for pain to serve as a bridge for religious experiences and identities within Christianity has shrunk – despite the previously mentioned comments of Pope John Paul II – to a zone of exceptionality outside the effective parameters of bio-medicine.

# 5

## The Aestheticization of Charisma

### Introduction

Charisma has long been recognized as a potentially potent bridge to religious experience, and no sociologist has done more to explore its capacities in this respect than Weber. Adapting the term from Sohm's theological analysis of the 'gift of grace', Weber (1968: 241) redefined charisma to mean a collectively recognized quality of personality whereby an individual is 'set apart' and 'treated as endowed with supernatural, superhuman, or at least specifically exceptional powers or qualities', becoming invested with authority over others. If Weber stripped charisma of its specifically Christian meaning, he nevertheless recognized that intimations of extraordinariness, manifest in the behaviour of unusual individuals, could stimulate social change, while also possessing the potential to enrich human experience and result in a sense of religiosity.

Having recognized its potential as a route to religious experience, however, Weber (1968) analysed charisma within an historical context that identified constraints on its scope and effectiveness. Arguing that charisma was the chief source of change in relatively undifferentiated pre-modern societies, Weber (1968: 244–5) distinguished its influence from the sanctity of tradition and the dominant force of legal rational rule in modernity. In this context, he acknowledged that the intensification of nationalism and imperialism could prompt a renewal of charisma, recognized that extraordinary individuals could emerge in the future, and demonstrated how charisma could combine with other forms of authority. Nevertheless, Weber also insisted that the fate of charismatic authority was tied most profoundly to the disenchantment wrought by Protestantism and the accelerated differentiation and bureaucratization of modern social life. Charisma receded alongside 'the development of permanent institutional structures', while modern rationalization meant that it could ultimately maintain its previous intensity 'only within the smallest and intimate circles, in personal situations, in *pianissimo*' (Weber, 1948 [1919a]: 155; 1968: 1133).

A century later, the revival of Charismatic and Pentecostal forms of Christian worship, and the pervasive deployment of the term 'charisma' within celebrity culture, stand not only as testament to Weber's analytical resurrection of the 'gift of grace' for modern times, but also as evidence that his conclusions need revisiting. The popularity of evangelical preachers on television, the profusion of politicians trained in impression management, and the growth of books, websites and audiotapes designed to help individuals cultivate charisma in order to accumulate social capital, suggest that the phenomenon remains significant (Gillespie and Warren, 2011; Leigh, 2011). Yet the frequently 'packaged' character of charisma, together with the media's growing role in constructing extraordinary affect (Massumi, 2002), also raises questions about whether charisma has become reduced to commercial stimuli and transient feelings of excitement (Rieff, 2007: 3, 5). Weber's suggestion was not, after all, that charisma would disappear, but that it would become diminished, incorporated as an adjunct into the functioning of institutions. The question here is whether charisma has become harnessed to bio-economic or bio-political forces, and can no longer serve as a general bridge to transcendent or socio-religious experiences.

In investigating this issue, we revisit Weber's reformulation of the term before arguing that there is a need to identify contrasting forms of charisma. The first, *pedagogic charisma*, was explored within Sohm's analysis of Early Christianity, but outlined much earlier by the apostle Paul. Differing from Weber's concern with the extraordinary individual, pedagogic charisma circulated between *all* who received Gods 'gift of grace' and assembled themselves into 'teaching communities' charged with assimilating and spreading the Word. Unconcerned with secular leadership, pedagogic charisma was associated with a transcendent conception of the sacred, focused upon the teachings of Christ, and demanded from the faithful preparedness to undergo persecution as a result of their engagement with other-worldly authority.

Weber's own focus on individuals who exhibit *charismatic personality*, are recognized as possessing extraordinary characteristics and are, consequently, able to exercise authority over others, constitutes the second formulation of this concept. Charismatic individuals can be religious or secular, but generate their appeal by offering to enhance the religious, political or even economic status of their followers. As Weber (1968: 243, 1114) argues, the 'divine mission' of charismatic personalities must prove itself 'by *bringing well-being*' to the 'faithful', while the demands of sacrifice are reversed. Rather than followers needing to confront the possibility of their own martyrdom, as in pedagogic charisma, any malfunction in the charismatic leader's sacred power can result in that individual bearing the penalties of failure.

Charismatic personalities persist even within rationalized economies, but typically evidence a substitution of other-worldly orientations to the divine for secular conceptions of the sacred. It is in this context that the rise of charismatic business leaders can illustrate the enduring relevance of Weber's conclusions about the routinization of the extraordinary alongside the advance of social differentiation. This development is also related to a third form of charisma – an *aesthetic charisma* that emerged alongside the growth of consumer culture in the second half of the twentieth century. Here, secular sacred experiences are stimulated through the material and interpersonal processes involved in branding; experiences bereft of any religious creedal basis (cf. Rieff, 2007: 4), but conducive to the authority exercised contemporarily by the bio-economic modality of the sacred.

Aesthetic charisma possesses affinities with both the interpersonal dynamics relevant to Weber's charismatic personalities (although it involves materiality as much as personality) and the circulation of grace in pedagogic charisma (although the content of what is circulated is different) (Pongsakornrungsilp and Schroeder, 2011). This is because the development of branding that is key to aesthetic charisma involves manufacturers and consumers in a pattern of co-production and co-recognition, resulting in a manufactured form of material charisma that circulates between these participants. The realization of aesthetic charismatic value also involves sacrifice, but this is a non-religious, *economic* sacrifice on the part of those seeking to share in the symbolic power and satisfactions of brands.

Pedagogic charisma, charismatic personalities and aesthetic charisma all involve intimations of extraordinariness in which embodied experiences are invigorated by an intentionality towards the metamorphoses offered respectively by eternal Christian life, by associating with exceptional personalities or by consuming brands. In each of its forms, the lived body is supplemented by what Merleau-Ponty (1962: 250) refers to as a virtual body, in being 'geared' to a future phenomenological place, a new 'perceptual ground' and a new 'general setting' in the world. Eschewing tradition and instrumental rationality, each charismatic form also involves relationships of authority, concerned variously with the contrasting referents of sacred teachings, extraordinary individuals and the seductive power of consumables.

Despite their similarities, however, the appeals, demands and transformative experiences associated with these charismatic forms vary. The supernatural promise of pedagogic charisma is religious, tied to other-worldly doctrines, while the charismatic personalities discussed by Weber exist increasingly outside religion. Here, the organization of experience has escaped the control of any single creed or institution and has become 'naturally unstable' (Weber, 1968: 1114). Aesthetic charisma can also be experienced as sacred; tied to material objects, however, it also often evidences material limitations. For all the creativity embedded in its production and circulation, aesthetic charisma possesses referents linked to the parameters of economic markets. Finally, these forms of charisma have different implications for the significance of sacrifice, ranging from potential martyrdom, to the costs borne by the failed charismatic personality, to the expenditure of economic resources. Each form of charisma can still be identified in the contemporary era, even if pedagogic charisma has undergone modification since its early Christian development, but the extension of aesthetic charisma within a globalizing economy is suggestive of both a spread of the bio-economic sacred and an increase in secularization.

## Pedagogic Charisma

Contemporary popular understandings of charisma refer to the unique qualities of individuals, but the etymology of the term can be traced back to the Greek word *charis* (grace or favour) and ancient concepts associated with the idea of spiritual gifts (Potts, 2009). As Smith (1956) explains, the basic idea is that there exists a God or gods who give favour to those in need, usually after personal appeal. The term charisma itself was first used influentially not by Weber (despite Talcott Parsons attributing the term to him), but by the Hellenistic biblical philosopher Philo Judaeus (BC20–AD50) (Smith, 1998: 36). The apostle Paul then developed this concept within his epistles, between AD50 and 60, employing it to refer to the bestowal of God's grace and the various spiritual and supernatural capacities that followed this gift (including powers of healing, miracle working, glossolalia [speaking in tongues] and spiritual wisdom) (Potts, 2009: 23). Paul's particular conception of charisma soon faded (its importance diminished by the institutionalization of grace within church offices), tending to feature only within theological debates. Nevertheless, after centuries of obscurity, it was his religious conception of the term that formed the basis for Sohm's (1970 [1892]) analytical revival of charisma.

Sohm was a Lutheran, disillusioned by the German authorities, who resurrected the concept by re-exploring Paul's epistles to the Corinthians (Smith, 1998). Central to Sohm's focus was the idea that the early Christian teaching of God's Word involved *pedagogic charisma* wherein those gifted with God's grace instructed the faithful into righteous ways of acting and thinking. Reiterating key aspects of Paul's analysis, Sohm argued that the focus for these pedagogues involved preparing the bodies of Christians to hear and internalize dispositionally the Word of God through such inter-corporeal practices as baptism and spiritual healing (Haley, 1980: 192; Brown, 1988). Combined with the divine power of charisma, these techniques undermined sinful habits and thoughts, instilling in the faithful through transformed experience a new, reinvigorated religious habitus.

Contrary to contemporary popular understandings of charisma, God's gift of grace attributed equality upon *all* who received it: all were given the gift of salvation and all were indispensable to the health of the teaching communities in which Christianity flourished. The existence of pedagogic charisma within these teaching communities, moreover, rendered this-worldly structures of governance among the faithful unnecessary. Christian teaching communities took their direction from God's commands: teacher and taught were united in learning and receiving divine instruction, and recognized that this transcendent source of authority should determine questions about individual ethical life (Haley, 1980). Charismatic 'rulers' were teachers, conveying a 'truth they have not invented' and leading 'without being elected', commanding and constraining, but themselves bereft of sovereignty as the only law 'is God's will' (Sohm in Lowrie, 1904: 101; Haley, 1980; Smith, 1998: 46). The suggestion that charisma might be associated with individual domination over others was thus entirely alien to the original meaning of the term (Potts, 2009).

If the Christian teaching communities in which pedagogic charisma was harnessed were unconcerned with imposing this-worldly authority, they were interested in escaping it. The era in which Paul advanced ideas about the 'gift of grace' was characterized by heightened anti-Semitism, and he sought to build a universal Christian fellowship which extended beyond the Jewish communities of the Hellenic and Roman world by promoting a new principal of *other-worldly authority*, contrary to both law and Jewish particularism, predicated upon the enchantment of the Word (Smith, 1998: 36, 40). As Harrison (2003) notes, however, the assertion that each member of the Christian community was uniquely gifted in terms of their relationship to the Word of God opposed prevailing social and political ideas and structures within the Roman Empire. This opposition met with considerable violence, posing dangers to those involved in pedagogic communities.

Roman emperors aware of the other-worldly commitments of Christian cults found it useful to scapegoat them in order to enhance their own power. The private meetings, often conducted at night, in which Christians discussed Christ's teachings also gave rise to popular suspicions that they practised black magic. Against this background, Emperor Nero blamed Christians for the great fire in Rome, and had Paul and Peter executed around AD65 to 67 (Potts, 2009: 28). Historians of that era also demonized Christianity: Suetonius, while critical of Nero's victimization of Christians, described them as a sect which promulgated a publically dangerous ideology, while Tacitus portrayed Christianity as a deadly superstition associated with degrading and shameful practices. The persecution and martyrdom of Christians was common in the first and second centuries, and meant that pedagogic charisma became associated with sacrifices that went far beyond giving up the habits and desires that predated the gift of grace, resulting often in the death of the believer (Brown, 1988; Potts, 2009). It was not until the fourth century that Christianity was legalized by the Roman Emperor Constantine.

This pedagogic charisma explored by Sohm was on the wane long before Christianity received official sanction, however, occurring largely because of the gradual rationalization of the Church. While prophecy and other gifts in Paul's time were considered to have divine legitimation, the routinization of church structures in the second century rendered this individualization 'redundant' and 'dysfunctional' (Potts, 2009). As Smith (1998: 37) argues, after its early establishment as an association of individuals, in which those possessed of the gift of grace engaged with the transcendent kingdom of God, the Church evolved into a 'rule-bound hierocracy' operating on the basis of 'impersonal *office charisma* rather than a charisma associated with the personal and interpersonal spreading of the word'. Teaching the Word remained, but there now existed an institutional authority to interpret and disseminate it. While it is possible to map the continuation of pedagogic charisma within the history of Christian mysticism, developments in the mainstream church did little to revive it. Not even Protestantism, with its focus on the individual, changed the situation. Luther rejected claims to direct revelation in 1520, asserting instead the absolute authority of scripture, and individual displays of charisma were met with distrust (Potts, 2009: 103).

## Charismatic Personality

There is at first glance little in common between pedagogic charisma and Weber's concern with the charismatic personality. Weber (1968: 1112, 1143) refers to Sohm's analysis as 'one-sided' and identifies pedagogic charisma as a limited form of this phenomenon. He also extracts charisma from its exclusive location within the religious realm, recognizing it as a 'universal' phenomenon that is 'self-determined and sets its own limits', and argues that even when charisma is not evident in its pure, most vibrant state, it can persist in routinized forms.

By removing the concept from its Christian milieu and identifying it primarily as an attribute of *individuals*, Weber emptied the 'gift of grace' of creedal meaning. Charisma for Weber can occur equally within prophet or priest, magician or madman. The exhibition and recognition of charisma is made possible not by the circulation of God's Word among teachers and taught gifted with grace, but because of the psycho-physical apparatus of humans. For Weber (1968: 1116), this apparatus is shaped by the routine experiences of everyday life, and by an inherent predisposition that exists within humans to experience emotionally charged social interactions that point *beyond* the mundane to a supernatural sense of power.

Having stripped charisma of its specifically Christian meaning, Weber's suggestion that it possesses a universal basis in the psycho–physical properties of humans occurs alongside the recognition that charisma can still possess religious dimensions. Ironically, however, it is his focus on Jesus, as a paradigmatic example of charisma, that transforms the meaning of the term away from divine grace to an image of power residing in extraordinary leaders (Weber, 1968: 631; Potts, 2009: 122). One of the key characteristics of Weber's (1968: 244, 1116) charismatic personality in general, and Jesus in particular, is the ability to stand *apart from*, and openly *challenge*, group norms, 'transform[ing] all values' and thereby redirecting in specific ways cultural experiences. It is this power to impart directionality to communities that is key to the transcendent, other-worldly qualities of the charismatic – a directionality foreign to all rules, revolutionary in relation to the mundane, and enforcing inner subjection to the divine – and it is in this context that Jesus' proposition 'It is written … but I say unto you …' exemplifies for Weber (1964: 361) the charismatic personality. What is signalled here is not simply a counter-cultural stance, but an individual *authority* that challenges prevailing norms, demanding a new experiential orientation (Weber, 1968: 244–6, 1115).

After identifying Jesus as a paradigmatic example of the creative power of charisma to re-direct people's experiences, Weber (1968: 1112) identifies 'charismatic prophets' as a *recurring* feature of circumstances characterized by rapid change, and his approach has been used to identify extraordinary personalities across an increasing variety of social contexts. Charisma has been used to analyse Hitler and Mussolini, Hugo Chávez, Fidel Castro, Kwame Nkrumah, John F. Kennedy, Ayatollah Khomeini, and Osama Bin Laden – 'a figure right from the pages of Weber' (Turner, 2003: 20; Kets de Vries, 2004) – as well as recent American presidents including Clinton and Obama, and contemporary TV personalities (Lindholm, 1990; Potts, 2009). Designating such figures as charismatic personalities has led critics to argue that Weber encouraged subsequent analysis of the subject to be heterogeneous to the point of contradiction (Turner, 2003: 9; Rieff, 2007: 124, 241–2), yet the essential point about Weber's approach is his suggestion that all these figures exhibit similar qualities and capacities. The 'deliberate swindler' is different from the 'berserker' or 'demagogue', while revolutionaries and terrorists seek to destroy the constitutional forms defended by extraordinary democratic leaders, but in all cases the charismatic is able to act as a *focus* for collective emotions, and to *channel* them in specific ways (Weber, 1964: 359).

This concern with the capacity of extraordinary personalities to channel collective experiences makes charisma a form of authority for Weber, as for Sohm, but an authority deployed not by the Word of God, but by inter-corporeal techniques that steer the emotions and the actions of others, 'revolutionis[ing]' people 'from within' (Weber, 1968: 244, 1116). Such analysis raises questions about the relationship between the individual and the collectivity. For Weber (1968: 1115–7), charismatic power rests on 'personal devotion to' and the 'personal authority of' these apparently 'natural' leaders, yet charismatic authority is 'naturally unstable', with the individual vulnerable to losing their charisma, feeling 'forsaken' by their god, and appearing to their followers as if their powers have deserted them. Against the background of this contingency and in the context of Weber's remarks that charismatic personalities must prove themselves, above all, by bringing well-being to faithful followers, are these leaders not simply products of and subordinate to the collectivities from which they emerge? This is the conventional sociological view. Durkheim (1973; 1995: 213, 386), for example, argued that the emotional effervescence flowing between individuals congregating in the presence of sacred symbolism generates in them a delirium akin to 'the religious state', motivating them to pursue impersonal ends, and to *recognize as extraordinary* leaders who symbolize the collectivity. Lindholm (1990) reinforces this Durkheimian approach towards the emergence of charisma, highlighting the social structures out of which extraordinary leaders appear.

Weber's own writings, however, insist that charismatic personalities can impart a direction to social groups that *goes beyond* the existing character of these collectivities. This is indicated in his suggestions that charismatic leaders are most likely to emerge during times of crisis, anxiety and uncertainty, during which group identity is weak and fragmented, and that they possess extraordinary qualities. In relation to these qualities, while Weber does not address directly the mechanisms resulting in charisma's 'authority-producing character' – that is, the specific sociological processes that allow a person to develop and enact charismatic authority (Turner, 2003: 15) – he implies that charismatic personalities operate via exceptional knowledge of, and capacity to manipulate, the experiential dynamics within social life. This suggestion possesses an affinity with the arguments of nineteenth-century theorists of crowd behaviour that 'a stone needs to be thrown' if patterns of suggestion, mimesis and contagion are to be initiated among crowds, and that certain exceptional individuals embody the potential to accomplish this channelling of experience.

Contrasting illustrations of this individual capacity can be found in the work of Girard. Girard's (2001: 56–63) first example occurs during a discussion of a Greek myth concerning the 'miracle worker' Apollonius of Tyana. Apollonius' power rests on his knowledge of the cathartic effects of a collective discharge of violence, and of the patterns of mimetic contagion that can overwhelm individual reservations about violence within emotionally aroused crowds. Getting someone to throw the 'first stone' is difficult, but, once he has aroused the crowd's anger and given them someone to blame for their misfortunes (a blind, harmless beggar who becomes a 'devil' in the mythical narrative), the first stone is thrown and quickly succeeded by hundreds; following this, the victim dies and social harmony is 'miraculously' restored.

Girard's second example involves his analysis of how, in the Biblical text John 8, Jesus breaks up a mob about to stone an adulterous woman. While 'it is written' in Jewish law of the time that stoning should be her punishment, Jesus halts it ('but I say unto you … let he who is without sin cast the first stone'). This statement disrupts violence by depriving the crowd of the mimetic model of the *first stone* through isolating each individual from the group, thereby effectively undermining a socio-religious scapegoating pattern enshrined in reli-gious law (Girard, 2001: 57). It is also based on a nuanced under-standing of the experiential dynamics of groups. Indeed, some of the minor details of the Biblical account (e.g. Jesus won't look the crowd in the eyes, but sits and speaks on the ground, writing in the sand) reinforce the sense that the charismatic authority he displays is emergent from a highly developed knowledge of inter-corporeal interaction. The Biblical story is telling us that Jesus is able to deploy this knowledge, through actions and words, to change the behaviour of others, even though that behaviour has the sanction of tradition: it is this deployment that allowed his early followers, and the authors of the New Testament text, to collectively recognize his charismatic authority.

These observations reinforce the value of Bass's (1981, 1985, 1999), Willner's (1984) and Gardner and Avolio's (1998) focus on the inspirational powers shared by charismatic leaders, manifest in various forms of 'impression management', including bodily posture, gestures and a range of verbal and non-verbal cues that stimulate particular experiences and actions in others (Lindholm, 1990: 45; Dawson, 2006: 19, 147). They also provide evidence for Sanders's (2000) conclusion that while a charismatic leader needs followers, these followers do not choose their leader at random. Indeed, Girard's examples provide clear insight into the charismatic persona-lity's 'authority-producing character' (Weber, 1964: 358). They are also perfectly suited to Weber's conception of the charismatic per-sonality (such as the innovative religious prophet) who receives recognition as an extraordinary individual outside of the formal structure of institutions, yet acknowledges the importance of the social milieu in which s/he operates. As both Mauss (1973a) and Foucault (1986, 1988a, 1988b) imply, in their analyses of 'techniques of the body' and 'technologies of the self', while charismatic person-alities may be exceptional and innovative, this does not stop there from being collectively sanctioned means of manifesting these qualities.

Weber is, then, insistent that the charismatic personality is an ini-tiator and director of group influence, even if he recognizes that we cannot explain this leadership without understanding the collectiv-ity itself. His attentiveness to the collective is evident, for example, in his writings on Judaism (Weber, 1952). Whereas Sohm identifies an infallible charisma, valid irrespective of the feelings or views of individuals, Weber here places charismatic authority in the context of *public consent*: it was the environments in which the prophets lived that furnished 'the problem central to the prophecy' (Weber,

1952: 300). More generally, Weber (1968: 1111–2) observes that charismatic figures appear as natural leaders in moments of distress 'whether psychic, physical, economic, ethical, religious, or political', manifesting to communities *on such occasions* 'their possession of specific gifts of body and mind'. As Smith (1998) argues, 'personal gifts may be pre-requisites of power', but they will fail to deliver it if, as Weber says, they are 'denied recognition'.

The importance of collectivity is emphasized further by Weber's understanding of the relationship between the charismatic persona-lity and sacrifice. It is charismatic personalities themselves, rather than those enveloped by the circulation of pedagogic charisma, who must atone in case of failure. As Weber (1968: 243) notes in the case of Chinese monarchs, droughts, floods, defeats in war, or other events considered unlucky forced acts of public penance. Failure constituted a loss of divine legitimation, and required reparation or abdication.

### Pure and routinized charisma

If Weber (1964: 361) insisted that charismatic authority is not the *creation* of a group, even if it becomes subject to collective elabo-ration through myth or ritual, his concern for the relationship between the charismatic personality and the collectivity did result in him distinguishing *pure* from *routine* charisma. The pure form of charisma possesses huge potential in terms of individually initi-ated and steered social creativity, while its appropriation within institutions routinizes charisma. Given that Weber (1964: 364) also sees charismatic leadership as 'a purely transitory' force unless routinized, but also conceptualizes routinization as *antithetical* to creativity, however, it is not surprising that critics have suggested that this distinction is inherently contradictory (Lindholm, 1990: 28; Adair-Toteff, 2005: 190). This apparent tension has led some to follow Parsons (1968) in assimilating charisma into a Durkheimian model of the socio-religious sacred (Shils, 1965). Collapsing its 'pure' into its 'routinized' forms, however, robs charisma of the task Weber assigned it; the role of accounting for social creativity and change initiated by specific *individuals* (Turner, 2003: 13).

Does Weber's analysis of routinization end his vision of the charis-matic personality? If so, perhaps his analysis possesses affinities with the historical fate of pedagogic charisma within Christian teaching communities. Having begun as a 'pure' gift of grace received from God directly by individuals, the Christian church institutionalized charisma, transforming it in Weber's terms from a pure to a routinized form. Rather than accept this conclusion, however, Feuchtwang

(2008) argues that both forms continue to coexist. Charismatic personalities exhibit the 'bringing into one person, a living body, a source of expectations of the extraordinary', while charismatic organizations make available to followers the capacities associated with this other-worldliness via such pedagogic means as prayer, meditation and altered consciousness (Dawson, 2006; Feuchtwang, 2008: 94). This does involve routinization, but constitutes an *extension* rather than the eradication of the extraordinary incorporated into charismatic practice; an analysis that is again consistent with Sohm's conception of pedagogic charisma and the charismatic organization (Palmer, 2008).

Despite Feuchtwang's (2008) attempts to view extraordinary individuals and organizations as two sides of charisma, however, Weber's (1964: 369) primary focus is on the *decline* of pure forms of charismatic personality and his work is ultimately fatalistic. Charisma is brutalized and manipulated in the last stages of its 'fateful historical course'; its waning social significance mirrored in 'the diminishing importance of individual action' within rational capitalism, and in its gradual capture by those seeking to legitimate their economic and social power (Weber, 1968: 1121–2, 1146–9). This manifestation of charisma remains evident in the contemporary era, although it may not be as instrumental as implied by Weber and can be explored further in the realm of business leadership. This serves as an introductory context in which to explore a third form of charisma, the secular *aesthetic charisma* attached to material products within contemporary consumer culture.

### From charismatic personalities to aesthetic charisma

Weber's (1968: 1146) account of the modern fate of charisma was predicated on his suggestion that rationalization prompted a collapse of pure into routinized forms. When this occurs, charisma exists merely as an institutionalized sacralization of this-worldly power: what passes as charisma in much of global modernity is not only devoid of religious character, but is also domesticated for utilitarian ends involving reconciliation to the status quo. Viewed in this light, it is tempting to assess the emergence over the last 20 years of models of charismatic leadership in business as an advanced stage in the bio-economic secularization of charisma.

Interest in charismatic leadership in business is relatively recent, with Conger and Kanungo noting in 1987 that organizational theorists had largely overlooked charisma. Since then it has become an influential aspect of 'effective leadership' models (Bass and Avolio, 1994; Ensari and Murphy, 2003; Hughes et al., 2003) that have arisen alongside those radical economic changes that occurred during the late twentieth century involving increased global competition, the need to respond quickly to accelerated flows of capital, the aestheticization of production, volatile shifts in consumption patterns, and the role of affect in marketing campaigns (Featherstone, 2010; Lury, 2011). If Weber is correct in thinking that charisma emerged during times of uncertainty, anxiety and challenge, these conditions appear to possess such characteristics in abundance.

Responding to these developments, models of charismatic business leadership identify key behavioural traits associated with the ability in volatile times to inspire and direct the experiences and actions of others. These include the capacity to communicate a powerful future vision at odds with the status quo, and the ability to become an exemplar through the embrace of personal risk and sensitivity to the needs of organizational members, yet possessed of the forcefulness of character to change people's views in line with this vision (Conger and Kanungo, 1987: 640–1; 1994; 1998; Ensari and Murphy, 2003: 53). The importance of such charismatic leadership to commercial organizations is reflected further by recent calls for businesses to recognize and nurture 'dispositional attributions' suggestive of charismatic authority among future leaders.

These discussions of charismatic leadership have been associated with characterizations of modern business organizations as 'emotional communities', a depiction likely to have prompted scepticism in Weber. Against this background, Shamir (1992) usefully highlights the endurance of utilitarian concerns in his warning that a 'leader is perceived as charismatic when the business is successful' (Ensari and Murphy, 2003: 53). Nevertheless, as the example of the late Steve Jobs of Apple illustrates – a leader known for ambitious visions of future products, a commitment to style, an erratic and sometimes aggressive approach to colleagues and a messianic demeanour (Isaacson, 2011) – the evolution of modern business practice has acknowledged the role of charisma as a potentially potent carrier of 'emotional contagion' that can generate specific experiences among employees *and* contribute to market successes (Wasielewski, 1985; Lewis, 2000). For Holt and Thompson (2004: 428) this opportunity has been exploited by 'supremely confident' leaders who 'pay no mind to industry conventions', 'struggle tenaciously against seemingly insurmountable odds, and improbably conquer the establishment' through 'creative destruction' that results in the creation of 'powerful new companies'. As Weber

(1968: 1117) argued, charismatic leadership can coexist with, and be utilized for profit by, economic organizations.

The existence of charismatic leadership in business provides further justification for Weber's determination to liberate its analysis from early Christianity and explore it within social and economic life more generally. However, it would be wrong to assume that charisma exists now only as a set of *personal* qualities that can be harnessed by companies, politicians and others for purposes of commercial or political gain. The third and final form of charisma we identify in this chapter, indeed, is manifest not by individuals, but is embedded within commodified products through a process of *aesthetic materialization*.

The etymology of 'aesthetic' can be traced to the ancient Greek term, *aisth*, meaning 'feeling through physical perceptions' (Strati, 2000: 16), and Gumbrecht (2004: 99–101) builds on Weber's comments about the psycho-social apparatus of humans in suggesting that the aesthetic experience of material and symbolic phenomena can provide us with feelings of *intensity* that exist at a distance from mundane existence. These feelings cannot be contained easily within existing frames of meaning, as they point *beyond* the everyday, but they are anchored in our responses to particular this-worldly events, performances and, crucially for our purposes, objects. These aesthetic experiences can therefore be characterized as sacred in a secular sense: they are part of, rather than forbidden to, daily life, yet inspire an excitement in people that we take to suggest that their material and symbolic referents are possessed of charismatic potential within a bio-economic modality of the sacred.

Rieff (2007: 4) and Potts (2009) have dismissed the idea of attributing charisma to inanimate objects in the contemporary era, but the affectual impact of aestheticized materials can be traced to prehistoric societies in which crafted objects were seen as possessing extraordinary powers that could engender wonder even when used in routine activities such as hunting. Recently, the existence and pervasiveness of this form of aesthetic charisma in the modern economy, via the rise of commercial brands, provides us with another reason to reconsider this dismissal.

The modern history of branding originates in the eighteenth century, but it was only after the Second World War that the proliferation of corporate logos and symbols, the spread of lifestyle consumerism and the growth of market research resulted in a situation whereby brands came to be seen as *distinct* from products and an essential element of company strategies to secure competitive advantage

(Arvidsson, 2007: 11). Branding involves various processes, but is centred upon the material aestheticization of consumption; the 'super-adding' of various tactile, visual, audible and other features and images to products purchased and utilized by consumers. As Lury (2004) notes, while brands are not reducible to specific objects, often circulating as symbols and images, they possess material elements in that they engage with and stimulate the senses in attempting to convey an impression of distinctiveness and extraordinariness.

The nature of this extraordinariness has been explored by Lury (2009: 77) in terms of the *typological characteristics* of brands: the distinctive space they simultaneously map and bring into being. This space is based upon theme, shape, sign, placing, performance, colour and even smell of products, and has been seen as a major determinant of a brand's marketing power (Gobe, 2001: xxxii). The topology of a brand is not intended to stop at the parameters of the product, but to reach out to and envelope potential consumers within a sensory experience structured by its folds and contours (Pine and Gilmore, 1999). As Nixon (1997) notes, this was especially evident in brand-led advertising from the 1980s that sought 'to construct for consumers an imaginary lifestyle within which the emotional and aesthetic values of the product were elaborated' (Schmidt et al., 2009). Extending this point further, Labrecque et al. (2011) argue that brand impact is maximized through the projection of a material sense that it offers escape from the mundane.

If these topographical dimensions of brands involve the novel, the extraordinary and the exceptional, any doubt that they would grow in importance was eradicated during the 1980s in a series of mergers and acquisitions that were accompanied by systems for measuring 'brand worth' and the suggestion that 'about 20% of bid prices were motivated by the value of brands' (Goodchild and Callow, 2001; Arvidsson, 2006: 5; Moor and Lury, 2011). This situation stimulated research into the development of successful brand identities. Just as there exist interpersonal techniques associated with the exercise of charismatic personality, so too are there particular strategies behind the construction of a brand identity possessed of aesthetic charisma: strategies involving the manner in which they are *performed*, and the particular *direction* in which these performances seek to structure consumer experiences and actions.

The staging of brands as performances resonates with Butler's (1990, 1993) suggestion that identities are constituted by their enactment in specific locales. In relation to one of the most successful recent brands, 'Nike towns' stimulate such performances by providing opportunities for consumers to play with and test out athletic gear. Sherry (1998) suggests that this environment encourages tactile and proprioceptive forms of 'getting to know' the essence of Nike. ESPN Zone, also in Chicago, possesses similar qualities. Owned by the entertainment conglomerate Walt Disney Co., ESPN invites consumers to an 'eat, drink, watch, play, and buy' experience structured by the manner in which its 35,000 square feet of retail space brings together sensations of spectating and enacting sporting performances (Sherry et al., 2001). More prosaic brand performances still allow for product identities to be enfolded onto the senses and actions of consumers. The carefully planned terrain of Apple stores encourages use and exploration, for example, while coffee shops such as Starbucks promote and encourage – through layouts, seating and Wi-Fi – particular images and ways of consuming drinks (Sherry, 1998; Arvidsson, 2006: 78–9; Lury, 2009).

The distinctiveness of brands is thus associated with performances possessed of *directionality* and involving what Massumi (2002) calls 'affect modulation', in that its messages, images and features 'tend to encourage particular modalities of use or ways of relating to other people by means of the object in question' (Arvidsson, 2007: 18; Sherry et al., 2001). The ESPN sports zone noted above, for example, appeals to many men because it structures consumption on the basis of a 'hedonistic playpen' that encourages a break from the responsibilities associated with male adult roles (Sherry et al., 2001; Holt and Thompson, 2004: 426). Focusing upon other branded products, Arvidsson argues that this directionality entails that 'it feels different to drive a BMW; with a Macintosh you are received as a creative person; [and] with the right kind of sneakers your status at school is enhanced' (ibid.).

Another way of analysing this directionality is to suggest that brands provide what Goffman (1974) referred to as a *frame* for action, *pre-structuring* consumer experience (Lury, 2004), and seeking to guide 'investments of affect' on the part of consumers (Arvidsson, 2006: 93). Nike, for example, sought to develop and utilize a counter-cultural cachet predicated upon 'street credibility' by associating its products with inner-city communities. In Britain, the energy drink Red Bull launched first in clubs and dance music venues, and was able in its subsequent marketing to draw on the image it developed through these associations (Arvidsson, 2006: 69). In summary, companies such as Coca-Cola, McDonald's, Nike and Apple do not just produce material objects, but possess a symbolic and emotional surplus that underpins, overlays and structures the consumption of their produce (Gobe, 2001).

According to Holt (2004), those brands that have become most successful, achieving truly iconic status, manage to weave their own distinctive message and presence into the mythical symbols and conscience of a people during particularly critical historical times, creating what Anderson (1983) referred to as an 'imagined community'. Coca-Cola has been particularly adept at this, becoming associated with the American troop rations during the Second World War (Macrae, 1991), but also by promoting themselves as agents of global reconciliation. Their campaign of the early 1970s – in which cola was symbolized as the drink effecting a harmonious coming together of multicultural young people performing 'I'd like to buy the world a Coke' – crystallized the nation's attempts to heal itself from the Vietnam war (Holt, 2004). If charismatic personalities arise during periods of change and uncertainty, the example of Coca-Cola suggests that the same conditions provide opportunities for the manufacture of materialized forms of charisma.

Deployed to steer the experiences and actions of individuals in particular directions, towards the consumption of particular products, it might be tempting to associate brands with Weber's demagogic examples of charismatic power. In the context of our conception of experience as involving the co-constitution of stimuli, feeling and classification/reflection, however, this would be a mistake. Brand-led and other companies may seek to structure and direct our experience through various strategies, such as those outlined above, but this does not rule out the possibility that we may reflect critically on our feelings when subjected to advertising and other commercially developed stimuli (Leys, 2011). Furthermore, theorists of branding have done much to demonstrate that the recognition and value of a brand is a *two-way* process of *co-creation* involving consumers as well as marketing departments (Arvidsson, 2006, 2007). This has obvious parallels with Weber's argument that charisma involves the *attribution* of extraordinary capacities or characteristics to a leader. If the charismatic personality was never a monadic individual, but always an inter-corporeal phenomena involving exchanges of energy and influence, the construction of brand values are not only related to production but also to consumers' 'perceptions and feelings about the brand' (Moor and Lury, 2011: 10).

In the context of this recognition of co-creation, research has been conducted into the subject of consumer motivations that feed into brand success. Beverland and Farrelly (2010) explore how individuals attempt to feel 'authentic' through consumption practices ranging from everyday shopping to tourist choices. Holt and Thompson

(2004) note how the leisure consumption of many men is informed by a pursuit of a self-formed individuality that harks back to the Puritan roots of modern America. Schouten and McAlexander (1995) argue that the success of the Harley Davidson brand is fuelled by the rebelliousness and sense of freedom with which it is associated. Archer et al. (2007) explore how sub-cultural groups generate a sense of worth through their active appropriation of the symbolism of Nike products. More generally, Kim and Yoo Jin Kwon (2011) suggest that young people, in both the East and West, may be developing emotional relationships with brands analogous to those they develop with their peers; relationships that include internet-based brand communities (Patterson, 1999: 410; Muniz and O'Guinn, 2001; Arvidsson, 2006: 83).

The importance of this two-way process of brand creation is illustrated by the determination with which companies engage in research on credit card spending, internet surfing habits and barcode scanner data that feeds back into design, production and marketing. Companies employ members of target consumer groups to investigate those same groups (Arvidsson, 2006: 71), while Entwistle's (2000, 2009) analysis of major clothes fashion manufacturers illustrates that brands evolve via research which focuses upon how consumers actually use/wear the products under question. It is not only manufacturers that recognize brand creation and development as a two-way process of co-creation, moreover, as anti-branding groups have interrogated the poor labour conditions and environmental damage associated with the production of certain branded goods, as well as highlighting their detrimental implications for consumer health (Holt, 2004). Critical reflection can indeed subvert what might otherwise become 'brand friendly' experiences.

There has been much talk of the sacralization or enchantment of consumption in recent years (Ferguson, 1992; Ritzer, 1999; Lyon, 2000), with Dechant (2002) identifying consumer culture as the new religion of America. The processes involved in creating aesthetic charisma, however, can help us understand what is really happening here. This emotional identification with powerful symbols in secular 'cathedrals of consumption' (Ritzer, 1999) is not a simple manifestation of collective norms, but involves individuals assembling for themselves particular identities through the purchase of specific brands that exist within a broader bio-economic modality of the sacred. For Rieff (2007: 222) this is part of a therapeutic process in which individuals strive to become their own charismatic prophets with the assistance of consumables that stimulate in them feelings 'without a message'.

The appeal of aesthetic charisma to the potentially transient preferences of consumers seeking products that can enhance their well-being contains affinities with Weber's analysis of the interactional basis of charismatic personality. This form of consuming manufactured forms of aesthetic charisma, moreover, is not without sacrifice. What is at stake here, though, is not preparedness to tolerate persecution or martyrdom for one's faith, but a willingness on the part of consumers to make an *economic sacrifice* to buy into this experience of extraordinariness. The manufacturers of products into which aesthetic charisma is invested do not escape the prospect of sacrifice either. Similar to Weber's charismatic personalities, if they fail to deliver the expected promise of brand appeal, they stand to be deserted by their followers who will look elsewhere for excitement and satisfaction.

The economic focus of these sacrifices also highlights the scope and influence of aesthetic charisma. Pedagogic charisma involved an other-worldly authority that accepted a secular sphere, while possessing widespread implications for the this-worldly behaviour of those engaged in learning the Word of God. Political and religious charismatic personalities possessed, at least in times past, a revolutionary potential that could stretch across the socially differentiated sectors of a society. Aesthetic charisma, in contrast, is involved in a highly differentiated and segmented experience of the extraordinary within the (enormously powerful) realm of commodified products.

### The branding of religious forms

Branding is increasingly pervasive. As Rinallo et al. (2012) argue, the burgeoning market for spiritual products, services, experiences and places has led to the branding of religions and religiosities in a process whereby religious institutions, leaders, marketers and consumers interact and co-create spiritual meanings (Gobe, 2001: 290). This may also be seen as a version of aesthetic charisma, though it is important to recognize the interactions that can occur between the bio-economic and religious modalities of the sacred here. The work of Morgan (2005), Orsi (2005), Meyer (2009) and others, for example, highlights how the commercialization and mediatization of religious symbols have been utilized by Christians, Muslims and others as aides in stimulating a religiosity related inextricably to transcendent or socio-religious goals (though we analyse this in Chapter 6 as an example of material fetishism distinct from aesthetic charisma in its orientation towards the other-worldly).

If such examples are indeed distinct from the bio-economic sacred in retaining an other-worldly orientation, their accommodation to a broader pattern of aestheticization suggests elements of marketization. The Muslim practice of veiling, for example, has become fashionable in countries even where once it was stigmatized. In the case of Turkey, young, urban and educated middle-class women in the early 1980s took to the practice of wearing 'a stylistically unprecedented form of covering' involving a large headscarf and a long loose fitting overcoat (Sandikei and Ger, 2010). It is arguable that this demonstrated not only the growing influence of Islam, but also its aestheticization, certainly in terms of the subsequent branding of this practice as a concern with style consistent with the Qur'an, and the development of a market keen to exploit demand for personalized forms of religious dress. This is not an unambiguous instance of the power of the socio-religious, but a suggestion that even religions that refuse to recognize a secular sphere are engaging increasingly with markets embedded in global practices outside of religious control.

## Conclusion

This chapter has explored charisma's capacity to constitute a route to religious experience by identifying three of its forms: the pedagogic charisma associated with early Christian teaching communities, Weber's conception of charismatic personality, and our conception of a material and manufactured aesthetic charisma. These forms are involved in the construction of extraordinary experiences that energize the lived bodies of individuals by super-adding to them what Merleau-Ponty (1962) refers to as virtual bodies: visions and intimations of metamorphosis.

Despite such similarities, these forms of charisma are associated with different types of authority, are predicated upon contrasting sacrifices, and also result typically in divergent experiences. Pedagogic charisma is tied to the experience of a particular, other-worldly creed, with the gift of grace stimulating extraordinary feelings that circulate among those dedicated to teaching and learning about God's Word. Charismatic personalities can also be associated with the promotion of religiosity, although they are in the modern world more commonly bound up with this-worldly excitements of celebrity culture, or those occasional outbreaks of enthusiasm that Weber (1968: 1130) associates with political 'heroes' who stand against 'the mundane power of the party organization.' Aesthetic charisma, in contrast, offers a thoroughly secularized form, albeit one able to stimulate extraordinary experiences via the bio-economic sacralization of the brand.

Aesthetic charisma may have become dominant in the modern age. Yet despite circulating between producer and consumer, and among consumers themselves, in a manner suggestive of limited affinities with pedagogic charisma, critics have suggested that the promise of 'redemption through consumption' it offers is particularly thin. In comparison with its pedagogic antecedent, it offers little in the way of overall guidelines about how to live, let alone morally serious engagements with human potentiality and finitude (Bauman, 2002; Mellor, 2004: 40; Campbell, 2005). The contrasting profundity of these forms of charisma can also be highlighted by Ladkin's (2006) suggestion that the charismatic encounter involves the individual in an experience of the sublime, whereby an encounter provokes an other-worldly experience which is both disturbing and invigorating. While Ladkin senses the sublime in charismatic leadership in general, it would not ordinarily be associated with the experiences of stimulation occasioned by material products within consumer culture, though an important caveat here concerns the marketization of religious products that assist individuals in maintaining or enhancing their faith.

Charisma has long been seen as a potential bridge to religious experience and action. In contrast to the force of tradition or of legal rational authority, charismatic belief and excitement revolutionizes people 'from within' (Weber, 1968: 1116). For Weber (1968: 1120), however, every type of charisma 'is on the road … to a slow death by suffocation under the weight of material interests', a conviction that has suppressed our recognition of the continued vibrancy of charismatic forms both within and outside the economy. Whether charisma can still constitute a bridge to religion is a more complex question, and one, perhaps, appropriate to Weber's pessimism. The appearance of the extraordinary in daily life continues in a manner he did not anticipate, but it does so within a bio-economic modality of the sacred that enframes experiences of the extraordinary within an aesthetic materialism of brands, consumerism and affect modulation that marginalizes the religious modalities with which it co-exists. If this tension between worldly and other-worldly modalities is evident with regard to experiences of charisma, however, it is arguably even more acute in relation to *eroticism*, as we shall now discuss.

# 6

## The Materialization of Eroticism

### Introduction

In the last few chapters we examined how contemporary experiences associated with intoxication, pain and charisma can be enframed in various ways, with contrasting consequences for their capacity to serve as bridges to religious identities. The extraordinary authority and influence exercised by bio-economic and bio-political forces in these key areas of human experience is neither complete nor uncontested, but it is sufficient to cast doubt on the conclusions of those who argue that religion remains a pervasive force across differentiated levels and sectors of society. This does not justify deterministic conclusions about the 'triumph of secularization', or assertions that there do not exist conditions in which forms of religious habitus can be constructed. It does raise questions about religion's capacity to shape people's lives in a global context characterized by secular modalities of the sacred that undermine other-worldly oriented dispositions and identities.

This chapter continues to address these questions by exploring *eroticism*, another sphere of human experience that assumes important material forms in global modernity. In contrast to those secular charismatic processes involved in the branding of consumer goods, however, the material fetishism associated with religious icons provides us with evidence of religion's continued, if limited, influence. This particular form of eroticism still competes for attention with secular attractions within consumer culture, but its other-worldly manifestations offer something distinctive in the wider market place.

In terms of those classical sociological resources that continue to illuminate our contemporary concerns with embodied experience as a route to religion, it is Weber's (1948) writings that attribute most importance to eroticism. Engaging with Comte's (1853: 190) suggestion that fetishism promoted in people spiritual values conducive to human development, Weber's interest builds upon philosophical and historical resources that established the significance of eroticism for other-worldly religious purposes as well as secular priorities. Plato's association of eros with the human yearning to be unified with higher ideals, for example, suggested there could be transpersonal as well as personal benefits from eroticism (that from a sociological perspective might serve to predispose individuals towards religious forms), while the Ancient Greek concern with the desires and longings of erotic love highlighted the capacity of these experiences to make life profoundly and even transcendentally meaningful for individuals.

Despite its significance, however, neither Weber nor indeed Bataille (the other major figure related to sociology who explored the subject in detail) endorsed eroticism as unambiguously beneficial for individuals or societies, choosing instead to remain sensitive to its classical associations with 'mad love' (*theai mania*, or 'madness from the gods') and recognizing it as personally and socially destabilizing. Irrespective of their contrasting concerns with the fates of the transcendent sacred and the socio-religious sacred in modernity, moreover, both Weber and Bataille identified eroticism as possessing a thoroughly ambivalent power, and focused as much upon its containment as on its other-worldly and this-worldly potentialities.

Why was there this focus on the ambivalent consequences of eroticism, on its potential to be destructive and not just religiously re-vitalizing? The disquieting consequences of erotic experiences lay significantly in their capacity to undermine both the model of autonomous selfhood associated with modernity, and those integrative values and meaning-giving qualities central to religious and social organizations. In relation to the former, eroticism was linked to an erasure of the mind/body distinction underpinning Western notions of individuality (that assumed one of its most influential forms with the Puritan 'elect', viewed as *the* harbingers of the modern habitus, who were obligated to *reflect* ceaselessly upon whether they were doing sufficient to 'work for God's glory in the world' [Dumont, 1985: 115–16; Mauss, 1985]). In terms of the latter, eroticism could extend beyond the borders of love and sensuality into either epiphanies and mysticism that turned people *away* from established religions and society, or in the exercise of possessiveness and violence that questioned the basis of *any* normative framework.

The apparent potency of eroticism would appear to make it of considerable continued sociological significance, yet recent suggestions that it has been domesticated within 'confluent love', or commodified into such forms as pornography, raise doubts about whether Weber's and Bataille's focus on the excessive, uncontainable and religious aspects of eroticism remain relevant. It is against this background that we now analyse how the capacity of eroticism to constitute a route to religious experiences and identities has become a site of contestation in contexts characterized by competing secular as well as religious modalities of the sacred.

Our argument develops in three stages. First, we outline eroticism's importance for Weber and Bataille, examining the partial convergence that exists between their depictions of physical and emotional eroticism as sacralizing experiences possessed of the capacity to facilitate an *escape* from everyday life. Second, we explore recent writings that suggest eroticism has been regulated alongside, or reduced to, the economic exploitation of bodies and biological responses within modern societies. These analyses rarely deal with the ambivalence of eroticism in a manner akin to their antecedents, but accentuate the recognition by Weber and Bataille that erotic experiences can be mediated in ways that impart a degree of organization and meaning to their energies and excesses. Third, we focus in more detail on the capacity of eroticism to be steered by mediating forms. Here, we build on Bataille's suggestion that material phenomena can be fetishized as erotic other-worldly forms (recognized as possessing particular powers, edicts and interdictions) that continue to promote religious experiences, but also recognize that there has been an unprecedented profusion of these images, icons and objects in the global media age (Meyer, 2009). This enhances the potential audience for those who promote religion through these media, but it also means that these phenomena compete for attention with each other, as well as having to contend with charismatic products designed to stimulate and seduce the senses towards secular consumer culture.

## Weber, Eroticism and Religious Regulation

Weber conceptualized eroticism as a vibrant embodied experience that could exceed the borders of mundane human experience and stimulate a sense of the other-worldly, and he analysed it in the context of his concerns about the secularization of modern life. Erotic experience, one might think, would have considerable attraction for Weber given that his vision of modern life, influenced by Nietzsche's writings on the 'death of God', is so bleak. As eroticism linked embodied experience to a sense of the transcendent that bypassed the rational thought Weber associated with truly human action, however, he advocated that it be regulated by religious institutions or confined to the private sphere. Thus, in choosing between the bleak but rationally ordered parameters of this world and the vertiginous attractions of other-worldly experience, Weber opts ultimately for the former.

Weber's approach towards eroticism arose in the context of his conviction that while the human search for rational meaning devalued 'this-worldly' activity, aesthetic or emotional responses to this situation possessed limited potential or posed an even greater threat to people's well-being. Christianity was central to this devaluation of worldly activity for Weber as it encouraged individuals to become engaged in an introspective search for personal salvation based on other-worldly considerations that relativized the intrinsic value of earthly achievements (Chowers, 1995), yet the search for meaning became even more difficult for those condemned to living in a 'disenchanted' world without faith (Weber, 1991). Trapped in the 'iron cage' of modernity, characterized by the rationalization of life-spheres unconnected by overarching values (Whimster, 1995: 449–50), life appeared devoid of significance.

In seeking remedies for this situation, Weber (1948 [1915]) scrutinized the meaning-restoring capacities of various 'value-fields', and his views on eroticism emerge from this analysis of art, intellectualism, politics and religion. Art could be experienced as a charismatic 'salvation' from 'routines', while intellectualism marshalled people's energy (and the experience of what James (1956) referred to as a feeling of sufficiency) into rational achievement, albeit one that contributed eventually to disenchantment (Weber, 1948 [1915]: 342, 350). Both were restricted by their elitism, however, and by a culture in which the proliferation of 'self-contradictory and mutually antagonistic' values led to relativism and a 'devastating senselessness' (Weber, 1948 [1915]: 356–7). Politics provided wider opportunities for individuals to join meaningful causes transcendent of the self, reaching its culmination during war (ibid.: 335). There were limits to such nationalism, however, becoming clear to Weber with Germany's military defeat and the retreat of values associated with national greatness (Bologh, 1990: 193). Religion, in contrast, devalued this-worldly pursuits, with its world-denying forms causing the largest clashes with these and other 'value-spheres', even if the churches still comforted those unable to 'bear the fate of the times' and still sought wider regulatory functions across differentiated sectors of society (Weber, 1948 [1915]: 330; 1948 [1919a]).

It is against this background of the fragility of meaning that Weber considered erotic experiences. Weber (1948 [1915]: 345, 347) refers to eroticism as 'an embodied creative power' that facilitates sensual experience of 'unique meaning' through a 'boundless giving of oneself' that is opposed to rationality. Erotic relationships offer a 'complete unification' of individuals who would otherwise be separated by the impersonality of bureaucracy (ibid.: 347), and take two forms. *This-worldly* erotic relationships possess an intense physical and emotional character that effaces individuality, offering the experience of being 'rooted in the kernel of the truly living', and 'an inner, earthly sensation of salvation by mature love' (ibid.: 347). This-worldly eroticism is therefore immanent rather than transcendent, but is nonetheless possessed of a salvific, sacred character. *Other-worldly* eroticism exists in Weber's writings on mysticism, wherein a search for individual salvation is pursued via an emotional state in which love for all results in unification with the divine.

Eroticism for Weber thus constitutes a flight from rationalized society, but does not effect a complete detachment from organized life or from the organic conditions of human beings that would prevent it from being harnessed to religious or secular forms. This is because the mystical search for loving absorption into the divine invests life with at least a degree of meaning *in relation to* this transcendent goal, while the intense physical and emotional character of this-worldly eroticism maintains links with biology even while rejecting the 'naïve naturalism' of animal sex and consciously cultivating sexuality as this-worldly contact with the sacred.

Having identified its links to this-worldly, embodied life, Weber explores how eroticism has been subject to social and religious attempts to regulate the forms it takes and the significance attributed to it. Historically, the cultural organization of sex includes religious endorsements of sacred harlotry, the eroticization of young males in Ancient Greece, Medieval troubadour love poetry, salon culture, and modern extra-marital affairs (Weber, 1948 [1915]: 345–6). Sexual eroticism has also found validation as a route to enlightenment within such mystical forms as Vajrayana Buddhism, through strategies which challenge the separation of the spiritual and the sexual, while there is a tradition within Christianity of highly eroticized descriptions of holy men and women encountering Christ (Bynum, 1987: 246–59; Kripal, 2001). More common within Christianity for Weber, however, were those censorious regulations revolving around the Church's attempt to remove sex from religious celebrations and contain it within marriage.

Despite the attraction of eroticism as a response to the 'icy darkness and hardness' of modernity (Weber, 1948 [1919b]: 128), Weber's own position is aligned to previous attempts to regulate it. He was convinced that mystical eroticism treated people as mere *means* to the end of cosmic bliss, while the 'fusing of souls' within intimate erotic relationships threatened religious and social orders, such as the religious 'ethic of brotherhood', in their exclusivity and potential 'brutality' (Weber, 1948 [1915]: 348). Such threats were manifest not only in a 'will to possession' that excludes others, but also in an egoistic 'enjoyment of oneself in the other' involving 'the most intimate coercion of the soul' of the weaker partner (ibid.). This is why Bologh (1990: 204, 217–8) can depict the erotic relation as 'a patriarchal arrangement in which the stronger party accepts and expects the devotion of the weaker one', and in which the will and subjectivity of the other is effaced.

Ultimately, then, Weber remains ambivalent about the religious potential of eroticism. He argues that erotic experiences can provide a joyous 'sensation of an inner-worldly salvation from rationalization', constituting an alternative to organized religion or the 'warrior ethic' as a source of meaning (Weber, 1948 [1915]: 346; 1948 [1919a]). However, Weber remained wary of the spiritual violence associated with erotic relationships, and did not view eroticism as a general foundation for religious or secular orders (Mitzman, 1971). In the final version of his 1915 'intermediate essay' on 'Religious rejections of the world', indeed, Weber seeks to confine eroticism to three contrasting manifestations in three distinctive locations. These involve a *religiously sanctioned physical eroticism* (in the Lutheran notion of God's allowance of marital sex), a *religiously sanctioned emotional eroticism* (in the Quaker submergence of eroticism within modernized egalitarian marriages) and a *secular physical eroticism* (in extra-marital relations and affairs) (Whimster, 1995: 459). Paradoxically, despite his argument that Christianity devalued this-worldly meaning, Weber concludes by attributing religion with a key role in limiting eroticism's damaging potential, and in ordering its expression within religiously sanctioned relationships. Despite its meaning-giving and revitalizing potential, the effects of eroticism were too unpredictable and potentially destructive to be sanctioned in unleashed forms.

## Bataille, Eroticism and Religious Sacrifice

Bataille (1992) analyses eroticism from the perspective of the socio-religious sacred, in contrast to Weber's concerns with its impact on the transcendent sacred, yet there remains a limited convergence between their analyses. Bataille, like Weber, associated modernity with the devitalization of religion and meaning occasioned by

Christianity in general and Protestantism in particular. In making this argument, though, Bataille (1988: 124; 1993) followed Durkheim (1995) in attributing Puritanism with the responsibility for prohibiting those sacred effervescent energies that connected people to a reality beyond organic need (Richardson, 1994: 75). It is in this context that Bataille (1996: 179) talks about the devitalizing consequences of a 'world that cannot be loved to the point of death', a world Protestantism and capitalism reduced to the bio-economic demands of 'self-interest and the obligation to work', a world in which the endurance of the sacred energies of eroticism and their religious potential become a key issue.

In a definition comparable to Weber's, Bataille treats eroticism as 'an exuberance of life'; a commitment to living as vitally as possible up to death, in which the boundaries associated with the 'discontinuity' of individual existence are dissolved (Bataille, 1987: 11). The whole point of erotic experiences and relationships is to destroy the self-contained character of participants and the mundane social contexts in which they live (ibid.: 17). Whatever form it takes, indeed, eroticism involves a 'burst of energy', but also a 'state of crisis' in which this-worldly concerns no longer appear important, and in which there is an opening out of the limits of the possible (ibid.: 42). Thus, while Bataille identifies three types of eroticism (physical, emotional and religious), these share the capacity 'to substitute for the individual isolated discontinuity a feeling of profound continuity' in which life becomes deeply meaningful, but also disorienting (ibid.: 15).

*Physical eroticism* involves a passionate conjoining of flesh in a dance of desire and consummation in which the sacrificial violation of individual being is experienced, resulting in a glimpse of the possibility of infinity (Richardson, 1994). Here, nakedness constitutes a prelude to a fusion that is also a destruction of mundane life, culminating in the temporary obliteration of difference. Physical eroticism is not immersion in unmediated biological life, though, but mirrors Weber's 'cultivated sexuality', a *human* return to animal life (Bataille, 1987: 11, 29; 1993: 342).

*Emotional eroticism* involves the joining of hearts in which 'the lover perceives the loved' in their totality, extending physical eroticism into interpersonal communion (Richardson, 1994: 109). The 'fusion of lovers' bodies persists on the spiritual plane', but this does not end the violation of individual being (Bataille, 1987: 20). Indeed, the search for fusion can result in an anguished 'urge to possess', entailing a partner preferring to kill rather than lose their lover.

Bataille explains this by noting that only in the destruction 'through death if need be, of the individual's solitariness can there appear that image of the beloved object which in the lover's eyes invests all being with significance' (ibid.: 21).

Resonating with Weber's discussions of mysticism, Bataille's third, *religious*, form of eroticism involves a spiritual revelation of continuity above the discontinuity of individual existence. Historically, this has been exemplified by religious sacrifice in which individual separateness is violated by a ritualized violence that fuses participants together: the victim dies, the spectators share in what death reveals. As Bataille (1987) explains, the sacredness of this 'is the revelation of continuity through the death of a discontinuous being to those who watch it as a solemn rite'.

What is particularly important about religious eroticism for Bataille is the sense in which its sacrificial aspect underpins *all* forms of eroticism. Urban (1995) illustrates this in relation to the sexual eroticism of the Kapalikas. This South Indian cult combines ritual sex with outsiders and other acts of transgression, based upon sacrifices of self and others, that are undertaken not merely to escape from a cycle of karma and re-birth, but also to achieve 'an ecstatic experience of sexual bliss at the cosmic level' (Urban, 1995: 81). There is, for Bataille, always a violation of individuality in eroticism, involving a socio-religious experience of meaning that reaches beyond the this-worldly present, and there is always a sacrificial component in the possession and merging central to erotic experiences and relationships.

Bataille's comments about religion and sacrifice suggest that eroticism might be compared with that effervescence central to Durkheim's account of how individuals are forged into collectivities. In each form identified by Bataille, however, eroticism constitutes an obliteration of self and others *without limits*, involving an emotionally disorientating 'void' associated with 'the bottomless and boundlessness of the universe' (Bataille, 1993: 168). Discontinuous identities are 'blown apart' as the experience of life confronts death. The anguish that Bataille (1989) associates with our awareness that we are incomplete is removed, only to be replaced by a limitless abyss. While effervescence for Durkheim *adds to* the individual, typically securing them to a collectivity, eroticism for Bataille *obliterates* the individual, propelling them beyond the socio-religious and towards non-existence.

Bataille's account of the ambivalence of eroticism engages with Durkheim's (1995: 213) 'impure' sacred. In contrast to the 'pure' sacred that involves for Durkheim an elevation of *homo duplex* into a socio-religious sphere, this 'low' sacred resists all efforts at such incorporation, involving instead a return to the animal and to the baseness, violence and inevitable death of organic existence. For Bataille, eroticism's force is bound indelibly to its doubled-edged character in encompassing both the pure and impure sacred in facilitating an escape from discontinuity that places one *beyond* comfort and comprehension. The meaning provided by erotic continuity is, then, compromised by its opening onto an experience *beyond* meaning (Bataille, 1987: 211, 244). Additionally, Bataille recognizes there is something 'heavy', 'sinister' and male-dominated about how physical eroticism destroys 'the self-contained character of the participants' (ibid.: 19). Reminding us of the ubiquity of sacrifice in eroticism, he observes that 'The lover strips the beloved of her identity no less than the blood stained priest his human or animal victim. The woman … is despoiled of her being' (ibid.: 90). As Simone de Beauvoir (1993) argues, it is the body of the woman reduced to immanence that provides for the transcendence of the man.

If the ambivalence of eroticism for Weber revolves around its potential to mitigate modern disenchantment, Bataille's considerations are based on a re-evaluation of Durkheim's analysis of the socio-religious sacred. Despite this, both identify Christianity as central to the increased importance of eroticism. By disenchanting the world, blocking the circulation of surplus energy and restricting contact with the sacred, Puritanism accentuates problems associated with the meaning of life and the anguish people experience living with knowledge of certain death. In this context, Bataille and Weber view the various forms of eroticism as modes of transporting individuals beyond isolated, routinized life. Eroticism here is a *positive* force. It is the extent of this transportation, though, that highlights its ambivalence.

For Weber, immersion within erotic relationships is socially ambivalent because of their restricted, often dyadic, size, or, in the case of mysticism, because of its negation of worldly relationships insofar as earthly experience is no more than a means to an end. The potency of erotic experiences here is such that they can become *radically* otherworldly, eluding a transcendent sacred enframing of the worldly within an other-worldly orientation. For Bataille, eroticism opens individuals to the shared experience of meaningful continuity, yet this is more disorienting than ordering in its consequences, and can override the socio-religious regulation of the sacred (Mayne, 1993: 16–17). Neither theorist then, despite developing their perspectives with regard to distinct modalities of the sacred, associates eroticism with the creation or consolidation of religions. Relatedly, both recognize the brutalizing potential of physical eroticism, an eroticism in which female identity is effaced. As Bologh (1990: 218) argues, erotic couplings may involve sacrifice from both parties, but women bear the brunt of violation in its physical and emotional forms.

## Contemporary Sociology and Material Eroticism

Weber and Bataille associated both Protestantism and rational capitalism with a reduction in the space available for erotic experiences and relationships, but still identified these as existing in several forms, possessing unpredictable consequences. Mainstream sociological analyses that have engaged with these issues tend to confirm that there has been a diminution of eroticism in the contemporary era, with two developments in particular suggesting it has been regulated alongside, and commodified by, bio-economic forces.

The first of these developments is reflected in the sociological suggestion that intimate relationships have been reformed in line with the individualization of workers and consumers in modern capitalism; a tendency that has diminished the importance attached to previously dominant markers of status such as 'husband' and 'wife'. Within this context, the merging, de-differentiating qualities of eroticism are to be found only rarely in analyses that focus on the extent to which partners remain individuals within modern dyads. This is most pronounced in Giddens's (1992), Beck and Beck-Gernsheim's (1995) and Bauman's (2003) visions of 'pure relationships' and 'liquid love' as superseding past forms of eroticism. No longer volatile, eroticism has been tamed into a manageable, negotiable resource subordinate to secular projects of the self or to the concern to find a liveable space between 'freedom and security'. Individuals remain separate within this dominant framework for modern intimacy; a framework suited ideally for the possessive individualism characteristic of the bio-economic sacred, and facilitated by the growing bio-political control of reproduction, fertility and 'sexual health'.

The second area in which the potency of eroticism has been challenged is reflected by those analyses of the 'sexualization' of the public sphere in which physical eroticism has become appropriated by consumer culture; a culture focused as never before on creating value from people's bodily experiences and biologically grounded responses to stimuli (Garber, 2000: 23; McNair, 2002; Paasonen, 2007). Physical communion has here been rationalized and commodified, emptied of what Weber and Bataille regard as its potential for life-affirming, transcendental meaning. This is manifest in the commercial exploitation of sex and sexuality that has proceeded via the entertainment industry's importing of pornographic aesthetics, scenarios and conventions into music videos, cosmetic advertisements and fashion photography (McNair, 2002: 12, 86; Paasonen, 2007; Sarracino and Scott, 2010). Online porn itself is not only increasingly centred on virtual 'communities' of shared fetishes, but also part of a broader set of lifestyle choices centred on the eroticization of body modification, tattooing, piercing and scarification (Farvazza, 1996: xviii; Klesse, 2000: 16), as well as sexual subcultures oriented towards pain, sadomasochism and other explorations of the experiential possibilities inherent to the biological materiality of bodies (Torgovnick, 1995; Klesse, 2000).

The use of pornographic images in contemporary culture is a particularly suggestive example of how physical eroticism has been instrumentalized. As Hunt (1993: 10) argues, the 'shock' of sexual depiction was until the mid-nineteenth century tied ordinarily to other aims. This was evident in the French Revolution when politically motivated pornography helped undermine the legitimacy of the ancient regime (ibid.: 31). Explicit images of the Queen's body had a symbolically levelling effect by insisting upon her accessibility (and, by implication, the social body) to everyone. Political uses of pornography faded during the nineteenth century, however, and photographic advances aided the production for monetary gain of images designed purely to provoke sexual excitement. Exceptions to this situation remain, but the general influence of twenty-first century pornographic images, texts and aesthetics can easily give the impression of reducing the power of physical eroticism to styles of sexual display and performance (e.g. Brown and Dehvine, 2011).

If sociological analysis of intimate relationships and the sexualization of consumer culture suggest that the bio-economic has increasingly displaced transcendent and socio-religious modalities of the sacred in enframing eroticism, other studies have focused on the *continuation* of religious dimensions of eroticism. Analyses of the global rise of religious extremism, for example, have drawn upon Bataille's focus on the erotic abandonments associated with sacrifice and engaged pessimistically with Weber's interest in the generalizability of an ethic of brotherly love, particularly with regard to the destruction that can follow unconditional commitments to sacred causes in which other people are reduced to sacrificial objects (e.g. Catherwood, 2003; Juergensmeyer, 2003).

In contrast to the apparent regulatory effects of modern individualized intimacy and commodified sexuality, this concern with religious violence challenges us to consider further the circumstances in which erotic experiences might still form a bridge to the establishment of religious identities. In exploring this question, we turn to an additional form of eroticism identified as important not only by Batailles, but also by the founder of sociology, Comte. *Material eroticism* consists of fetishistic investments in icons, images, texts and objects possessed of the potential to stimulate intense *other-worldly* experiences resonant with religious meanings. It differs from the aesthetic charisma examined in Chapter 5 in terms of this other-worldly directionality.

## The Fetishistic Power of Material Eroticism

Bataille's focus upon physical, emotional and religious eroticism acknowledges the fetishistic power of material images, icons and objects to stimulate and sometimes guide the direction in which erotic experience occurs. This material eroticism is apparent in the images that permeate his fiction: evocations of the pure and impure sacred mix in stories involving socio-religious images of the sun, moon, sexual violation and decapitation (Ades and Baker, 2006). More generally, material eroticism has long been recognized as possessing the capacity to animate, or move people beyond the parameters of rational action. In the case of sexuality, for example, Dennis (2009: 1) notes that 'in the 5th century BCE, young men hid out on the Greek island of Knidos until dark in order to embrace a nude statue of Aphrodite, leaving what Pliny none too discreetly referred to as a "stain" on the goddess's marble derriere'. Centuries later, several Venetian patricians were brought to trial in the 1630s for copulating with a statue of Christ (Dennis, 2009: 1, 60). Here, physical eroticism is stimulated by material images possessed of other-worldly significance.

The fetishism that lies at the heart of material eroticism has usually been viewed negatively. Derived from the Portuguese *feitico*, the name given to a popular and often heretical talisman in the Middle Ages, the word fetish developed subsequently to mean fated, charmed or bewitched (Gamman and Makinen, 1994). First used in English during the seventeenth century, it became popular anthropologically as a result of the writings of E.B. Tylor and others on 'primitive cultures'. An object was a fetish when it was considered to have a spirit incorporated into or acting through it. These anthropological explanations have tended to be ethnocentric – assuming that the use of such objects betrayed an epistemological error, a forgetting that imaginary powers had been projected onto the material – contained within narratives suggesting a wider lack of civilization (Mitchell, 1986). The most damning indictment of fetishism, however, came from the writings of Marx, for whom this process involved a projection and alienation of human powers and relationships onto illusionary religious or commodified objects.

These critical perspectives on fetishism vary, but each echoes the Platonic complaint that the affectual stimulation provoked by images, symbols and objects can result in errors of understanding and even a loss of self, and could be safeguarded against only by maintaining rational distance from such 'imitations' (Mitchell, 1986: 5; Dennis, 2009: 24–5). Yet not everyone viewed fetishism negatively. Comte (1853: 190) identified in this practice something enduring about the emotional, intellectual, moral and *religious* nature of humans, insisting that not even our 'high intellectual culture' can prevent us from being plunged into a state of 'radical fetishism' by phenomena that stimulate in us overwhelming emotions. It was the power of fetishism to take people *beyond* their individual selves and egoistic concerns that appealed to Comte in his argument that material eroticism could 'rejuvenate people's emotional life', bringing reason, feeling and action into a harmony that promoted a socially emboldening religion of humanity (Comte, 1858: 46–51; Wright, 1986: 19; Pickering, 1993: 698–9; Scharff, 1995: 77).

Comte's assessment of the social and individual consequences of fetishism is opposed to that of Marx and others. Nevertheless, where these thinkers converge is in recognizing that intense experiences of transcendence can be provoked and steered not only by intimate personal relationships, or by the *idea* of a mystical oneness with the divine, but also by images, icons, texts and other material objects. This is supported by the Christian belief that the power of images originates in God's ability, as reported in Genesis, 'to produce a creature in his own image and to breathe life into him', and developed via His production of other images, such as the holy Shroud, created without human intervention (Mondzain, 2002: 324–6). Most importantly, it was because Christ had been sent in the embodied image of humanity, with the mission of saving enfleshed mortals, that the Church provided 'century after century, a doctrine that not only accounted for spiritual redemption, but also shared salvation with the entire visible and therefore sensible world' (Mondzain, 2002: 326).

This association of the human form with archetypal religious imagery exerted an enduring influence in the Christian tradition, ranging from medieval notions of the 'King's two bodies' to the many communities for whom the pure body was a visible image of religiosity. Finch's (2010) analysis of early New England Reformers, for example, highlights how 'plainness' manifest in bodily appearance was experienced and perceived as reflecting inner goodness and helped separatists identify who were true and authentic Christians. It is not just Christianity, however, that has treated images as sacred. Subsequent to the Old Testament's condemnation of sacrilegious images, Islamic *hadith* proscribed 'the effigy' (with the international controversy over the Danish cartoons of Muhammad illustrating the passions that can be stirred when such interdictions are ignored) (Frodon, 2002: 221). These examples show that the fetishistic sacralization of images need not result in their positive valuation, while Calvin's attack on religious imagery from within the Christian tradition can help us understand the general sensitivities surrounding other-worldly associated imagery. Calvin (1960 [1536]) 'feared the power of a visual figure to enthral, contain, or constrain his own concept of the deity' and quoted Augustine's warning that 'infirm minds' can be led astray by the animate capacity of images (Kibbey, 1986; Morgan, 2005: 142).

Despite the controversies that have surrounded the idolatrous worship of images and objects – charges that Protestantism levied against Catholicism, and that Christianity had earlier laid at the door of paganism – all religions use some form of material fetishism to stimulate a sense of the sacred within the embodied subject, even if this is that of the written text. As Morgan (2005: 10) notes, sortilege (the random selection of a passage from a sacred text such as the Bible, Torah or Qur'an) 'as a special message to the seeker, is one such practice', while creating amulets engraved with sacred inscriptions is another. Even Calvin's claim 'that the biblical Word is the only proper image of the Word' provides us an example of how material phenomena are fetishized as possessing special powers within religion (Morgan, 2005: 12). Ordinarily, however, the uses of materiality extend way beyond the Word. The life of the Counter-Reformation Saint Teresa of Avila provides a particularly striking example here, envisioning a statue of Christ she had seen in a monastery courtyard before being entered physically by the Lord and engulfed in him in a state of delirium and bliss (Kristeva, 2009). Contemporarily, the Orthodox Church views icons as a means of revelation, of sacred knowledge and as a method of communication with God: as 'channels of grace ... icons are sacramental, different from ordinary material objects' (Howes, 2007: 7).

The significance attached to religious icons, images and objects may share the aim of stimulating in people a sense of transcendent escape from the mundane world of daily affairs, but the power over such fetishistic means has been highly contested within and between religions. Mitchell (1986: 6), for example, highlights issues of 'statues and other material symbols in religious ritual' that were central to the English Civil War. Such conflicts are no less intense today. What Latour (2002: 37) refers to as the 'state of emergency', proclaimed after the terrorism of 9/11, focuses on how we deal with images of all sorts in 'a frantic search for the roots of fanaticism'. As Latour (2010: 31) notes, what is happening today in the modern attempt to impose logic and rationality over the fetishistically charged images of 'extremists' is not novel: it has antecedents ranging from 'the Greeks who abandoned the idols of the Cave but put Ideas on pedestals; to the Jews who broke the Golden Calf but built the Temples, the Christians who burned pagan statues but painted icons; to the Protestants who white-washed frescos but brandished the true text of the bible from the pulpit'. Despite all attempts to prohibit them, there appears 'no way to stop the proliferation of mediators, inscriptions, objects, icons, idols, image, picture, and signs' (Latour, 2002: 23).

Evidence of the continued power of religious fetishes is plentiful. As Luhrmann (2004) argues in the case of contemporary evangelical Christianity, for all the emphasis placed on language and the Word, images deployed in rituals seek to invoke in believers an emotional intensity in which God's presence becomes real and immediate. This conclusion is reinforced by Meyer's (2010a: 751) analysis of the 'aesthetics of persuasion' within Pentecostalism wherein 'sensational forms' that draw on images and objects, as well as music, invoke and organize access to the transcendental through the generation of 'repeatable patterns of feeling and action'. Morgan's (1998: 179–83) research into American Protestants also suggests that many followers 'find a central place for images in their piety', especially when these 'invoke the faculty of memory' or enable them to 'help the individual assemble a personal spiritual narrative'. Members of this relatively individualist faith use popular religious images, such as Sallman's 'Head of Christ', in order to stimulate a shared sense of belonging within a transcendent community (Morgan, 1998: 204).

Orsi's (2005) analysis of Catholicism in mid-twentieth-century America demonstrates further how materially eroticized objects are used as media of transcendent presence in order to shape one's own dispositions and actions as well as the responses of others. Holy cards, beads, relics, statues and images as well as blessed waters and oils were viewed as holding the power of the holy figure or the sacred place and as making it 'present' in the living subject as an aspect of their own sense of themselves as one of the faithful (Orsi, 2005: 49). This 'corporealization of presence' enabled individuals to find the strength to act in ways they would otherwise have found impossible in living with distress and challenging secular authorities (Orsi, 2005: 50, 74).

Each of these fetishistic investments expresses what Gumbrecht (2004: xv, 98) refers to as 'moments of intensity' within a broader desire for transcendent presence in which objects provide a material instantiation for meanings that could otherwise be abstract, and proffer an interesting contrast to the early Protestant theological emphasis on treating as metaphors the body and blood of Christ in the Eucharist and elsewhere. They also lend support to Morgan's argument that religious images, icons and objects can be used to enhance the 'collective "orchestration" of the habitus' of religious groups. In seeking a common focus – whether this be using prayer mats to facilitate common prayer, a particular version or translation of the holy book, or a particular holy image – individuals and groups can stimulate religious presence and maintain religious identities that possess a particular content and direction in relation to this-worldly and other-worldly matters.

These fetishistic attachments can and have been the subject of disagreement, debate and conflict: there is a long history of religions, nations and individuals battling over and replacing one set of images, icons, objects and texts with another, but their power to move and animate individuals is indisputable. Material eroticism, while it is analytically distinct from the physical, emotional and religious eroticism identified by Weber and Bataille, can transform people as they pass 'into one state and out of another', criss-crossing the various sensory thresholds of the human body and involving various combinations of 'touch, sight, smell and sound, but also memory, intuition, and imagination' that open up the embodied subject to transcendent forces (Morgan, 2010: 12). As Mitchell (1986: 26) makes clear, the words in religious texts stimulate images in the minds of readers, while the visual imagery of a painting or sacred object can guide thought in a particular direction.

## The Contested Economy of Fetishism

This focus on the embodied basis of material eroticism is relevant not simply for understanding fetishistic investments in religion, but for appreciating the manner in which the spread of bio-economic forces (via consumer culture and global media) means that religion must, in the modern age, compete for interest and emotional investment with a huge range of non-religious images and objects. One example of this competition, and the embodied basis with which it is associated, is evident in the actions of Christian groups who view themselves as struggling to maintain their sexual integrity amidst the instrumentalization and commodification of eroticism via the sexualization of consumer culture. Prominent here, in issues we discussed earlier, are controversies involving the spread of pornography and the proper location of sex in society.

The prominent evangelic pastor Mark Driscoll's (2009) tract *Porn-Again Christian* usefully summarizes some of the common concerns here, in a manner that demonstrates the continued relevance of Weber's analysis of the religious regulation of physical eroticism. Quoting from Genesis 2:24 to 25, Driscoll (2009: 4, 8) states that sex 'as God intends it is for one man and one woman in marriage with the overarching purpose of oneness', that sexual activity or excitement outside of this context is a sin, and that as Paul's letters to the Corinthians (5:9–11) make clear, righteous Christians should not associate with anyone 'guilty of sexual immorality'. Identifying 'common pornography' as highly addictive in its capacity to stimulate key neurobiological zones associated with compulsive behaviour, Driscoll (2009: 35) also argues that there exists a strong connection between addiction to pornography and violence. If it is to result in desired forms of transcendence, and not the illegitimate 'loss of self' that characterizes discussions of pornography addiction, physical eroticism needs to be experienced within the authorized confines of marriage or in sublimated form through the ecstatic forms of intoxicating worship evident in Charismatic churches.

Driscoll's contemporary exhortations to avoid 'undesirable' sources of visual stimuli possess an affinity with a long line of other guardians of morals, such as Clement of Alexandria who, in the second century, admonished the Greeks for defiling their ears and prostituting their eyes with seductive and arousing profane images (Dennis, 2009: 59). They also reinforce other attempts to regulate Christian sexuality within the confines of marriage (such as the virginity pledge movement initiated in 1993 by the Southern Baptist Convention and involving over 2.5 million young people; Bearman and Brückner, 2001), and possess parallels with the condemnation of homosexuality in many Islamic and Pentecostal Christian communities today (Kugle and Hunt, 2012; Van Klinken, 2013). Such actions signify an opposition to illegitimate sources of stimuli, but they also reflect a concern to *maintain the affectual charge* of those religiously authorized material texts, icons and images in the global marketplace.

Maintaining the fetishistic charge of such other-worldly directed phenomena involves a considerable challenge that can be approached via Durkheim's (1995) depiction of how material signs accumulated their power in traditional societies via the contagious circulation of effervescent emotions that consolidated the group within itself. Sacralization emerged through processes that were 'natural' in that they appeared to arise spontaneously without intent or design. In global modernity, however, the conditions underpinning group formation have changed: it is less likely that any organization seeking to reproduce a particular type of habitus in new generations can rely simply on unimpeded, organic processes of group membership. Individuals not only confront a profusion of competing signs and symbols within and outside of religious and consumer cultures, purporting to represent them and their 'belonging' to a particular lifestyle, but also exist as members of collectivities that are often more socially differentiated and geographically mobile than ever before.

In these circumstances 'natural' sacralization is no longer sufficient to ensure that particular images or objects are invested with extraordinary powers. Instead, there is a need for individuals and groups to engage deliberately and reflexively in practices and strategies that enhance the importance and capacity of particular materials to stimulate experiences of transcendence supportive of a particular theology or personal commitment. This involves attempting to maintain the status of material objects as extraordinary and worthy of continued fetishistic investments through processes of 'enhanced' sacralization. Enhanced sacralization is not unique to the modern world, but it has become more common as groups and individuals are increasingly aware that there exists a marketplace within which these material signs compete.

The strategies that have been used to effect enhanced sacralization vary widely, but many groups are prepared to engage in conflict and violence in order to elevate the status of that materiality prized within, or rendered sacrilegious by, their own religion. This is clear when we realize that positive attempts to enhance the value of 'authorized' religious materials are often accompanied by actions intended to denigrate those of their competitors as either idolatrous or decadent (e.g. the destruction of the Bamiyan Buddhas by the Taliban in Afghanistan, and the furore created by Reverend Terry

Jones's plans to stage a Qur'an-burning protest on the anniversary of 9/11). One of the more recent examples of this involved the notorious 'Innocence of Muslims' film clips that were circulated around the globe using YouTube and other media in September 2012. Portraying Muhammad as a fraud, a womanizer and a child molester, many thousands of Muslims engaged in violent protests against these sacrilegious images. In responding to the 'symbolic violence' of the film, an attack on the US consulate in Benghazi resulted in the death of the US Ambassador to Libya and three of his colleagues, while buildings were set on fire and Western flags burnt in protests from Khartoum to Cairo and Jakarta.

If 'enlightened' Westerners remained puzzled at this furore, a very different but nevertheless illuminating case occurred in the same month when the British Royal Household took legal action against the publication in Europe of topless pictures of the Duchess of Cambridge. While the religious connotations of the public criticism that followed these pictures were much more implicit than those in the case of the *Innocence* film clips (focused on the transgression of a Royal body and the sacred value of 'privacy'), there was a general sense in Britain that a line had been crossed and that the publication of such imagery justifiably 'moved' the Royal Family to legal action possessed of the potential to result in the imprisonment of offenders. Such examples illustrate that the economy of fetishistic signs and symbols is not bound globally by any universally agreed rules of competition. It can involve and has promoted conflict and violence, and is a reason why some critics have sought to reconstruct the bases on which eroticism can contribute to radically reformed types of religiously enhanced experiences and identities.

## Conclusion

Weber and Bataille identified eroticism as a socially ambivalent phenomenon, with the capacity to be life-enhancing and a route into a religious habitus, but also able to stimulate forms of oppression, undermine institutional religion and destabilize social relationships. Recent writings, in contrast, have explored the bio-economic routinization and exploitation of eroticism, while also acknowledging that images, icons, texts and other material phenomena continue to possess the capacity to be fetishized in a manner that harnesses erotic experience to the promotion of religious experiences and identities.

In assessing the opportunities associated with this material eroticism, we noted that the other-worldly referents of religious icons still have to compete with instrumentalized and commodified forms of eroticism and with other secular products imbued with an aestheticized charisma in global modernity. In the light of this, our suggestion that Christian anxieties over pornography, and the Muslim challenges to what are perceived to be sacrilegious materializations of the sacred, can be said to signal how other-worldly fetishism and this-worldly aesthetic charisma have now become a site of contestation between competing religious and secular modalities of the sacred.

It is in this context that religious movements have had to confront the challenge of operating within a variety of bio-economic marketplaces, seeking to maintain the appeal and the competitive edge of their products by engaging in processes of 'enhanced' sacralization; something particularly evident in cases of religious conflict and violence. While such processes are arguably reflective of adaptation to a broader materialization of eroticism within global culture, they are also indicative of the increasing *reflexive* character of contestation between different modalities of the sacred, given the need for religious individuals and groups to engage deliberately in practices and strategies that mark them out as religious in a secular context. In the following chapter, we assess the implications of this turn to reflexivity for how we can conceptualize the instauration of a religious habitus today.

# 7

## Instauring the Religious Habitus

### Introduction

Having explored in Chapters 1 and 2 how debates about religion can be advanced by examining the significance of contrasting modalities of the sacred for secularization, social differentiation, religious authority and embodied experience, we focused in Chapters 3 to 6 on the last of these variables. This is not because issues related to embodied experience render redundant the emergent structural contours of global modernity. It is because recent developments associated with modernization, differentiation and the proliferation of competing religious and secular authorities raise questions about the extent to which contemporary enframings of experience can still result in stimuli, feelings, classifications and reflections conducive to religious views and identities. This subject is, therefore, of crucial significance to issues concerning secularization and the revitalization of religion: the existence or absence of appropriate levels and intensities of religious experience in present and future generations provide or problematize the crucial embodied bases on which religious forms are reproduced, strengthened or undermined in the future.

It was in this context that we focused on those experiential bridges explored by Durkheim and Weber as historically central to religious identities. Intoxication, pain, charisma and eroticism are not the only phenomena we could have studied, but they remain of great importance to human life and provide useful case studies of how experiences can be differentially shaped. Our arguments here, which go to the heart of the embodied bases of secularization and de-secularization processes, suggest an overall trajectory towards the dominance of this-worldly bio-political and bio-economic enframings of embodied existence, but one wherein certain forms of religion nonetheless thrive. Before assessing the implications of our analysis in terms of conclusions to be drawn about secularization and the sacred, however, this chapter extends our assessments of particular types of experience by exploring the conditions in which it is still possible to construct forms of religious habitus.

Focusing on the religious habitus entails that we move away from interrogating the conditions conducive to the promotion of *particular* religious experiences. It requires instead that we examine more generally the extent to which these and other stimuli, feelings and thoughts can coalesce and become crystallized into relatively stable and enduring *embodied dispositions* and *orientations* towards religion. Of particular note to our concern with these general embodied conditions on which religious commitments are forged is the growing necessity of *reflexivity* in the contemporary global age. The frequency and importance of deliberations about and reflections on one's reactions, inclinations and views, and the increasingly complex conditions in which these are formed, has grown to unprecedented levels as new media and accelerated flows of information and migration have made more people more aware than ever before of the co-existence of competing religions, politics, lifestyles, and economic choices and options (Archer, 2003).

Religious orientations may once have developed via the traditional cultivation of habits, but increasingly have to be pieced together, crafted, or, following Latour's (2011) development of the term, instaured, through a deliberative process in which individuals are forced to navigate options and choices and come to terms with the doubts and uncertainties these can stimulate. In explicating this situation, and its implications for the religious habitus, our discussion is framed within a critical interrogation of Bourdieu's notion of this term. This is not only because Bourdieu has provided the most influential theoretical account of the habitus, but also because the pervasiveness of reflexivity in modernity poses significant challenges to it, and to the view of religious orientations with which it is associated.

## Bourdieu and the Habitus

Bourdieu's notion of the habitus has exerted enormous influence in sociology (e.g. Bourdieu and Wacquant, 1992: 18–20; Shilling, 1993; King, 2000; Pickel, 2005; Sayer, 2005; Adams, 2006), with his analysis of the religious habitus increasingly evident in theoretical and substantive analyses of religion (e.g. Bourdieu, 1991; Berlinerblau, 1999; Collins, 2002; Verter, 2003; Rey, 2004, 2007; Lee, 2010; Mellor and Shilling, 2010b). For Bourdieu (1987: 124; 1991: 16), the religious habitus is aligned closely to its societal context, and is associated not with reflexivity but with *pre-reflexive dispositions* towards experience, action and understanding that 'modify, in a deep and lasting fashion, the practice and world-view of lay people' by 'justifying their existence' as 'occupants of a determinate social position'. What distinguishes these as *religious* orientations is that they are facilitated by exchanges, involving goods of salvation between religious specialists and laypeople, and that they provide a distinctive mode of social justification and normalization that involves misrecognizing the structure of the social world as the natural/supernatural structure of the cosmos (Bourdieu, 1977: 129; 1991: 14, 19–22). Religion is a cultural adjunct to social and governmental structures, providing theodicies of good fortune for the privileged and suffering for the dispossessed, and reconciling individuals to the social fields that structure their conditions of experience: 'theodicies are always sociodicies' (Bourdieu, 1991: 16).

This account of the religious habitus and the field of religion possesses value since, historically, many of its forms have buttressed hierarchical divisions and inequalities by contextualizing them within cosmological systems of meaning, but it has been criticized. There are two major sets of reasons for this dissatisfaction. The first concerns Bourdieu's (2000: 103, 124, 240, 245) identification of the religious habitus as historically anachronistic, and his insistence that the modern state has taken over from religion the function of consecrating inequalities. This recalls simplistic versions of the secularization thesis in being unable to account for the revitalization of religion and religious identities since the end of the twentieth century. It also ignores the importance of religious orientations for those most exposed to the insecurities of life associated with 'globalization processes occurring above the level of the state and localized reactions and fragmentation below it' (Engler, 2003: 455). If we accept that religion consecrates experiences, values and identities for people marginalized from the sectors of governmental largesse and influence, moreover, we might also want to follow analysts who have explored, *contra* Bourdieu, how it can offer a resource for forging identities and claiming rights *in opposition* to the state (Gauchet, 1997; Bruce, 2003; Braeckman, 2009).

The second dissatisfaction with Bourdieu's notion of the religious habitus concerns its socially reproductive consequences and the relative passivity with which it is inculcated in its recipients (Calhoun, 1993; Archer, 1995; Jenkins, 2002). In relation to the former, Bourdieu's (1994, 2000) focus on the exchanges occurring within and between the religious and other social fields – in which agents struggle for distinction and ownership of spiritual, economic, cultural and social capital – recognizes that the contexts in which forms of habitus develop alter over time. Nevertheless, he emphasizes homologies rather than disjunctions between types of habitus and the fields in which they develop, and has recognized that his formulations tend to normalize social reproduction (Bourdieu and Wacquant, 1992). His conception of the religious habitus, in other words, remains essentially conservative irrespective of the dynamism that sometimes appears in his analysis of those fields implicated in relationships between state and corporate actors. In terms of the related concern that the religious habitus is inculcated automatically, Bourdieu (1984: 466) argues that dispositions operate 'beyond the reach of introspective scrutiny or control by the will', with misrecognized experiences becoming sedimented in the bodies of subjects, immune to critical reflection and reconciling them to their surroundings. Social stasis and individual acquiescence dominate, and we get little sense of the deliberative and reflexive work dimensions of experience that are involved in cultivating identity-transforming religious 'techniques of the body' (Mauss, 1973a), 'technologies of the self' (Foucault, 1986) or 'body pedagogics' (Mellor and Shilling, 2010a).

These criticisms have not prevented Bourdieu's conception of the religious habitus from being applied productively to socially reproductive class conflict in such regions as Latin America (Maduro, 1977), but they have contributed to a number of adaptations of it. Csordas (1994) ameliorates the tendency of the habitus to recapitulate social structures by focusing on the variable phenomenological dimensions of lived religious orientations. Martin (2000) explores the capacity of forms of religious habitus to generate narratives of resistance to prevailing power structures. Urban (2003) utilizes the concept to reveal how religious groups can challenge economic norms. Each adaptation develops by uncoupling routinized religious orientations from a necessary causal relationship with the social milieu in which they develop, acknowledging also the need to differentiate between the norms of state and economy, on the one hand, and the dispositions that actually develop within individuals and families, on the other. Each is also predicated on the recognition that Bourdieu ignores the potential of the religious habitus to transform experience and provoke social change within and beyond the differentiated field of religion as a result of its association with an 'authority higher than any available in this world' (Bruce, 2003: 11; Lau, 2004: 373).

Bourdieu's notion of the religious habitus faces an even greater challenge as a result of the proliferation of social conditions antithetical to the regularized dispositions at its core. Viewing the religious habitus as a set of pre-reflexively established habits and world-views, Bourdieu recognizes non-routinized contemplative deliberation only as an *exceptional* response to *exceptional* situations (Bourdieu and Wacquant, 1992: 40, 131; Adams, 2006). His analysis is here predicated on an aversion to the 'intellectualist tradition' that holds reflexivity to be a common mode of engagement with the world (Bourdieu, 1990: 68–9; 1998: 81). In its place, the habitus mediates external structures and personal subjectivity through its existence as 'society written into the body', 'a socialized body, a structured body, a body which has incorporated the immanent structures of the world … and which structures the perception of that world' (Bourdieu, 1998: 81). Nowadays, however, the pace of social change, the proliferation of new media and the quantities of information that circulate globally appear to militate against the maintenance of firmly routinized dispositions to action and thought (Sayer, 2005; Elder-Vass, 2007; Archer, 2012). Indeed, Archer (2012) goes so far as to suggest that such conditions encourage a pervasive extension of reflexivity that *fatally undermines* habitual schemas and Bourdieu's approach.

In what follows, we focus on this under-explored issue of the relationship between reflexivity and the religious habitus, accepting elements of Archer's influential critique but also identifying its limitations. We do this by drawing on the writings of Latour (2011) to reconceive the religious habitus as a phenomenon that is actively re-made, or instaured, through the deliberations of individuals intent on cultivating a repertoire of religious orientations, techniques, feelings and beliefs within religious modalities of the sacred. This reconceptualization enables us to include reflexive considerations alongside religious dispositions and avoids the connotations of social reproduction and individual passivity within Bourdieu's analysis. In their place, the idea that forms of religious habitus are instaured sensitizes us to the variable relationships that exist between these orientations and those social and cultural milieus in which they are forged.

We illustrate our argument with reference to the forms of religious habitus associated with Christian Pentecostalism and Islamic Revivalism. These can be characterized respectively by individualized decisions to 'open' the body to the transcendent power of the Holy Spirit (an approach that builds on a tradition of individuals deliberating reflexively on their relationship with God and with this-worldly matters), and by efforts to create a disciplined religious identity fitted to its socio-religious context through an intense scrutiny of the self (an approach that has in recent decades assumed increasingly individualized reflexive components). These forms of religious habitus exist within contrasting modalities of the sacred, but highlight in different ways the importance of intentionality and reflexivity to the instauration of religious identities in the current era. Both also enable us to highlight the varied and contingent relationships that can exist between religious orientations and societal norms.

## Modernity, Reflexivity and the Habitus

Irrespective of its limitations, Bourdieu's analysis of routinized embodied orientations and world-views has been accepted by even his strongest critics as suited to traditional societies underpinned by low levels of structural differentiation and 'ideational diversification' (Archer, 2010: 280–4). In such circumstances, the habitus and its religious variants persist within stable modes of socialization that equip people with techniques and dispositions that are effective within their environment. In global modernity, however, a growing number of scholars have suggested that high levels of social stability, integration and contextual continuity are increasingly absent. People are confronted more than ever before with alternative ways of experiencing the world around them. These circumstances mean that traditional socialization processes have become more diverse and less significant compared to the capacity to respond actively to fast-changing circumstances, making routinized dispositions and orientations unviable (Giddens, 1991; Beck, 1992; Calhoun, 1993: 82; Robertson, 1993; Archer, 2010, 2012; Herbert, 2011).

It is not just these general features of modernity that suggest reflexive engagement with change is unavoidable, but also developments that have occurred *within* the field of religion – especially in relation to religious authority (Maqsood, 2013). As Chaves (1994: 766) notes, whereas in traditional societies religious edicts and interdictions could be routinized as a result of the limited character of social change, the differentiated fields with which religions now interact have prompted their leaders to deliberate upon and institute considerable changes to the structures of religious power. These have resulted in a pluralization and horizontalization of religious authority; a situation in which religious legitimacy is increasingly diverse and contested (Edgell, 2012: 258). Such circumstances do not entail that religion is unable to flourish, but cast doubt on whether traditional modes of religious socialization, reproduction and habitus can endure unaffected, and increase those situations in which individuals have to *choose* from where to receive religious guidance (Wilson, 1985; Dobbelaere, 1988, 1989; Starrett, 1998; Turner et al., 2009; Herbert, 2011; Speck, 2013).

Those acknowledging that modernity has stimulated an increase in deliberative engagements with religion and other phenomena, yet wishing to make creative use of 'the religious habitus' and its secular variants, have added to Bourdieu's conception a greater sense of the active, contemplative dimensions of people's dispositions. They have done this either by recognizing the enduring significance of the habitus in reflexive contexts (Sayer, 2005; Elder-Vass, 2007; Fleetwood, 2008) or through attempts to hybridize routinization and deliberation, such as in the notion of a 'reflexive habitus' centred on a disposition towards reflexivity itself (Sweetman, 2003; Adams, 2006). Casting doubts on these attempts at reconciliation, however, Archer (2010) emphasizes the difficulties in combining conceptually the pre-reflexive orientations central to Bourdieu's notion, and the conscious, interrogative, deliberative reflection on and questioning of the self she views as stimulated by and essential to surviving and prospering in the modern era.

For Archer (2003, 2007, 2010), the role of habit in the social world is necessarily replaced, because of the frequency with which it encounters obstacles and blockages, by the 'internal conversation'. Proceeding via an inner dialogue based upon listening and responding inwardly to thoughts and feelings about the self, wherein dispositions, reactions, emotions and circumstances are scrutinized in the light of an individual's aims and preferences, these interior conversations sometimes result in decisions to act *against* inclinations and habits and seek *change*. Reflexivity has a retrospective character when directed towards existing habits, but can take on a prospective quality when projecting possible versions of the self into the future. It is not monadic, moreover, as it involves drawing on and interpreting the views of significant others (albeit not a single generalized other), and uses the public resource of language (Mead, 1962; Archer, 2010: 2–5).

This highly influential account of the necessity and pervasiveness of reflexivity in the current era – an account possessed of a strong affinity with Elias's (2000) argument that thought has become an increasingly important factor historically in the formation of experience – suggests it would be difficult to justify retaining even an adapted version of the concept of a religious habitus. Despite Archer's criticisms of Bourdieu's work, however, she follows him in associating the habitus with *pre-reflexive habit* (Bourdieu, 1984:

466). It is this that allows her to draw upon Durkheim (1983: 79–80) and Weber (1927: 355; 1968: 321) in identifying modernity with an overcoming of the disposition towards tradition and habit – an overcoming developed patchily throughout the twentieth century, but which has reached a stage where 'unthinking habit' of the sort envisaged by Bourdieu is non-viable (Archer, 2010: 280).

Others writing long before Bourdieu, however, provide a more future-oriented understanding of dispositional habits as possessed of a 'potential energy' with the capacity to re-make the individual alongside the emergence of new circumstances; an understanding intended to maintain the utility of the concept for the modern era (e.g. James, 1900; Dewey, 2002: 44). In what follows, we build on this insight by suggesting that the idea of the religious habitus retains utility contemporarily but requires re-conceptualizing in order to signify how individuals and groups seek to actively and reflexively re-make, craft or instaur their embodied experiences and subjectivities in line with religious prescriptions. The religious habitus assumes various forms, depending on the 'religious repertoires' available within distinct traditions (Martin, 2005; Edgell, 2012), and can have significantly more complex relations to broader social contexts than those suggested by Bourdieu.

## Religious Engagements with the Habitus

Bourdieu's (1990: 54) conceptualization of the habitus as 'the active presence of past experiences' may be limited, but usefully signifies the importance of history for understanding the term. It was Aristotle's (2000) notion of *hexis* – referring to an acquired moral character, central to virtue in that it directs an individual's feelings, desires and actions as a result of habituation – that was first translated into Latin as *habitus*. Imparted with a Christian inflection in the thirteenth century within Aquinas's *Summa Theological*, medieval Islamic thinkers from the eleventh to the fifteenth century also engaged with the religious implications of Aristotle's work and the role of regularized habits in Muslim life.

In Christian theology, Aquinas's development of the habitus incorporated a distinction between acquired and infused virtues, maintaining space for human merit and divine grace (Wisse, 2003; Mathieu, 2009). Rather than promoting a passive assimilation of prevalent norms, Aquinas conceives the habitus as a medium for *overcoming* 'unthinking habit' by placing 'one's activity under more control than it might otherwise be': the religious habitus is a means to ensure that *deliberative choices* for the good become *dispositions* towards the good (Davies, 2003: 124–5). This strategic incorporation of Aristotelian philosophy into Christian theology was mirrored in medieval Islamic thought by such figures as Abu Hamid al-Ghazali, al-Miskawayh, Ibn Rush and Ibn Khaldun, who explored the importance of regularized habits in Muslim life (Mahmood, 2005). For Muslim writers the *malaka* approximated to the habitus in building within the individual a faith affirming quality, deriving from scrutiny, disciplined practices and experiences that follow from these (Lapidus, 1984: 55–6; Mahmood, 2005: 137).

The broader religious contexts for these analyses were not identical in Islam and Christianity. Grace did not occupy the same importance for salvation within Islamic thought as in Christian theology, but remained significant: religiously pure habits were *always* dependent on good works, but also required the grace of Allah. Similarly, while Christianity's focus on *orthodoxy* addressed the relatively individualized and voluntaristic forging of a Christian habitus through a focus on belief, Islam's much stronger focus on *orthopraxy* contextualized issues of individual dispositions, character and ethics in a collective regulation of action embracing a *whole society* via religious law, a common language (Arabic) and common patterns of worship across its different forms (Bruce, 2003: 234–5, 242).

Despite these differences, the common concern in Islam and Christianity for *overcoming* unthinking habit and forging a *new* mode of being, itself based on an orientation towards the *transformative power* of the divine, is not easily contained within Bourdieu's (1987: 124; 1990: 167) model. In terms of forging a new mode of being, we can see in both religions analogies with Foucault's (1988a: 18) interest in the conscious cultivation of techniques, habits and practices designed to instil in the self or other new patterns of acting. In terms of the transformative dimensions of this mode of being we should also note that its sources are based in religious traditions, the parameters and effects of which pre-date and are, *contra* Bourdieu, irreducible to the extant structures of society. The religious habitus is thus forged in people not only through the discipline and training emphasized by ancient philosophy (Aristotle, 2000), but also via an orientation to other-worldly forces (be these grace, divine law or other). The challenge for any reconceived notion of the term is to incorporate these active, deliberative orientations at its centre (Wisse, 2003: 21–2).

## Instauring the Religious Habitus

In addressing this task, we turn to Latour's (2011: 9) interest in the active crafting or instauration of new bodily dispositions, orientations and modes of being. This process is for Latour informed by a 'multi-realist' recognition that individuals are able to 'bring together' and work upon ideas and materials, each possessed of their own qualities, to instaur new spheres of activity, cognition and being which can decisively shape human experience in *particular* ways.

In unpacking these notions of instauration and multi-realism, Latour (2011) draws on Souriau's (1943: 44) illustration of a sculptor: a craftsperson who does not create something from nothing, but who forges or instaurs from the potentialities of clay a vision that combines the intrinsic properties of the material with an idea of what it could become. This is not a 'social' construction. Instead, it results from the combination of multiple elements, with the sculptor also being shaped through her activity in terms of the development of skills, muscle tensions and the experience gained from working on the task. Both sculptor and clay are instaured in this process of working and being worked on.

Other examples could be drawn from the 'instauration of music', in which the evocation of sounds from materials led to the development of instruments and the composition of music; music possessed of the capacity to affect the mood of those who listen to it and to transport the individual to places and experiences irreducible to the properties of sound-waves (DeNora, 2000). Each of these instaurations draws on multiple elements of the environment to create new ways of being or dwelling in the world that are more than their constituent parts (Latour, 2011: 307).

Sculpture and music may be simple examples of instauration, but we can apply this mode of analysis to the more complex case of religion by highlighting the intentional and active elements in religious affiliation as identified by Aristotle's theological interpreters. In this context, we define the instauration of a religious habitus as crafting a mode of human being that locates stimuli, feeling and thought at the intersection of worldly and other-worldly realities by *enframing* the former in the latter, and thereby *transforming* embodied experience in a way that imparts a particular directionality to life. Emphasizing particularity in this definition allows us to take into account diverse forms of religious habitus, reflecting the different repertoires encoded within contrasting religious 'traditions' (Asad, 1986: 14; Latour, 2011: 12, 14), and remaining sensitive to the various ways in which they may interact with surrounding social and cultural structures.

In exploring the utility of this definition, Christian Pentecostalism and the Islamic piety movement provide us with contrasting examples of how the religious habitus can be instaured within contrasting religious modalities of the sacred. Our focus on the active and deliberative aspects involved in the construction of religious identities does not suggest that concern for routinized habits is unimportant. Instead, developing Aristotle's and Aquinas's concerns, we highlight those intentional attempts to cultivate routines congruent with bodily openness, on the one hand, and disciplined virtue and piety, on the other, while also exploring their relationship with the societies in which they are formed.

### Crafting the Open Religious Habitus

Historically, one of the central features of the transcendent sacred Christian cultural 'repertoire' has been a focus on individuals being *drawn out* of their societies (by opening their bodies and minds to an other-worldly sphere), while also maintaining a worldly existence in which sectors of society are recognized as governed by non-religious criteria (Martin, 2005). In this context, Christians are meant to develop a relationally-defined, but unique, sense of personhood arising from the experience of communion with God (Zizioulas, 2004), while also acquiring from this communion the enhanced capacity to reflect upon, interrogate and deploy their individual conscience in engaging morally with, and identifying religious potential within, secular society (albeit often in conjunction with the guidance of the Church) (Seligman, 1992: 135).

This distinction between the spiritual (other-worldly) and the temporal (worldly), and the associated capacity of Christians to reflect on earthly matters by utilizing their communion with God as a source of guidance, was evident in the work of Aquinas and Augustine, but took different forms within the religious field over time. The medieval hierarchical division of the church into other-worldly focused religious virtuosi and this-worldly grounded masses, for example, was deconstructed by the Reformation's promotion of an emergent 'worldly asceticism' for *all* (Weber, 1948 [1915]: 274–6; Troeltsch, 1976; McKinnon, 2010). This entwined other-worldly and worldly matters within an intense reflexive scrutiny of personal dispositions and activities made all the more urgent by the Puritan rejection of priestly absolution (Weber, 1991). Despite such variation, however, this Christian location of the individual at the intersection of the worldly and other-worldly has long required the faithful to *cultivate consciously* techniques and habits designed to open their bodies to spiritual forces.

One such early Christian technique of instauration is baptism. This required initiates to embark on a lengthy programme of self-directed preparation and education prior to being received into the Church (Brown, 1988), and has assumed renewed visibility with the modern Pentecostal focus on conversion (Poloma, 2003; Meyer, 2010a). Klaver and van de Kamp (2011), for example, examine this Pentecostal opening of the body as a conversional creation of a 'born-again subject', centred on the bodily dynamics of becoming and remaining a convert, involving techniques of prayer, pure living, and a reflexive interrogation of the self across every aspect of life as believers prepare their bodies to be receptive to the Holy Spirit. Physical images and objects are used in this preparation by churches but also by individuals as 'sensational forms' in attempts to nurture a materially mediated religious eroticism that is also intended to distance people from those secular attractions of consumer culture analysed in Chapter 6 (Meyer, 2010b). Possession, having been self-consciously sought, is manifest variously by individuals speaking in tongues, fainting and finding themselves unable to control tears, laughter or fits (Poloma, 2003). There is much reflexively scruti-nized attention directed towards the embodied presence of God in Pentecostalism, much deliberative concern 'with the stuff of the physical' in terms of divine and demonic forces, and a recognition that 'all born-again believers are able and entitled to embody the Holy Spirit' in this active instauration of a Christian habitus (Meyer, 2010a: 753).

This focus on opening the body to other-worldly forces is not a wholly reflexive process: deliberative attempts to prepare the body are engaged in as a means to being 'taken over' and inhabited viscer-ally, *mind and body*, by the Holy Spirit. Nevertheless, the reflexive preparation of the body is important and does not accord with a simple routinization of previously inculcated dispositions towards religion. Furthermore, while Christianity's investments in other-worldly communion have not been accompanied by investments of comparable religious worth in earthly, secular matters (as reflected for Martin [2005: 142] in the New Testament's relative neglect of law, war and politics), this is not the same as suggesting that religious orientations *legitimate* social realities. Such a suggestion obscures analytically important questions about the *ambiguity* pertaining to

Pentecostalism in this regard. Here, we can not only contrast Troeltsch's (1976) and Weber's (1991) discussions of Puritanism's elective *affinity* with modern capitalism to their Marxist critics who, in the manner of Bourdieu, argued that there existed a simple *accommodation* of religion to capitalism, but we can also note the significance of such competing claims today.

In what might be called the broadly Weberian camp, most accept that Pentecostalism promotes habits and practices uniquely well adapted to contemporary global conditions, but are resistant to viewing it as 'a mere reflex of the modern' and have argued that it continues to exert an independent effect on capitalism's development (Coleman, 2000: 3; Droogers, 2001: 54; Robbins, 2004: 137; Martin, 2005: 141). This is evident in Poloma's (2003) study of Christian revivalism in the 1990s. The experience of repentance and divine healing was prominent among those attending the services Poloma studied, together with the determination to live according to the inspiration and Word of God. Emboldened as individuals, in their individual relation to God, these worshippers did indeed return with renewed enthusiasm to their workaday lives. Nevertheless, as suggested in Chapter 3, their priority was to maintain the powerful sense they possessed of being part of a moral community (Poloma, 2003). These experiences possessed only a contingent relationship with current economic priorities, focusing as they did on searching for God's guidance in their daily affairs and maintaining their orientation to being *called out of the world* (Poloma, 2003: 23, 30–2, 89–91, 95; see also Csordas, 1990).

Such conclusions about the independent significance of Pentecostalism are reinforced by studies that identify its astonishing growth in South Korea as an important factor in that country's modernization (Freston, 2001: 61; Buswell and Lee, 2006: 1; Baldacchino, 2012: 368) and that have identified the cultivation of Pentecostal orientations in 'mega-churches' as a method which utilizes 'commercialized' places of worship to cultivate *distance from* prevailing mores and practices (Ellingson, 2010; Maddox, 2012). Following Weber, furthermore, Korean scholars have noted how the previously dominant Confucianism *hindered* modernization (Hong, 1973: 111; Lee, 1982: 5; Lie, 1998: 78–9). Baldacchino (2012) draws on these observations to emphasize further the continued importance of the *particular* beliefs and practices of Protestantism (including hard work, honesty and clean living) for the progress of modernization and capitalism: the deliberative instauration of specific religious orientations and habits becomes the means through which worldly economic activity is infused with other-worldly significance (Baldacchino, 2012: 373–7).

Critics of this broadly Weberian camp, in contrast, conclude that Pentecostalism displays a thoroughgoing *accommodation* to capitalism involving a collapse of the transcendent into the secular (Bruce and Voas, 2007: 13; Ellingson, 2010: 263). Utilizing Benjamin's (2004: 288–91) suggestion that capitalism has become the 'unassailable global religion', Maddox (2012: 155), for example, locates Pentecostalism within a broader, secular sacred re-enchantment of the world, akin to what we have referred to as the bio-economic sacred, rather than a revival of a religious form that might challenge it. Such an argument suggests that the reflexively cultivated dispositions involving hard work, sobriety and integrity represent no more than an ideological appropriation and celebration of qualities and embodied techniques central to contemporary capitalism (Bruce and Voas, 2007; Maddox, 2012).

Given that Christianity has historically facilitated flexible approaches to worldly matters, however, its capacity to embrace constructively key elements of secular culture is not necessarily a sign of its dissipation into it. As Baldacchino (2012: 382) notes, it may be the case that, in time, Pentecostalism follows the trajectory of ascetic Protestantism in this regard. Yet for the moment, 'we are at the level of elective affinity' in that it is exercising a decisive influence upon the deliberations and habitus of significant numbers of individuals in many parts of the world, as well as influencing the nature and development of societies (Baldacchino, 2012: 382). Questions about the longer-term resilience of the Pentecostal habitus remain open, but this openness is connected to the flexibility it provides to adherents to engage reflexively with the secular aspects of worldly life.

## Crafting the Disciplined Religious Habitus

In contrast to Christianity's distinction between the 'spiritual' and 'temporal', Islam's cultural repertoire has historically been associated more commonly with commitment to a 'total society' consistent with a socio-religious rather than transcendent modality of the sacred (Black, 1993: 59; Volpi and Turner, 2007). If Christianity promotes flexibility in its dealings with the secular, the Islamic insistence on the application of sharia to this-worldly matters forms part of a legal-moral tradition in which all worldly behaviour is proscribed and judged by religious categories (Asad, 1993: 212). These differences, alongside the Islamic focus on group rights as opposed to the Christian emphasis on personal rights (Siedentop, 2000), help account for Salvatore's (2006) critical view of those such as Tietze (2001) who argue that individualism, voluntarism and reflexivity have become increasingly important among Muslims. For Salvatore (2006), such arguments under-estimate the continued significance of *early socialization* and the development of 'traditional' *routinized experiences* and *identities* in Islam.

Salvatore's (2006) critique is consistent with Bourdieu's (1990: 55) emphasis on the significance of early experiences for integration into a habitus and Weber's (1964: 152–3) suggestion that these are particularly important in societies characterized by the monopolistic exercise of control over access to the sacred. It is reinforced by Kühle's (2012: 120) argument that while religion has, for many in the West, become a choice, 'research on Muslim minorities in Western societies consistently claims that for individuals with a Muslim background identities cannot be freely chosen' (Schmidt, 2002; Cesari, 2004, 2007; Peek, 2005; Spielhaus, 2010; Voas and Fleischmann, 2012). Recent census data, revealing exceptionally high degrees of inter-generational religious continuity among Muslim minorities in Europe, can also be used to support such conclusions (Kühle, 2012: 122; Scourfield et al., 2012: 99).

Despite these arguments, however, there is a strong case for refusing to view as opposites the early socialization associated with Bourdieu's conception of the habitus, and the focus on reflexivity and deliberation criticized by Salvatore (2006). Many young European Muslims celebrate as *reflexive choices* their religious identities, in making them distinctive within their host societies, even if there are strong constraints on them (Jenkins, 2000: 23; Kühle, 2012: 121–3). Similarly, given that monopolistic control over access to the sacred is becoming increasingly rare in Muslim-majority societies, as well as elsewhere, socialized and routinized forms of religious habitus are likely to face significant challenges to their viability (Kühle, 2012: 126). These challenges have been documented by Archer (2010) in terms of the rise of contextual discontinuity, and involve – in Bourdieu's terms – increasing levels of change and differentiation within and between social fields. Either way, they require for their successful negotiation increased levels of reflexivity even on the part of agents wishing to maintain the status quo in terms of their lives and beliefs.

These points should perhaps make us pause before juxtaposing reflexive Christian cultivations of an 'open body' to an Islamic insistence that followers 'close' their bodies to all but fixed patterns of externally prescribed ritual behaviour designed to instil habitual obedience to an immutable religious law (Asad, 1993: 56–7; Falk, 1994). So too should recent analyses identifying the resurgence of an ascetic form of Islam predicated upon a reflexive return to the this-worldly socio-political ethic of the Prophet Muhammad (Turner, 1974; Robinson, 2004). In this respect, Mahmood's (2005) study of the Islamic piety movement in Egypt provides an excellent illustration of how individual reflexivity can scrutinize and deepen religious orientations and dispositions through a focus on this-worldly behaviour guided by a deliberative focus on religious principles.

The piety movement forms part of the Islamic Revival or Islamic Awakening that has pervaded the Muslim world since the 1970s. Those active in it seek to inform their actions and society 'with a regulative sensibility that takes its cue from the Islamic theological corpus rather than from modern secular ethics' (Mahmood, 2005: 2, 42–3, 47). This is not a matter of following traditional habits, but of 'honing one's rational and emotional capacities so as to approximate the exemplary model of the pious self' based upon the conduct of the Prophet and his Companions (Mahmood, 2005: 31). Such intentional work on the embodied self was pervasive among the Egyptian women Mahmood studied as they sought to cope with people 'who constantly placed them in situations that were far from optimal for the realization of piety in day-to-day life', and with 'the internal struggle they had to engage in within themselves in a world that constantly beckoned them to behave in impious ways' (Mahmood, 2005: 156).

These Muslim women met these challenges by seeking to cultivate through dress, demeanour and actions an exterior and interior self that approximated to Islamic norms. As Mahmood (2005: 161) explains, since they regarded outward bodily markers as ineluctable means of stimulating the virtue of modesty and fear of God, 'the body's precise movements, behaviours, and gestures were all made the object of their efforts to live by the code of modesty'. The decision to fast, outside as well as within Ramadan, was a key method of taming and shaping the inner self, for example, while veiling was *the* means through which an interior state of modesty was acquired. As one respondent explained, 'you must wear the veil, first because it is God's command ... and ... with time, because your inside learns to feel shy without the veil, and if you take it off, your entire being feels uncomfortable' (Mahmood, 2005: 157). This normalizing of

the body towards a model of Islamic piety did not involve traditional socialization or the unthinking, autonomous responses evident
in Bourdieu's conception of the habitus. It did incorporate a deliberative and intentional disciplining through what Mahmood (2005:
123, 157) views as a cumulative process of pedagogy that aims to
harmonize the exteriors and interiors of the body, consistent with
broader aspects of Islamic practice. The correct execution of *salat*
exemplifies this, involving, as Mahmood's (2005: 137) respondents
emphasized, not only 'an intention to dedicate the prayer to God',
'a prescribed sequence of gestures and words', 'a physical condition
of purity' and 'proper attire', but a duty that should be performed
'with all the feelings, concentration and tenderness of the heart
appropriate to the state of being in the presence of God – a state
called *khushu'*.

This attempt to craft a pure and uncompromised religious identity involved developing an 'inner quality' through 'outer practice
which makes practice a perfect ability of the soul of the actor'
(Lapidus, 1984: 54; Mahmood, 2005: 137). Its practitioners also
drew on material cultural artefacts, including the veil, as part of a
religiously fetishistic 'aesthetics of persuasion' designed to discipline
the body in line with the subject's reflexive intentions (Meyer,
2010a: 751). Such reflexively driven reformations of the habits and
identities of Mahmood's respondents were consequential not only
for their self-identities, moreover, but also for their views and
actions in relation to work, relationships, marriage and employers in
Egypt. These did not simply reinforce societal norms, but scruti-
nized and often adopted a critical orientation to them on the basis
of their capacity to assist pious living; an approach that prompted
the Egyptian authorities to monitor their private meetings and
which takes on particular significance in the context of recent and
current conflict in the country.

These women of Egypt's Islamic Revival movement are not an
isolated example of how the Muslim habitus is being instaured in
the modern age. Gökariksel's (2009) exploration of the reflexive
adoption of piety by Muslim women in Turkey replicates Mahmood's
analysis in this respect, reinforcing key elements of Göle's (1996,
2010) accounts of women's adoption of the Islamic headscarf in
France, Turkey and the Middle East. Maqsood's (2013) study of
religious consumption in urban Lahore makes the more general
point that increased literacy and global media have led young
Muslims to discuss and reflect upon their religious beliefs. Their
increasing familiarity with doctrinal debates has meant that many

do not rely on traditional religious elites for guidance, but increasingly 'learn and make decisions about their individual practices by themselves' (Maqsood, 2013). In each case, the personally and socially transformative nature of religious habits is emphasized. In each case, its development occurred in a reflexive, evaluative and potentially transformative engagement with secular culture.

In Latour's (2011) terms, these forms of Islamic habitus can be seen, like their Pentecostal counterparts, to involve the instauration of a religiously-based *multi-realism* rather than the *mono-realism* envisaged by Bourdieu. This is because they involve not an absorption of the social by the religious, but a bringing together of distinctive phenomena, possessed of contrasting principles, productive of something new. The practices and identities developed by the Muslim women considered by Göle (1996, 2010), Mahmood (2005) and Gökariksel (2009), for example, were not 'traditional' in any simple sense. The adoption of the veil is often understood to be key to maintaining a Muslim habitus, for example, but it is a symbol of 'tradition' reflexively constructed in opposition to the secular: in countries such as Malaysia, the veil is not traditional at all, but a contemporary development (Turner, 2010b: 19). Similarly, in France, its adoption by Muslim women is a reflexive process, articulating an ambivalent attitude towards the prevailing culture, where it is perceived as an 'iconic' representation of the threat of Islam to secular modernity, 'a symbolic colonization of the public space … supposed to be free of religion' (Salvatore, 2006: 1017).

If the veiling of women's bodies is more ambiguously 'traditional' than it might seem, however, it can also be said that, like Christian Pentecostalism, the relationship of the Islamic piety movement to contemporary capitalism is not free of ambiguity. Turner (2010b: 19), for example, notes increasing religious consumerism and individualism, evident within a rapidly developing global Muslim market for particular services relating to pilgrimage, dress, education, holidays and food, suggesting a more thoroughgoing reflexive reconstruction of tradition than its apparent anti-secularism implies (Speck, 2013). The degree of reflexivity evident in these contexts is such that Göle (2010: 264) associates it with Taylor's (2007) account of the 'post-Durkheimian' nature of contemporary culture, noting it is 'personally pious' and 'publicly visible', but more 'voluntary and mental' than traditional forms of Muslim habitus. Indeed, with regard to Europe and Muslim-majority societies across the globe, a strong emphasis on the re-formation of Islam is notable across a range of studies, covering increasing pluralism, greater reflexivity and choice by individuals, and changing patterns of social organization (Babès, 1997; Saint-Blancat, 1997; Roy, 1998; Tietze, 2001; Maqsood, 2013).

## Conclusion

Bourdieu's conception of the religious habitus has become increasingly influential in sociological studies of religion. It has also faced criticism for its tendency to equate religion with tradition and social reproduction, and its inability to account for modern conditions that render problematic habitual approaches towards social life, necessitating that reflexivity and deliberation become increasingly important dimensions of human experience. In this chapter, we have supplemented the writings of those who have engaged with Bourdieu's concerns by suggesting that the religious habitus is viewed most productively as something crafted or instaured by individuals. The context for this argument relates not only to those global changes that undermined situations of contextual continuity (Archer, 2010), but also to complementary trends in the pluralization and horizontalization of religious authority (Chaves, 1994).

The roots of these changes are deeply embedded. In the Christian West, for example, there were from the early modern era challenges to the ecclesiastical authority of the Catholic Church from the growth of Protestant sects as individuals could, at least in principle, choose between competing paths to religious truth. Recent issues regarding the proliferation and credibility of religious authority have, moreover, moved centre stage at a time when political changes, new technologies and modes of intervening in and extending human life and reproductive capacities have flourished. In the case of Islam, for example, Turner et al. (2009: 14) suggest that contemporary social media have created a situation in which 'almost any local teacher or *mullah* can issue a *fatwa* to guide a local community by setting himself up with his own blog (see also Herbert, 2011).

In this context, as emphasized in previous chapters, the relations between religious and secular modalities of the sacred are interactive and often competitive, necessitating an increasingly reflexive approach to the instauration of a religious habitus. In the light of this, we have highlighted the significance of active and deliberative dimensions to the construction of religious identities evident in both transcendent and socio-religious modalities of the sacred. Here, we have not rejected the significance of habit and equilibrium, but have emphasized how the active and conscious development of religious identities often involves the *reflexively chosen cultivation of routinized habits*; a reflexivity that will have to be engaged in anew each time such habits are obstructed in the future. A logical consequence of this view is the need to recognize that the habitus does not routinely operate in a way that is hidden entirely from, or impervious to, the reflexive capacities of the embodied subject (Dewey, 1980; Adams, 2006; Elder-Vass, 2007).

This argument reaches back to Aristotle and Aquinas, and also relates to pragmatists such as Dewey (2002), who view reflexivity and deliberation on the one hand, and habit, on the other, as related modes through which individuals negotiate their environment on the basis of religious and other priorities (Shilling, 2008). Habits do not have to be unthinking routines socialized in individuals without their conscious awareness, but can result from self-directed 'intentional responsive activities' aimed at the achievement of particular goals (Siegfried, 1996: 96). In such cases, the reflexive instauration of a particular religious habitus unifies the embodied subject with the world and cosmos in particular ways, forging modes of connection that enable a certain command to be achieved over the self and environment (Dewey, 1969; 2002: 15, 26). In developing this analysis, illustrated through our brief explorations of Christian Pentecostalism and Islamic Revivalism, we have been able to acknowledge certain convergences in, as well as differences between, transcendent and socio-religious modalities of the sacred as manifest in the construction of Christian and Islamic forms of habitus.

We sought to show that the early socialization associated with Bourdieu's conception of the habitus is not incompatible with subsequent attempts to instaur, or re-make, a habitus in line with reflexive engagements with contemporary notions of religious purity or religious traditions. The Egyptian women of the Islamic Revival in Mahmood's (2005) study, for example, were not engaged in voluntaristic decisions regarding whether to continue or discard Muslim identities acquired in early childhood; they were engaged in a reflexively articulated scrutiny of how they could *re-make* and purify their bodies and minds in a manner that would most effectively advance their Islamic selves. Similarly, 'born again' Pentecostals dedicated to maintaining their openness to spiritual forces in Poloma's (2003) study were deliberating not whether to continue with their religious identities, but how to advance them.

Important differences remain in the patterns by which religious identities are first assumed in contrasting religions, but this does not prevent reflexive and active approaches toward the re-creation of such identities from being increasingly important in the current age. It is, though, important to note the differences that were reflected in the illustrative examples and discussions employed in this chapter. Pentecostal intent and deliberation is focused on being receptive to the transcendental inspiration of the Holy Spirit, while Islamic piety is concerned with reflexively instauring a disciplined and pure body and self fit for existence in a socio-religious realm. It is also important to acknowledge, in line with our analyses of experience in previous chapters, that certain stimuli associated with pain or eroticism, for example, retain the capacity at times to overwhelm reflexive deliberations irrespective of the different identities cultivated by embodied subjects.

In summary, we have suggested that the 'religious habitus' remains a useful concept – in identifying the cumulative impact of experiences resulting in religious dispositions and identities that facilitate the enframing of this-worldly matters in other-worldly concerns – insofar as it is freed from the assumptions about its essentially conservative function. Building on Latour's (2011) analysis to conceive of the religious habitus as a series of reflexively informed acts involving the instauring of orientations towards the other-worldly, also allows us to avoid any sense that religion is acquired and maintained merely through unthinking processes of acculturation and socialization. Far from forms of the religious habitus necessarily serving to reproduce and legitimate social structures, moreover, the particular way in which this enframing steers the thoughts, experience and actions of the faithful allows us to analyse the actual and potential contingencies and ambiguities of its relationship with the society in which it was forged.

While this attentiveness to the reflexivity now endemic to the instauration of a religious habitus allows us to take seriously the resurgent vitality of certain manifestations of socio-religious and transcendent forms of the sacred, however, it also directs our attention to the fact that ostensibly 'traditional' religious beliefs and practices are far more modern than they might appear to be. This does not necessarily imply secularization, though our reflections on the instauration of a habitus in Christian and Islamic contexts suggest an increasingly ambiguous relationship to the bio-economic modality of the sacred in particular. Here, we noted that Pentecostalism mirrors earlier Protestant forms in suggesting an elective affinity with global capitalism. While the nature of the transcendent sacred allows for flexibility with regard to secular spheres of social life, it is not clear whether, in time, this affinity might be transformed into a more straightforward pattern of accommodation rather than reflexive adaptation.

In the case of Islam, indicators of such adaptation and, potentially, accommodation are perhaps more surprising, given that the socio-religious sacred, which it to some degree exemplifies, seeks to incorporate all areas of social life within patterns of religious regulation. Questions concerning the degree to which this religious form is, in contrast, increasingly becoming infused with patterns of consumerism suggest that the reflexive instauration of a religious habitus does not occur in isolation from patterns of bio-economic secularization. In our concluding chapter, we reflect further upon such questions, highlighting what we see as the key issues arising from our assessment of the interaction between contrasting modalities of the sacred in global modernity today.

# 8

## Conclusion

At the beginning of this book we mapped out four key positions relative to the secularization thesis, each representing apparently incommensurate claims regarding the relationships between religion, the sacred and the secular today, and proposed that their convergences and differences could form part of a broad theoretical synthesis toward the subject. Subsequent chapters then developed this framework, centred on an engagement with the enframing of embodied experience within distinct worldly and other-worldly modalities of the sacred, through analyses concerned with investigations of the continued vitality of religion, on the one hand, and the expansion of multiple processes and levels of secularization, on the other. Having done so, we can now reflect back on what is at stake in re-theorizing debates about secularization in this way. In what follows, we summarize our conclusions in relation to three key issues: the implications of removing the sacred from an exclusive association with religion in the way we have outlined; the significance of our focus on experience; and the potential value of our theoretical approach for making sense of the secularizing features of global modernity today.

### Reconfiguring the Sacred

A key motivation behind our engagement with ostensibly contradictory arguments about secularization has been an attempt to transcend what Beckford (2003: 68) has termed the 'dialogue of the deaf' that frequently characterizes debate on this issue in the sociology of religion. What he is referring to are factors such as an unwillingness to engage seriously with alternative points of view, the re-specifying rather than the creative reconstruction of meanings invested in fundamental concepts, the selective utilizations of 'data' relative to theory, and the misrepresentation of arguments that might relativize or undermine a particular approach (Beckford, 2003: 70–1). In a similar vein, Gorski and Altinordu (2008: 58) have noted how key arguments for and against secularization simply define alternative views out of existence. For example, since the rational choice approach 'defines secularization as a decline in religious demand, and because it defines religious demand as a constant', secularization is rendered impossible. What we have attempted to do, in contrast, is to offer a theoretical model comprehensive enough to include a range of divergent perspectives, but which advances debate by facilitating the investigation of secular as well as religious modalities of the sacred and by sensitizing us to how these enframe embodied experiences in the contemporary era.

Utilizing the category of the sacred in an inclusive yet analytically differentiated manner, we followed the examples of both Durkheim and Weber. Both sociologists used the term to signal phenomena that can be considered sacred as a result of their distinctive and extraordinary status within a society, but also provided resources for recognizing divergent forms of it. Developing key aspects of their work, we removed the sacred from an exclusive association with religion, and identified four distinct modalities of the sacred characterized by variable positions vis-à-vis issues of worldly and other-worldly orientation, and differentiating or de-differentiating aspects of social structure. It is these variations, we suggest, that allow us to illuminate the different characters and trajectories of religious and non-religious embodiments of the sacred today, and the variable factors that impact upon their interactions, accommodations, reflexive adjustments or conflict.

As a clarification of how this reconfiguring of the sacred transforms some common assumptions in debates about secularization, and the simple polarization of Weberian and Durkheimian perspectives often underpinning them, we can return to Bruce's (2002) outline of a number of 'mistakes of method' evident in this context. Critiquing – from a broadly Weberian perspective – what he sees as misleading attempts to inflate the significance of religion in the present, Bruce highlights the neo-Durkheimian notion of 'implicit religion' as a particularly egregious example of this error. What this notion attempts to capture is the sense that certain social or cultural phenomena, while lacking an ostensibly religious character, nonetheless possess experiential, symbolic or functional aspects that suggest an implicitly religious nature. Related notions of 'invisible religion', 'quasi-religion' or 'para-religion' follow a similar trajectory (Greil, 1993; Greil and Robbins, 1994; Demerath, 2000: 2). It is such an approach that allows football, for example, to be seen as a modern 'religion' (see Luckmann, 1967; Coles, 1975; Augé, 1982; Bailey, 1997; Hervieu-Léger, 2000). Aside from noting the over-eagerness of some sociologists of religion to claim evidence for the importance of their subject matter (sociologists of sport, in contrast, do not concern themselves with seeking out 'implicit sport'), Bruce's (2002: 203) primary critique of such approaches is that they overlook the differences between religion and football, to continue with this example of 'invisible' religion, that render such analogies or equations redundant. Ignoring, in particular, the moral seriousness and other-worldly orientations of religion, they eradicate secularization only methodologically, via an artificial inflation of the numbers of the 'unconventionally religious'.

Given the way in which we have, throughout this book, defined religion with reference to other-worldly orientations, we can readily agree with Bruce that phenomena such as football do *not* count as 'religion'. This is so not only because, as a number of writers have noted, football and religion occupy distinct social spheres, suggest contrasting phenomenological experiences or are characterized by a surfeit or lack of engagement with fundamental questions of life (Chandler, 1992; Hoffman, 1992; Hervieu-Léger, 2000; Higgs and Braswell, 2004). In the light of the arguments in this book, it is also because we are in a position to identify the potential for variable or non-existent *links* between football and religion, and equally variable *relationships* to the sacred more broadly. Thus, as we suggested in Chapter 3, phenomena such as sport can be seen as sites for interactions and contestations between different modalities of the sacred. Indeed, as we have argued more extensively elsewhere, we can identify the socio-religious sacred in how some Muslim groups seek to integrate sport into a total, other-worldly oriented form of life; in the transcendent sacred in Evangelical Christianity's recognition of sport as a 'secular' phenomenon that can be utilized for religious purposes; in the bio-economic sacred evident in the increasing commercialism of sports; and in the bio-political sacred manifest in the technological and medical management of bodies in the pursuit of limit performances (Shilling and Mellor, 2014).

In the context of this example we are not simply recognizing that phenomena such as football can be 'sacred' without being 'religious', but signalling how phenomena can be sacred in very different ways, and therefore have variable outcomes in terms of their roles and impact within global modernity. Here, de-conflating the sacred from an exclusive association with religion makes it possible to avoid engaging in an unwarranted expansion of what counts as religious. Identifying contrasting modalities of the sacred, however, also enables us to maintain the analytical utility and precision of discussions involving phenomena made extraordinary in relation to mundane life (Stark, 2001: 102). In so doing, it also provides us with a way of studying the operationalization of the sacred sociologically via a focus on the embodied experience of religious and secular life.

## Experiencing Religious and Secular Modalities of the Sacred

A key argument of this book has been that existing debates on secularization and the revitalization of religion have tended to ignore or treat partially the embodied bases on which these processes operate. Previously focused upon the viability of religious *belief* systems within modern technological societies, an approach which reduces our embodied existence to the Cartesian preoccupation with thought, theory has turned recently to issues regarding bodily senses and sensualities in engaging with sacred presence and the materiality of religion. Illuminating another dimension to extraordinary experience, these writings unfortunately often marginalize the creedal dimensions of religious practice. While both approaches highlight important issues, then, they tend to ignore the manner in which religions are concerned with mind *and* body, thought *and* feeling. In bringing these concerns together, we sought to encompass the strengths of both approaches by arguing that experience was co-constituted by the interactions that occurred among reflexive thought, feeling and stimuli. This approach enables us to avoid reducing experience of religious and secular modalities of the sacred to matters of either cognition or physicality, yet provides us with a relatively simple and flexible basis on which to explore the variety of embodied engagements with extraordinary phenomena.

Focusing on the diverse ways in which phenomena encountered as sacred can be experienced, indeed, opens up new ways of engaging with processes of sacralization that have tended to be neglected in relation to questions of secularization. Here, we examined how key bridging experiences – developed through a critical engagement with the writings of Durkheim and Weber – can be understood as means for nurturing particular embodied dispositions and practices that come to impart a particular religious directionality to social life. Exploring these experiences also highlighted how their potential to result in religious affiliation was contested increasingly by alternative enframings emergent from non-religious modalities of the sacred.

Thus, we noted that while the potential Durkheim identified for embodied *intoxication* to constitute a bridge to distinctively religious experiences and identities continues to be evident in a number of contexts, the capacities of both socio-religious and transcendent modalities of the sacred to enframe experiences of intoxication in the light of other-worldly criteria and modes of authority are constrained in relation to bio-economic and bio-political modalities of the secular sacred. This constraint is evident not only in various patterns of accommodation and adaptation, but also in the social significance of non-religious modes of emotional, chemical, collective and individual modes of intoxication. Examining how the development of social differentiation in (terms of identities and lifestyle options) has occurred alongside a de-differentiating bio-political regulation of bodies, we suggested that hyper-intoxicating forms of the religious sacred are not only seen as 'abnormal' within secular cultures at large, but also by significant numbers of those who identify as religious. The sacrificial killings practised and valorized in some Islamic groups can be read as such a hyper-intoxicating resurgence of the socio-religious sacred, for example, though the radically conflictual orientation towards global modernity such phenomena embody signals their marginal status vis-à-vis its core orientations and trajectories. We also noted a paradoxical tendency here, involving the reconfiguring of religious trajectories under the influence of secular developments: since sacrificial killing has arguably become a bio-political response to the increasing hegemony of secular bio-politics, there is a case for noting elements of accommodation to secular trajectories, despite its violently oppositional character. Either way, it is hard to conceive of these changes as anything other than a secularization of intoxication, significantly limiting its capacity to act as a bridge to a religious habitus, albeit one wherein a complex set of contestations and countervailing pressures continue to be evident.

Our exploration of changes relating to the enframing of experiences of *pain*, a phenomenon that can also be seen as a key bridging experience to the religious sacred emergent from the work of Durkheim, indicated a similar pattern of secularization, though one more straightforwardly associated with the extraordinary social significance of the bio-political management of bodies via bio-medical interventions. The dominant enframing of pain within modern bio-medicine, which is reinforced by sociological analyses that view pain as undermining of people's projects and identities, encourages both an intense sensitivity and aversion to pain tied to the historical marginalization of religion in modern societies. Indeed, we argued that religious approaches towards pain which retain credibility tend to do so when they exist in a zone of exceptionality in which they comple-ment rather than oppose the medicalized approach. This exists in stark contrast to those earlier contexts where religious communities sought to intensify the human engagement with pain within an other-worldly framework of orthodoxy and orthopraxy. The ability to engage positively with pain experientially, publicly and meaningfully has been lost, certainly within the Western part of global modernity, where the belief that the world could be saved *through* pain has entirely given way to the view that the world can be saved *from* pain. In short, the scope for pain to serve as a bridge for religious experi-ences and identities has shrunk to a zone of exceptionality outside the effective parameters of bio-medicine.

In turning to bridging experiences emergent from the work of Weber, we sought to broaden the understanding of *charisma*'s capac-ity to constitute a route to religious experience by identifying three forms of the phenomenon: the pedagogic charisma associated with early Christian teaching communities, Weber's well-known concep-tion of charismatic personality, and our own conception of a material and manufactured secular aesthetic charisma. These forms share a common orientation to the construction of a sense of the extraordi-nary that involves invigorating the lived bodies of individuals, but are associated with distinct patterns of authority and result typically in contrasting experiences. These range from the transformative encoun-ter with other-worldly grace, to the this-worldly excitement of celeb-rity culture, and to the thoroughly secularized phenomenon of aesthetic charisma, wherein the experience of the extraordinary is achieved via the bio-economic sacralization of the brand. The latter, in particular, is an increasingly central feature of global modernity and, therefore, the dominant form of charisma today. Representative of a broader commodification of culture, its centrality challenges Weber's pessimistic account of the trajectory of charisma in moder-nity, but nonetheless reinforces his attentiveness to the rational utili-zation of charisma in modern contexts, a utilization that, as we have noted across several chapters, increasingly marks religious as well as non-religious forms of life today.

If this tension between worldly and other-worldly modalities is evident with regard to experiences of charisma, it is even more acute in relation to *eroticism*. We began by examining how the analyses of both Weber and Bataille identified eroticism as a route to religious experience, albeit one frequently possessed of ambiguity in terms of its destabilizing potential. Further to this, we suggested that recent sociological writings focused upon its rationalization, domestication and consumerization need to be complemented with recognition of the fact that images, icons, texts and other material phenomena continue to possess the capacity to be fetishized. This provides continuing opportunities for institutions and individuals to harness erotic experience to the promotion of religious experiences and identities. In assessing the opportunities associated with this 'material eroticism', however, we noted that there has been an unprecedented profusion of these images, icons and objects in global modernity. This creates the potential for religion to enframe bodily experiences through the circulation and display of material fetishism, but also promotes a situation of competition between competing religious fetishisms and between religious fetishism and non-religious forms of aesthetic charisma designed to stimulate and seduce sensory feelings towards consumer culture. It was in this context that we argued that retaining the extraordinary status and affectual charge of their own images, icons and object has meant that religious movements have sought to maintain the appeal and the competitive edge of their products by engaging in processes of 'enhanced' sacralization – something particularly evident in cases of religious conflict and violence. While such processes are arguably reflective of adaptation to a broader materialization of eroticism within global culture, we also suggested that they are indicative of the increasingly *reflexive* character of contestation between different modalities of the sacred, given the need for religious individuals and groups to engage deliberately in practices and strategies that mark them out as religious in a secular context.

The importance of focusing on the above bridging experiences was not simply to explore the extent to which particular aspects of human life remained viable routes to religious feelings and thoughts. It was also to prepare the ground for a wider analysis of the extent to which it is still possible in the contemporary era for religious dis-positions and orientations to become sedimented into the identities of embodied subjects. This takes us beyond issues regarding specific experiences, to the wider bodily and cognitive ground on which religion is based and is an essential, if under-explored, issue in debates about secularization and the revitalization of religion.

In this context, we suggested that the notion of 'religious habitus' remains a useful concept in identifying religious dispositions and identities that facilitate the enframing of this-worldly matters in other-worldly concerns, but opposed Bourdieu's formulation of it as possessing a fundamentally conservative character. Building instead on Latour's analysis to conceive of the religious habitus as a series of reflexively informed acts involving the re-making or instauring of orientations towards the other-worldly, we noted how forms of the religious are produced from the bringing together of a variety of traditions, ideas, artefacts and beliefs. Taking account of the reflexivity now endemic to the instauration of a religious habitus allows us to take seriously the resurgent vitality of certain manifestations of socio-religious and transcendent forms of the sacred. It also directs our attention to the fact that ostensibly 'traditional' religious beliefs and practices are far more modern than they might appear to be, and have developed an increasingly ambiguous relationship to the bio-economic modality of the sacred in particular.

The importance we attributed to the religious habitus is not meant to occlude the importance of emergent structures, especially in differentiated societies wherein the impact of meso-level allegiances is circumscribed by macro-level arrangements that shield, at least partly, the value-fields of institutions (secular and religious) from each other. Nevertheless, embodied dispositions and orientations towards religion remain essential factors in establishing the future vitality of institutional forms, and also in determining the potential of societies to be infused with and even restructured on the basis of a resurgent and de-differentiating impact of socio-religious feeling. Debates about the revitalization or secularization of religion may restrict their intervention to particular issues or to certain 'levels' of society, but will remain partial accounts if they fail to engage with the ground on which forms of habitus can either assist or obstruct the future vitality of religious forms.

## Secularizing the Sacred

The theoretical framework we have developed, alongside our more specific investigations into particular bridging experiences and the more general embodied grounds on which forms of religious habitus are nurtured or obstructed, warn us against making determinist conclusions about irreversible processes. Nevertheless, incidences of the secularization of the sacred are evident not only in the increasing significance of secular relative to religious modalities for imparting particular forms of institutional and embodied directionality to global modernity, but also in the multiple ways in which bio-political and bio-economic modalities increasingly eat into socio-religious and transcendent attempts to enframe human experiences in relation to other-worldly orientations.

Such a process, referred to in the 'inherited' model of secularization as *internal* secularization, has long had a significant history in Christianity (tied as Christianity is to acceptance of and engagement with the secular as a social sphere distinct from religion) (Wilson, 1985: 17). That it can be seen to exist even within resurgent forms of Islamic piety, however, is testimony to how interactions between the religious and the secular are evolving in complex ways across the globe, even where theological commitments to a socio-religious orientation might appear to constrain them. This development reinforces the value of revisionist accounts of secularization that emphasize its social, cultural and geographical contingency, but also, nonetheless, suggests a broad overall trajectory towards continuing secularization. Such a trajectory calls into question Demerath's (2000, 2007) account of an oscillation between patterns of secularization and sacralization: while he does acknowledge that forms of the latter can advance the former, his overall vision of these as countervailing processes, checking each other and provoking symbiotic counter movements, is not borne out by our explorations of bridging experiences.

This trajectory is, of course, neither fixed nor irreversible, since it is an emergent outcome of the interactions, struggles and evolving preferences of human beings. In terms of the latter, and contrary to economistic assumptions about their stability, the changes pertaining to bridging experiences considered in this book not only suggest a significant degree of plasticity, but also, via the spread of the bio-economic sacred, indicate conditions under which preferences for certain types of experience over others are actively encouraged to evolve very rapidly. Our discussion of the opposition that exists between aesthetic charisma and material eroticism, for example, suggests that certain religious authorities have engaged in processes of enhanced sacralization in order to capture market share and distance their followers from the attractions of secular goods. This can help explain why religions such as Pentecostal Christianity and Islam, both of which have theologically strong models of orthodoxy and orthopraxy tied to key experiential foci, are resurgent globally, while more 'liberal' forms, namely those less clearly distinguished from secular orientations and values, appear to be in decline. It is not that secularization is 'self-limiting' due to the stable preferences of consumers for other-worldly compensators (Stark and Bainbridge, 1987), otherwise we might expect such religious forms to be even more significantly dominant globally than they are, but, rather, that the *evolving marketization of competing sacralizations actively encourages shifting preferences*. The much noted spread of both resurgent Islam and Pentecostal Christianity in societies as they undergo rapid modernization is suggestive of such transformations (Norris and Inglehart, 2004; Martin, 2005).

The implication of both other-worldly and worldly modalities of the sacred in patterns of rapid modernization signals, furthermore, their entanglement in processes of globalization more broadly. Some time ago, Lechner (1991) suggested that globalization rendered debates about secularization more complex but also reinforced their salience, since key features of the Western experience of modernity, particularly those relating to issues of differentiation and worldly/other-worldly tensions, were now of global scope and significance – a point reinforced in more recent theoretical accounts of the subject (Beyer, 2007). By interrogating these features in relation to the embodied bases upon which particular forms of habitus may or may not be constructed, and the variable patterns of contestation, interaction and influence affecting them, we have, following Latour (2011), offered a 'multi-realist' conception of the religious habitus centred on the recognition that individuals are able to 'bring together' and work creatively towards the instauration of new spheres of activity, cognition and being which can decisively shape human experience in particular ways. This has enabled us to take seriously the diversity of religious and secular engagements across a range of cultural and historical contexts, reinforced by our focus on distinct modalities of the sacred. What this attentiveness to diversity does *not* add up to, however, is a simple endorsement of the 'multiple modernities' thesis, that is, the claim that cultural differences across the globe are of such significance that what we call 'modernity' is actually a (potentially endless) series of distinct forms (Eisenstadt, 2000; Wittrock, 2000). In contrast, and in common with Schmidt (2006), we regard it as an open question whether we can talk of 'multiple modernities' or 'varieties of modernity'. Insofar as socio-religious or transcendent modalities of the sacred are able to determine the trajectories of the social contexts in which they are located, they would lend some support to the former position. Given that our book has indicated how complex and problematic such a pattern of determination is in the present, however, this is hardly a straightforward matter. Indeed, the ways in which bio-political and bio-economic modalities are able to complement each other in an increasingly global reconfiguring of experiences, orientations and identities in a secular frame problematize it further.

If questions concerning 'multiple modernities' remain open, however, our study has suggested that those relating to a 'post-secular' society do not. While it has been noted that advocates of this notion offer a series of frequently contradictory and ill-supported claims about the decline of the secular (Beckford, 2012), it has nonetheless become an increasingly popular assumption amongst many analysts of religion and society, alongside a selective engagement with Taylor's (2007) focus on the prospects for religion beyond the 'immanent frame' of secular modernity (Warner et al., 2010: 6). While, as we have emphasized, the ultimate future of religion in its various forms is indeterminate, we can conclude that it is one that will evolve via interactions with globally powerful secular modalities. What we have called socio-religious and transcendent modalities of the sacred will no doubt continue to foster the incorporation of individuals and groups into a religious habitus, but our analysis indicates that these will continue to be constrained, and to some degree re-shaped, by bio-political and bio-economic forces that enframe human experiences and steer the development of societies in this-worldly directions.

# References

Aalton, A. (2007) 'Listening to the dancer's body', in C. Shilling (ed.) *Embodying Sociology*. Oxford: Blackwell.

Abufarha, N. (2009) *The Making of a Human Bomb: An Ethnography of Palestinian Resistance*. Durham, NC: Duke University Press.

Adair-Toteff, C. (2005) 'Max Weber's charisma', *Journal of Classical Sociology*, 5(2): 189–204.

Adams, M. (2006) 'Hybridizing habitus and reflexivity: Towards an understanding of contemporary identity?', *Sociology*, 40(3): 511–28.

Ades, D. and Baker, S. (2006) *Undercover Surrealism: Georges Bataille and Documents*. London: Hayward Gallery Publishing.

Adogame, A. (2010) 'Pentecostalism and charismatic movements in a global perspective', in B.S. Turner (ed.) *The New Blackwell Companion to the Sociology of Religion*. Oxford: Blackwell.

Agamben, G. (1998) *Homo Sacer: Sovereign Power and Bare Life*. Stanford, CA: Stanford University Press.

Ahmed, A.S. (1991) 'Postmodernist perceptions of Islam: Observing the observer', *Asian Survey* 31(3): 213–31.

Albrecht, D (1999) *Rites in the Spirit*. Sheffield: Sheffield University Press.

Alexander, J.C. (1988) 'Culture and political crisis: "Watergate" and Durkheimian sociology', in J.C. Alexander (ed.) *Durkheimian Sociology: Cultural Studies*. Cambridge: Cambridge University Press.

Alexander, J.C. (1990) 'Must we choose between criticism and faith? Reflections on the later work of Benjamin Barber', *Sociological Theory*, 9(1): 124–30.

Anderson, B. (1983) *Imagined Communities: Reflections on the Origin and Spread of Nationalism*. London: Verso.

Appadurai, A. (1996) 'Grassroots globalization and the research imagination', *Public Culture*, 12(1): 1–19.

Archer, L., Halsall, A. and Hollingworth, S. (2007) '"University's not for me – I'm a Nike person": Urban working-class young people's negotiations of "style", identity and educational engagement', *Sociology*, 41(2): 219–37.

Archer, M. (1995) *Realist Social Theory: The Morphogenetic Approach*. Cambridge: Cambridge University Press.

Archer, M. (2003) *Structure, Agency and the Internal Conversation*. Cambridge: Cambridge University Press.

Archer, M. (2007) *Making Our Way Through the World: Human Reflexivity and Social Mobility*. Cambridge: Cambridge University Press.

Archer, M. (2010) 'Routine, reflexivity and realism', *Sociological Theory*, 28(3): 272–303.

Archer, M. (2012) *The Reflexive Imperative*. Cambridge: Cambridge University Press.

Arendt, H. (1998) *The Human Condition*, 2nd edn. Chicago, IL: Chicago University Press.

Aristotle (2000) *The Nicomachean Ethics*. London: Hackett.

Armstrong, D. (1995) 'The rise of surveillance medicine', *Sociology of Health and Illness*, 17(3): 393–404.

Arney, W. and Neill, J. (1982) 'The location of pain in natural childbirth', *Sociology of Health and Illness*, 7: 375–400.

Arvidsson, A. (2006) *Brands: Meaning and Value in Media Culture*. London: Routledge.

Arvidsson, A. (2007) *The Logic of the Brand*. Maggio. Dipartimento di Sociologia e Ricerca Sociale.

Asad, T. (1983) 'Notes on body pain and truth in medieval Christian ritual', *Economy and Society*, 12(3): 287–327.

Asad, T. (1986) *The Idea of an Anthropology of Islam*. Occasional Papers Series. Washington, DC: Center for Comparative Arab Studies at Georgetown University.

Asad, T. (1993) *Genealogies of Religion: Discipline and Reasons of Power in Christianity and Islam*. Baltimore, MD: Johns Hopkins University Press.

Asad, T. (2002) *Formations of the Secular: Christianity, Islam, Modernity*. Stanford, CA: Stanford University Press.

Atkinson, M. (2008) 'Triathlon, suffering and exciting significance', *Leisure Studies*, 27(2): 165–80.

Atkinson, M. and Young, K. (2008) *Deviance and Social Control in Sport*. Leeds: Human Kinetics.

Augé, M. (1982) 'Football: De l'histoire sociale à l'anthropologie religieuse', *Le Débat*, 19, February.

Babès, L. (1997) *L'Islam Positif: La Religion des Jeunes Musulmans de France*. Paris: L'Harmattan.

Bailey, E. (1997) *Implicit Religion: What Might it Be?* Professorial Lecture, Middlesex University, November.

Baker, W. (2007) *Playing with God: Religion and Modern Sport*. Cambridge, MA: Harvard University Press.

Baldacchino, J-P. (2012) 'Markets of piety and pious markets: The Protestant Ethic and the spirit of Korean capitalism', *Social Compass*, 59(3): 367–85.

Bancroft, A. (2009) *Drugs, Intoxication and Society*. Oxford: Polity Press.

Barton, C. (1994) 'Savage miracles', *Representations*, 45: 41–71.

Bass, B.M. (1981) *Stogdill's Handbook of Leadership*. New York, NY: Free Press.

Bass, B.M. (1985) *Leadership Performance Beyond Expectations*. New York, NY: Academic Press.

Bass, B.M. (1999) 'On the taming of charisma', *Leadership Quarterly*, 10(4): 541–53.

Bass, B.M. and Avolio, B.J. (1994) *Increasing Organizational Effectiveness Through Transformational Leadership*. Thousand Oaks, CA: SAGE.

Bataille, G. (1987) *Eroticism*. London: Marion Boyars.

Bataille, G. (1988) *The Accursed Share*, Vol. 1. New York, NY: Zone Books.

Bataille, G. (1989) *Theory of Religion*. New York, NY: Zone Books.

Bataille, G. (1992) *On Nietzsche*. London: Athlone Press.

Bataille, G. (1993) *The Accursed Share*, Vols 2 and 3. New York, NY: Zone Books.

Bataille, G. (1996) 'The Sacred Conspiracy', in A. Stoekl (ed.) *Visions of Excess: Selected Writings, 1917–1939*. Minneapolis, MN: Minnesota University Press.

Bauman, Z. (2002) *Society Under Siege*. Cambridge: Polity Press.

Bauman, Z. (2003) *Liquid Love*. Cambridge: Polity Press.

Bearman, P. and Brückner, H. (2001) 'Promising the future: Virginity pledges and first intercourse', *American Journal of Sociology*, 106(4): 859–912.

Bebbington, D. (1989) *Evangelicalism in Modern Britain: A History from the 1730s to the 1980s*. Grand Rapids, MI: Baker.

Beck, U. (1992) *Risk Society*. London: SAGE.

Beck, U. and Beck-Gernsheim, E. (1995) *The Normal Chaos of Love*. Cambridge: Polity Press.

Beckford, J.A. (1989) *Religion in Advanced Industrial Society*. London: Unwin Hyman.

Beckford, J.A. (2003) *Social Theory and Religion*. Cambridge: Cambridge University Press.

Beckford, J.A. (2012) 'SSSR presidential address. Public religions and the postsecular: Critical reflections', *Journal for the Scientific Study of Religion*, 51(1): 1–19.

Beckmann, A. (2001) 'Regarding consensual "Sadomasochism"', in R. Sykes, N. Ellison and C. Bochel (eds) *Social Policy Review 13*. London: The Policy Press.

Beckwith, S. (1996) *Christ's Body: Identity, Culture and Society in Late Medieval Writings*. London: Routledge.

Bell, C. (1992) *Ritual Theory, Ritual Practice*. Oxford: Oxford University Press.

Bell, D. (1976) *The Cultural Contradictions of Capitalism*. Champaign, IL: University of Illinois Press.

Bell, D. (1977) 'The return of the sacred? The argument on the future of religion', *British Journal of Sociology*, 28(4): 419–49.

Bell, D. and Kennedy, B. (2000) (eds) *The Cybercultures Reader*. London: Routledge.

Bendelow, G. and Williams, S. (1995) 'Pain and the mind–body dualism: A sociological approach', *Body & Society*, 1(2): 83–103.

Bendelow, G. and Williams, S. (1998) 'Emotions, pain and gender', in G. Bendelow and S. Williams (eds) *Emotions in Social Life*. London: Routledge.

Benjamin, W. (2004) *Walter Benjamin: Selected Writings, Volume 1: 1913–1926*. Cambridge, MA: Harvard University Press.

Bennett, J. (2001) *The Enchantment of Modern Life: Attachments, Crossings and Ethics*. Princeton, NJ: Princeton University Press.

Bentham, J. (1789) *An Introduction to the Principle of Morals and Legislations*. Oxford: Blackwell.

Berger, P. (1967) *The Sacred Canopy*. New York, NY: Free Press.

Berger, P. (1999) (ed.) *The Desecularization of the World*. Michigan, MI: Eerdmans.

Berger, P. (2006) 'Interview with Peter Berger', with Charles T. Mathewes, *The Hedgehog Review* 8(1–2): 152–61.

Berlinerblau, J. (1999) 'Ideology, Pierre Bourdieu's doxa, and the Hebrew Bible', *Semeia*, 87: 193–214.

Beverland, M. and Farrelly, F. (2010) 'The quest for authenticity in consumption: Consumers' purposive choice of authentic cues to shape experienced outcomes', *Journal of Consumer Research*, 36(5): 838–56.

Beyer, P. (1993) *Religion and Globalization*. London: SAGE.

Beyer, P. (2007) 'Globalization and glocalization', in J.A. Beckford and N.J. Demerath III (eds) *The SAGE Handbook of the Sociology of Religion*. London: SAGE.

Black, A. (1993) 'Classical Islam and medieval Europe: A comparison of political philosophies and cultures', *Political Studies*, XLI: 58–69.

Bleich, E. (2006) 'On democratic integration and free speech: Response to Tariq Modood and Randall Hansen', *International Migration*, 40(5): 17–22.

Bloom, M. (2007) *Dying to Kill: The Allure of Suicide Terror*. New York, NY : Columbia University Press.

Bloor, M., Monaghan, L., Dobash, R. and Dobash, R. (1988) 'The body as a chemistry experiment', in S. Nettleton and J. Watson (eds) *The Body in Everyday Life*. London: Routledge.

Boeve, L. (2008) 'Religion after detraditionalization: Christian faith in a post-secular Europe', in G. Ward and M. Hoetzl (eds) *The New Visibility of Religion: Studies in Religion and Cultural Hermeneutics*. London: Continuum.

Bologh, R. (1990) *Love or Greatness? Max Weber and Feminist Thinking – A Feminist Inquiry*. London: Unwin Hyman.

Bonner, M. (1992) 'Some observations concerning the early development of Jihad along the Arab–Byzantine frontier', *Studia Islamica*, 75: 5–31.

Bonner, M. (1996) *Aristocratic Violence and Holy War*. New Haven, CT: American Oriental Society.

Boothroyd, D. (2006) *Culture on Drugs*. Manchester: Manchester University Press

Bourdieu, P. (1977) *Outline of a Theory of Practice*. Cambridge: Cambridge University Press.

Bourdieu, P. (1984) *Distinction*. London: Routledge and Kegan Paul.

Bourdieu, P. (1987) 'Legitimations and structured interests in Weber's sociology of religion', in S. Lash and S. Whimster (eds) *Max Weber, Rationality and Modernity*. London: Allen and Unwin.

Bourdieu, P. (1990) *Logic of Practice*. Stanford, CA: Stanford University Press.

Bourdieu, P. (1991) 'The genesis and structure of the religious field', *Comparative Social Research* 13: 1–43.

Bourdieu, P. (1994) *The Field of Cultural Production*. New York, NY: Columbia University Press.

Bourdieu, P. (1998) *Practical Reason*. Stanford, CA: Stanford University Press.

Bourdieu, P. (1999) *The Weight of the World*. Stanford, CA: Stanford University Press.

Bourdieu, P. (2000) *Pascalian Meditations*. Cambridge: Polity Press.

Bourdieu, P. and Wacquant, L.J.D. (1992) *An Invitation to Reflexive Sociology*. Chicago, IL: University of Chicago Press.

Bourgois, P. and Schonberg, J. (2009) *Righteous Dopefiend*. Berkeley, CA: University of California Press.

Bowker, J. (2007) *Beliefs that Changed the World*. London: Quercus.

Braeckman, A. (2009) 'Habermas and Gauchet on religion in postsecular society: A critical assessment', *Continental Philosophical Review* 42: 279–96.

Braidotti, R. (2008) 'In spite of the times: the postsecular turn in feminism', *Theory, Culture & Society*, 25(6): 1–24.

Brouwer, S., Gifford, P. and Rose, S. (1996) *Exporting the American Gospel: Global Christian Fundamentalism*. London: Routledge.

Brown, D. and Dehvine, S. (2011) *Carry Yourself Like a Lady, Fuck Like a Porn Star*. Ebook.

Brown, P. (1988) *The Body and Society*. London: Faber and Faber.

Bruce, S. (2002) *God is Dead: Secularization in the West*. Oxford: Blackwell.

Bruce, S. (2003) *Politics and Religion*. Cambridge: Polity Press.

Bruce, S. (2006) 'Secularization and the impotence of individualized religion', *The Hedgehog Review* 8(1–2): 35–45.

Bruce, S. (2010) 'Secularization', in B.S. Turner (ed.) *The New Blackwell Companion to the Sociology of Religion*. Oxford: Blackwell.

Bruce, S. (2011) *Secularization: In Defence of an Unfashionable Theory*. Oxford: Oxford University Press.

Bruce, S. and Voas, D. (2007) 'Religious toleration and organisational typologies', *Journal of Contemporary Religion*, 22(1): 1–17.

Burdsey, D. (2010) 'British Muslim experiences in English first-class cricket', *International Review for the Sociology of Sport*, 45(3): 315–34.

Burkitt, I. (1999) *Bodies of Thought*. London: SAGE.

Buswell Jr, R.E. and Lee, T.S. (2006) *Christianity in Korea*. Honolulu, HI: University of Hawaii Press.

Butler, J. (1990) *Gender Trouble*. London: Routledge.

Butler, J. (1993) *Bodies That Matter*. London: Routledge.

Bynum, C.W. (1987) *Holy Feast and Holy Fast*. London: University of California Press.

Bynum, C.W. (1989) 'The female body and religious practice in the later middle ages', in M. Feher, R. Nadaff and N. Tazi (eds) *Fragments for a History of the Human Body*. New York, NY: Zone Books.

Caillois, R. (1950) *L'Homme et le Sacré*. Paris: Gallimard.

Calhoun, C. (1993) 'Habitus, field and capital: The question of historical specificity', in C. Calhoun, E. Lipuma and M. Postone (eds) *Bourdieu: Critical Perspectives*. Oxford: Polity Press, pp. 61–88.

Calvin, J. (1960 [1536]) *Institutes of the Christian Religion*, 2 vol. Philadelphia, PA: Westminster Press.

Camerer, C. F. (2007) 'Neuroeconomics: Using neuroscience to make economic predictions', *The Economic Journal*, 117(519): C26–C42.

Campbell, C. (2005) *The Romantic Ethic and the Spirit of Modern Consumerism*. Oxford: Blackwell.

Carmichael, K. (1988) 'The creative use of pain in society', in R. Terrington (ed.) *Towards a Whole Society*. London: Richmond Fellowship Press.

Carrette, J. and King, R. (2004) *Selling Spirituality: The Silent Takeover of Religion*. London: Routledge.

Carruthers, J. and Tate, A. (2010) (eds) *Spiritual Identities: Literature and the Post-Secular Imagination*. Bern, Switzerland: Peter Lang.

Casanova, J. (1994) *Public Religions in the Modern World*. Chicago, IL: University of Chicago Press.

Casanova, J. (2006) 'Religion, European secular identities and European integration', in T.A. Byrnes and P.J. Katzenstein (eds.) *Religion in an Expanding Europe*. Cambridge: Cambridge University Press.

Casanova, J. (2011) 'Religions, secularizations and modernities', *European Journal of Sociology*, 52(3): 425–46.

Casanova, J. (2012) 'Are we still secular? Explorations on the secular and the post-secular', in P. Nynäs, M. Lassander and T. Utriainen (eds) *Post-Secular Society*. New Brunswick, NJ: Transaction.

Catherwood, C. (2003) *Christians, Muslims, and Islamic Rage*. London: Zondervan.

Cesari, J. (2004) *When Islam and Democracy Meet: Muslims in Europe and the United States*. New York, NY: Palgrave Macmillan.

Cesari, J. (2007) 'Muslim identities in Europe: The snare of exceptionalism', in A. Al-Azmeh and E. Fokas (eds) *Islam in Europe: Diversity, Identity and Influence*. Cambridge: Cambridge University Press.

Chandler, J. (1992) 'Sport is not a religion', in S. Hoffman (ed.) *Sport and Religion*. Champaign, IL: Human Kinetics.

Chandler, T. (2002) 'Manly Catholicism: Making men in Catholic public schools, 1945–80', in T. Chandler and T. Magdalinski (eds) *With God on their Side. Sport in the Service of Religion*. London: Routledge.

Charmaz, K. (1983) 'Loss of self: A fundamental form of suffering in chronic illness', *Sociology of Health and Illness*, 5: 168–95.

Chaves, M. (1994) 'Secularization as declining religious authority', *Social Forces* 72: 749–74.

Chesnut, R. A. (1997) *Born Again in Brazil: The Pentecostal Boom and the Pathogens of Poverty*. New Brunswick, NJ: Rutgers University Press.

Chidester, D. (1996) 'The church of baseball, the fetish of Coca-cola, and the potlatch of rock 'n' roll: Theoretical models for the study of religion in American popular culture', *Journal of the American Academy of Religion*, 64 (Winter): 743–65.

Chidester, D. (2005) *Authentic Fakes: Religion and American Popular Culture*. Berkeley, CA: University of California Press.

Chowers, E. (1995) 'Max Weber: The fate of homo-hermeneut in a disenchanted world', *Journal of European Studies*, 25: 98–123.

Coakley, S. (1997) (ed.) *Religion and the Body*. Cambridge: Cambridge University Press.

Coakley, S. and Shelemay, K. (2007) (eds), *Pain and Its Transformations: The Interface of Biology and Culture*. Cambridge, MA: Harvard University Press.

Cohen, E. (1995) 'Toward a history of European sensibility: Pain in the later middle ages', *Science in Context*, 9(1): 47–74.

Cohen, E. (2000) 'The animated pain of the body', *The American Historical Review* 105: 36–68.

Coleman, J.S. (1990) *Foundations of Social Theory*. Cambridge, MA: Harvard University Press.

Coleman, S. (2000) *The Globalisation of Charismatic Christianity*. Cambridge: Cambridge University Press.

Coles, R. (1975) 'Football as a surrogate religion', in M. Hill (ed.) *A Sociological Yearbook of Religion in Britain*. London: SCM Press.

Collins, P.J. (2002) 'Habitus and the storied self: Religious faith and practice as a dynamic means of consolidating identities', *Culture and Religion: An Interdisciplinary Journal*, 3(2): 147–61.

Comaroff, J. and Comaroff, J.L. (1999) 'Occult economies and the violence of abstraction: Notes from the South African postcolony', *American Ethnologist*, 26: 279–303.

Comaroff, J. and Comaroff, J.L. (2000) 'Millennial capitalism: First thoughts on a second coming', *Public Culture*, 12: 291–343.

Comte, A. (1853) *The Positive Philosophy of Auguste Comte*, Vols I and II. Translated by H. Martineau. London: John Chapman.

Comte, A. (1858) *The Catechism of Positive Religion*. Translated by Richard Congreve. London: John Chapman.

Conger, J.A. and Kanungo, N. (1987) 'Toward a behavioral theory of charismatic leadership in organizational settings', *Academy of Management Review*, 12: 637–47.

Conger, J.A. and Kanungo, N. (1994) 'Charismatic leadership in organizations: Perceived behavior attributes and their measurement', *Journal of Organizational Behavior*, 15: 439–52.

Conger, J.A. and Kanungo, N. (1998) *Charismatic Leadership in Organizations*. Thousand Oaks, CA: SAGE.

Conrad, P. (2007) *Medicalization of Society: On the Transformation of Human Conditions into Treatable Disorders*. Baltimore, MD: Johns Hopkins University Press.

Conrad, P. and Schneider, J. (1992) *Deviance and Medicalization*. Philadelphia, PA: Temple University Press.

Cooper, A. (1998) *Playing in the Zone*. New York, NY: Shambhala.

Cotterrell, R. (1999) *Emile Durkheim: Law in a Moral Domain*. Stanford, CA: Stanford University Press.

Cox, H. (2001) *Fire from Heaven: The Rise of Pentecostal Spirituality and the Shaping of Religion in the Twenty-First Century*. Cambridge, MA: De Capo Press.

Csikzentmihalyi, M. (2008) *Flow*. London: Harper-Perennial.

Csordas, T. (1988) 'Elements of charismatic healing and persuasion', *Medical Anthropology Quarterly*, 2: 121–42.

Csordas, T.J. (1990) 'Embodiment as a paradigm for anthropology', *Ethos*, 18(1): 5–47.

Csordas, T.J. (1994) *The Sacred Self: A Cultural Phenomenology of Charismatic Healing*. Berkeley, CA: University of California Press.

Curry, T. (1993) 'A little pain never hurt anyone: Athletic career socialization and the normalization of sports injury', *Symbolic Interaction*, 16(3): 273–90.

Dalferth, I.U. (2010) 'Post-secular society: Christianity and the dialectics of the secular', *Journal of the American Academy of Religion*, 78(2): 317–45.

Damasio, A. (2000) *The Feeling of What Happens*. London: Vintage.

Davie, G. (2010) 'Resacralization', in B.S. Turner (ed.) *The New Blackwell Companion to the Sociology of Religion*. Oxford: Blackwell.

Davies, B. (2003) *Aquinas*. London: Continuum.

Davis, K. (2003) *Dubious Equalities and Embodied Differences*. London: Rowman and Littlefield.

Dawkins, R. (2006) *The God Delusion*. Boston, MA: Houghton Mifflin.

Dawson, L.L. (2006) 'Psychopathologies and the attribution of charisma: A critical introduction to the psychology of charisma and the explanation of violence in new religious movements', *Nova Religio*, 10(2): 3–28.

D'Costa, G. (2010) 'Preface', in J. Carruthers and A. Tate (eds) *Spiritual Identities: Literature and the Post-Secular Imagination*. Bern, Switzerland: Peter Lang.

de Beauvoir, S. (1993) *The Second Sex*. London: Everyman.

de Boeck, F. (2004) *Kinshasa: Tales of the Invisible City*. Ghent: Ludion.

Dechant, D. (2002) *The Sacred Santa: Religious Dimensions of Consumer Culture*. London: Pilgrim Press.

Deleuze, G. and Guattari, F. (1972) *Anti-Oedipus*. London: Continuum.

Demerath III, N.J. (2000) 'The varieties of sacred experience: Finding the sacred in a secular grove', *Journal for the Social Scientific Study of Religion*, 39(1): 1–11.

Demerath III, N.J. (2007) 'Secularization and sacralization deconstructed and reconstructed', in J.A. Beckford and N.J. Demerath III (eds) *The SAGE Handbook of the Sociology of Religion*. London: SAGE.

Demian, M. (2004) 'Seeing, knowing, owning: Property claims as revelatory acts', in E. Hirsch and M. Strathern (eds) *Transactions and Creations: Property Debates and the Stimulus of Melanesia*. Oxford: Berghahn Books.

Dennis, K. (2009) *Art/Porn: A History of Seeing and Touching*. London: Berg.

DeNora, T. (2000) *Music in Everyday Life*. Cambridge: Cambridge University Press.

Dewey, J. (1969) *Democracy and Education*. New York, NY: Macmillan.

Dewey, J. (1980) *Art as Experience*. New York, NY: Perigee.

Dewey, J. (2002) *Human Nature and Conduct*. New York, NY: Dover.

Dewsbury, J.D. (2003) 'Witnessing space: "Knowledge without contemplation"' *Environment and Planning A*, 35: 1907–32.

Dobbelaere, K. (1981) 'Secularization: A multi-dimensional concept', *Current Sociology* 29: 1–216.

Dobbelaere, K. (1985) 'Secularization theories and sociological paradigms: A reformulation of the private–public dichotomy and the problem of societal integration', *Sociological Analysis*, 46: 377–87.

Dobbelaere, K. (1987) 'Some trends in European sociology of religion: The secularization debate', *Sociological Analysis*, 48: 107–37.

Dobbelaere, K. (1988) 'Secularization, pillarization, religious involvement, and religious change in the Low Countries', in T.M. Gannon (ed.) *World Catholicism in Transition*. New York, NY: Macmillan, pp. 80–115.

Dobbelaere, K. (1989) 'The secularization of society? Some methodological suggestions', in J.K. Hadden and A. Shupe (eds) *Secularization and Fundamentalism Reconsidered*. New York, NY: Paragon House, pp. 27–43.

Driscoll, M. (2009) *Porn-Again Christian*. Re:Lit Publishers.

Droogers, A. (2001) 'Globalisation and pentecostal success', in A. Gorton and R. Marshall-Fratani (eds) *Between Babel and Pentecost*. Bloomington, IN: Indiana University Press, pp. 41–61.

D'Souza, S.M. (2012) 'Quran copy burning in Afghanistan and the US "exit" strategy', *Institute of South Asian Studies Insights*, No. 158, 5 March.

Dumit, J. (2012) *Drugs for Life*. London: Duke University Press.

Dumont, L. (1985) 'A modified view of our origins: The Christian beginnings of modern individualism', in M. Carruthers, S. Collins and S. Lukes (eds) *The Category of the Person: Anthropology, Philosophy, History*. Cambridge: Cambridge University Press.

Durkheim, E. (1898) 'Individualism and the intellectuals', reprinted in R. Bellah (ed.) *Emile Durkheim on Morality and Society*. Chicago, IL: Chicago University Press.

Durkheim, E. (1952) *Suicide*. London: Routledge.

Durkheim, E. (1953) *Sociology and Philosophy*. London: Cohen and West.

Durkheim, E. (1961) *Moral Education*. New York, NY: Free Press.

Durkheim, E. (1973) 'The dualism of human nature and its social conditions', in R. Bellah (ed.) *Emile Durkheim on Morality and Society*. Chicago, IL: Chicago University Press.

Durkheim, E. (1982) *The Rules of Sociological Method*. London: Macmillan.

Durkheim, E. (1983) *Pragmatism and Society*. Cambridge: Cambridge University Press.

Durkheim, E. (1984) *The Division of Labour in Society*. London: Macmillan.

Durkheim, E. (1992) *Professional Ethics and Civic Morals*. London: Routledge.

Durkheim, E. (1995) *The Elementary Forms of Religious Life*. New York, NY: Free Press.

Edge, A. (2007) *Faith of our Fathers*. London: Two Heads.

Edgell, P. (2012) 'A cultural sociology of religion: New directions', *Annual Review of Sociology*, 38: 247–65.

Eichberg, H. (1998) *Body Cultures*. London: Routledge.

Eisenstadt, S.N. (1989) 'Max Weber on Western Christianity and the Weberian approach to civilizational dynamics', *The Canadian Journal of Sociology/Cahiers canadiens de sociologie*, 14(2): 203–23.

Eisenstadt, S. N. (2000) 'Multiple modernities', *Daedalus*, 129: 1–29.

Elder-Vass, D. (2007) 'Reconciling Archer and Bourdieu in an emergentist theory of action', *Sociological Theory*, 25(4): 325–46.

Eliade, M. (1959) *The Sacred and the Profane: The Nature of Religion*. London: Harcourt Brace Jovanovich.

Eliade, M. (1963) *Myth and Reality*. New York, NY: Harper and Row.

Elias, N. (1991) *Symbol Emancipation*. London: SAGE.

Elias, N. (2000 [1939]) *The Civilizing Process*, 2 vols. Oxford: Blackwell.

Ellingson, S. (2010) 'New research on megachurches', in B.S. Turner (ed.) *The New Blackwell Companion to the Sociology of Religion*. Oxford: Blackwell, pp. 245–66.

Engler, S. (2003) 'Modern times: Religion, consecration and the state in Bourdieu', *Cultural Studies*, 17(3/4): 445–67.

Ensari, N. and Murphy, S.E. (2003) 'Cross-cultural variations in leadership perceptions and attribution of charisma to the leader', *Organizational Behavior and Human Decision Processes*, 92: 52–66.

Entwistle, J. (2000) *The Fashioned Body*. Oxford: Polity Press.

Entwistle, J. (2009) *The Aesthetic Economy of Fashion*. London: Burke.

Escohotado, A. (1999) *A Brief History of Drugs*. Rochester, VT: Park Street Press.

Esposito, J. (2002) *Unholy War: Terror in the Name of Islam*. Oxford: Oxford University Press.

Falk, P. (1994) *The Consuming Body*. London: SAGE.

Farvazza, A.R. (1996) *Bodies Under Siege*. Baltimore, MD: John Hopkins University Press.

Featherstone, M. (1991) *Consumer Culture and Postmodernism*. London: SAGE.

Featherstone, M. (2010) 'Body, image and affect in consumer culture', *Body & Society*, 16(1): 193–221.

Feder, M., Naddaff, R. and Tazi, N. (1989) *Fragments for a History of the Human Body*, 3 vols. New York, NY: Zone Books.

Fenn, R.K. (1978) *Toward a Theory of Secularization*. Society for the Scientific Study of Religion, Monograph Series, no. 1.

Fenn, R.K. (1982) *Liturgies and Trials: The Secularization of Religious Language*. London: Pilgrim Press.

Ferguson, H. (1992) *The Religious Transformation of Western Society*. London: Routledge.

Fernandez, J. (1990 [1972]) 'Tabernanthe iboga: Narcotic ecstasis and the work of the ancestors', in P. Furst (ed.) *Flesh of the Gods: The Ritual Use of Hallucinogens*. London: Waveland.

Feuchtwang, S. (2008) 'Suggestions for a redefinition of charisma', *Nova Religio*, 12(2): 90–105.

Fields, H. (2007) 'Setting the stage for pain: Allegorical tales from neurocscience', in S. Coakley and K.K. Shelemay (eds) *Pain and Its Transformations*. Cambridge, MA: Harvard University Press.

Finch, M. (2010) *Dissenting Bodies: Corporealities in Early New England*. New York, NY: Columbia University Press.

Flake, C. (1992) 'The spirit of winning: Sports and the total man', in S. Hoffman (ed.) *Sport and Religion*. Champaign, IL: Human Kinetics.

Fleetwood, S. (2008) 'Structure, institutions, agency, habit and reflexive deliberation', *Journal of Institutional Economics*, 4: 183–203.

Foucault, M. (1979) *Discipline and Punish*. Harmondsworth: Penguin.

Foucault, M. (1983) 'Le combat de la chasteté', *Communications*, 35.

Foucault, M. *(1986) The Care of the Self.* New York, NY: *Pantheon.*

Foucault, M. (1988a) 'Technologies of the self', in L. Martin, H. Guttman and P. Hutton (eds) *Technologies of the Self.* Amherst, MA: University of Massachusetts Press.

Foucault, M. *(*1988b*)* 'The ethic of care for the self as a practice of freedom', in J. Bernauer and D. Rasmussen (eds) *The Final Foucault.* Cambridge, MA: MIT Press.

Foucault, M. (1997) *Il Faut Defender la Societé. Cours au Collège 1975–1976.* Paris: Seuil.

Foucault, M. (2004a) *Securité, Territoire, Population. Cours au Collège 1977–1978.* Paris: Seuil.

Foucault, M. (2004b) *Naissance de la Biopolitique. Cours au Collège 1978–1979.* Paris: Seuil.

Frank, A. (1995) 'As much as theory can say about bodies', *Body & Society* 1(1): 184–7.

Frank, A. (1997) *The Wounded Storyteller.* Chicago, IL: Chicago University Press.

Franks, D. (2010) *Neurosociology.* New York: Springer.

Freston, P. (2001) *Evangelicals and Politics in Asia, Africa and Latin America.* Cambridge: Cambridge University Press.

Freston, P. (2007) 'Evangelicalism and fundamentalism: The politics of global popular protestantism', in J.A. Beckford and N.J. Demerath III (eds) *The SAGE Handbook of the Sociology of Religion.* London: SAGE.

Freund, P.E.S. (2006) 'Socially constructed embodiment: Neurohormonal connections as resources for theorizing about health inequalities', *Social Theory and Health,* 4: 85–108.

Freund, P.E.S. (2011) 'Embodying psychosocial health inequalities: Bringing back materiality and bio-agency', *Social Theory and Health,* 9: 59–70.

Friedland, R. and Alford, R.R. (1991) 'Bringing Society Back in: Symbols, Practices, and Institutional Contradictions', in W.W. Powell and P.J. DiMaggio (eds) *The New Institutionalism in Organizational Analysis.* Chicago, IL: University of Chicago Press, pp. 232–66.

Frodon, J.M. (2002) 'The war of images, or the Bamiyan paradox', in B. Latour and P Weisbel (eds), *Iconoclash.* Cambridge, MA: MIT Press.

Gamman, L. and Makinen, M. (1994) *Female Fetishism.* London: Lawrence and Wishart.

Garber, M. (2000) *Bisexuality and the Eroticism of Everyday Life.* London: Routledge.

Gardner, W.L. and Avolio, B.J. (1998) 'The charismatic relationship: A dramaturgical perspective', *Academy of Management Review,* 23: 32–58.

Garland, D. (1990) *Punishment and Modern Society.* Oxford: Oxford University Press.

Gatrad, A. (1994) 'Muslim customs surrounding death, bereavement, postmortem examinations, and organ transplants', *British Medical Journal,* 309: 521–3.

Gauchet, M. (1997) *The Disenchantment of the World.* Princeton, NJ: Princeton University Press.

Gauchet, M. (2002) *La Démocratie Contre Elle-Même.* Paris: Gallimard.

Gauchet, M. (2005) *La Condition Politique.* Paris: Gallimard.

Gay, J. (1939 [1731]) 'Dissertation concerning the fundamental principle of virtue or morality', in Edwin A. Burtt (ed.) *The English Philosophers From Bacon to Mill.* New York, NY: Modern Library.

Gellner, E. (1992) *Postmodernism, Reason and Religion.* London: Routledge.

Geraci, R. (2010) *Apocalyptic AI*. Oxford Scholarship Online.

Giddens, A. (1991) *Modernity and Self-Identity*. Oxford: Polity Press.

Giddens, A. (1992) *The Transformation of Intimacy*. Oxford: Polity Press.

Gifford, P. (2004) *Ghana's New Christianity: Pentecostalism in a Globalising African Economy*. Bloomington, IN: Indiana University Press.

Gillespie, D. and Warren, M. (2011) *Charisma: Get What the Greats Have Got*. London: Hodder.

Gimlin, D. (2012) *Cosmetic Surgery Narratives: A Cross-National Comparison of Women's Accounts*. Basingstoke: Palgrave Macmillan.

Girard, R. (1977) *Violence and the Sacred*. Baltimore, MD: John Hopkins University Press.

Girard, R. (1987) *Job: The Victim of His People*. London: Athlone.

Girard, R. (1995) *Violence and the Sacred*. London: Athlone.

Girard, R. (2000) 'Violence renounced: Response by Rene Girard', in W.M. Swartley (ed.) *Violence Renounced*. London: Pandora.

Girard, R. (2001) *I See Satan Fall Like Lightning*. Maryknoll, NY: Orbis.

Girard, R. (2004) 'On Mel Gibson's *The Passion of the Christ*', *Anthropoetics*, X(1).

Girard, R. (2008) Apocalyptic thinking after 9/11: An interview with René Girard. *SubStance*, 37(1): 20–32.

Giulianotti, R. and Klauser, F. (2012) 'Sports mega-events and terrorism', *International Review for the Sociology of Sport*, 47(3): 307–23.

Giulianotti, R. and Robertson, R. (2012) 'Mapping the global football field', *British Journal of Sociology*, 63(2): 216–40.

Glucklich, A. (2001) *Sacred Pain*. Oxford: Oxford University Press.

Gobe, M. (2001) *Emotional Branding*. New York: Allworth Press.

Godazgar, H. (2007) 'Islam versus consumerism and postmodernism in the context of Iran', *Social Compass*, 54(3): 389–418.

Goffman, E. (1974) *Frame Analysis*. London: Harper & Row.

Gofman. A. (1998) 'A vague but suggestive concept: The "Total Social Fact"', in W. James and N.J. Allen (eds) *Marcel Mauss: A Centenary Tribute*. New York, NY: Berghahn Books.

Gökariksel, B. (2009) 'Beyond the officially sacred: Religion, secularism, and the body in the production of subjectivity', *Social and Cultural Geography*, 10(6): 657–74.

Göle, N. (1996) *The Forbidden Modern: Civilization and Veiling*. Michigan, MI: University of Michigan Press.

Göle, N. (2010) 'Manifestations of the religious-secular divide: Self, state and the public sphere', in L.E. Cady and E. Shakman Hurds (eds) *Comparative Secularisms in a Global Age*. London: Palgrave, Macmillan.

Goodchild, J. and Callow, C. (2001) *Brands: Visions and Values*. London: John Wiley & Sons.

Goodger, J. and Goodger, B. (1989) 'Excitement and representation', *Quest*, 41: 257–72.

Gorski, P.S. and Altinordu, A. (2008) 'After secularization?', *American Review of Sociology*, 34: 55–85.

Greil, A.L. (1993) 'Explorations along the sacred frontier: Notes on para-religions, quasi-religions and other boundary phenomena', in D.G. Bromley and J.K. Hadden (eds) *Religion and the Social Order*, Vol. 3, Part A. Greenwich, CT: JAI Press.

Greil, A.L. and Robbins, T. (1994) 'Introduction: Exploring the boundaries of the sacred', in D.G. Bromley and J.K. Hadden (eds) *Religion and the Social Order, Vol. 4: Research and Theory on Quasi-Religion*. Greenwich, CT: JAI Press.

Griffith, R.M. (2004) *Born Again Bodies: Flesh and Spirit in American Christianity*. Berkeley, CA: University of California Press.

Gumbrecht, H. (2004) *The Production of Presence*. Stanford, CA: Stanford University Press.

Gusfield, J. (1996) *Contested Meanings*. Madison, WI: University of Wisconsin Press.

Habermas, J. (2008) *Between Naturalism and Religion. Philosophical Essays*. Cambridge: Polity Press.

Habermas, J. (2010) 'A reply', in N. Brieskorn, J. Habermas, M. Reder, F. Ricken and J. Schmidt (eds) *An Awareness of What is Missing: Faith and Reason in a Post-Secular Age*. Cambridge: Polity Press.

Haggerty, P. and Boyle, K. (2012) 'Planning for the worst', *British Journal of Sociology*, 63(2): 241–59.

Halbwachs, M. (1930) *Les Causes du Suicide*. Paris: Alcan.

Halbwachs, M. (1980) *The Collective Memory*. London: Harper and Row.

Haley, P. (1980) 'Rudolph Sohm on charisma', *The Journal of Religion*, 60: 185–97.

Hammond, P.E. (1985) 'Introduction', in P.E. Hammond (ed.) *The Sacred in A Secular Age*. Berkeley, CA: University of California Press.

Hammond, P.E. (2000) *Dynamics of Religious Organizations: The Extravasation of the Sacred and Other Essays*. Oxford: Oxford University Press.

Hankinson, R. (ed.) (2008) *The Cambridge Companion to Galen*. Cambridge: Cambridge University Press.

Hargreaves, J. (1994) *Sporting Females*. London: Routledge.

Harkness, G. and Islam, S. (2011) 'Muslim female athletes and the Hijab', *Contexts*, 10(4): 64–5.

Harrington, A. (2007) 'Habermas and the "post-secular" society', *European Journal of Social Theory*, 10(4): 543–60.

Harris, S. (2006) *Letter to a Christian Nation*. New York, NY: Knopf.

Harrison, J. (2003) *Paul's Language of Grace in its Graeco-Roman Context*. London: Paul Mohr Verlag.

Haynes, N. (2012) 'Pentecostalism and the morality of money: Prosperity, inequality, and religious sociality on the Zambian Copperbelt', *Journal of the Royal Anthropological Institute*, 18: 123–39.

Hayward, C. and Madill, A. (2003) 'The meanings of organ donation: Muslims of Pakistani origin and white English nationals living in North England', *Social Science & Medicine*, 57(3): 389–401.

Heck, P.L. (2004) 'Jihad revisited', *Journal of Religious Ethics*, 32: 95–128.

Heelas, P. (1996) *The New Age Movement*. Oxford: Wiley-Blackwell.

Heelas, P. (2006) 'Challenging secularization theory: The growth of "new age" spiritualities', *The Hedgehog Review*, 8(1–2): 46–58.

Heelas, P. and Woodhead, L. (2005) *The Spiritual Revolution: Why Religion is Giving Way to Spirituality*. Oxford: Blackwell.

Hegland, M.E. (1998) 'Flagellation and fundamentalism: (Trans)forming meaning, identity and gender through Pakistani women's rituals of mourning', *American Ethnologist*, 25(2): 240–66.

Heidegger, M. (1993) 'The question concerning technology', in D. Krell (ed.) *Martin Heidegger: Basic Writings*. London: Routledge.

Henkel, H. (2005) 'Between belief and unbelief lies the performance of salat: Meaning and the efficacy of a Muslim ritual', *Journal of the Royal Anthropological Institute*, 11: 487–507.

Herbert, D. (2011) 'Theorizing religion and media in contemporary societies: An account of religious "publicization"', *European Journal of Cultural Studies*, 14(6): 626–48.

Herlinghaus, H. (2010) 'In/comparable intoxications: Walter Benjamin revisited from the Hemispheric South', *Discourse*, 32(1): 16–36.

Hervieu-Léger, D. (2000) *Religion as a Chain of Memory*. Cambridge: Polity Press.

Higgs, R. and Braswell, M. (2004) *An Unholy Alliance: The Sacred and Modern Sports*. Macon, GA: Mercer University Press.

Hoffman, S. (ed.) (1992) *Sport and Religion*. Champaign, IL: Human Kinetics.

Hoffman, S. (2007) *Good Game: Christianity and the Culture of Sports*. Waco, TX Baylor University Press.

Hollinger, D. (1991) 'Enjoying God forever: An historical/sociological profile of the health and wealth gospel in the USA', in P. Gee and J. Fulton (eds) *Religion and Power Decline and Growth*. London: Sociology of Religion Study Group.

Holloway, J. (2006) 'Enchanted spaces: The séance, affect, and geographies of religion', *Annals of the Association of American Geographers*, 96(1): 182–7.

Holt, D. (2004) *How Brands Became Icons*. Harvard, MA: Harvard Business School Press.

Holt, D. and Thompson, C. (2004) 'Man-of-action heroes: The pursuit of heroic masculinity in everyday consumption', *Journal of Consumer Research*, 31(2): 425–40.

Hong, Y.S. (1973) *Korea's Self-Identity*. Seoul: Yonsei University Press.

Horne, J. and Manzenreiter, W. (2006) (eds) 'Sports mega-events', *The Sociological Review* (Monograph Series), Special Supplement 2.

Howe, D. (2004) *Sport, Professionalization and Pain*. London: Routledge.

Howes, G. (2007) *The Art of the Sacred: An Introduction to the Aesthetics of Art and Belief*. London: I.B. Taurus.

Hubert, H. and Mauss, M. (1964) *Sacrifice: Its Nature and Function*. Chicago, IL: University of Chicago Press.

Hughes, J. (2003) *Learning to Smoke*. Chicago, IL: Chicago University Press.

Hughes, R.L., Ginnett, R.C. and Curphy, G.J. (2003) *Leadership: Enhancing the Lessons of Experience*. New York, NY: Irwin McGraw-Hill.

Hunt, L. (1993) 'Introduction: Obscenity and the origins of modernity', in L. Hunt (ed.) *The Invention of Pornography 1500–1800*. New York, NY: Zone Books.

Hunt, S. (2005) *Religion and Everyday Life*. London: Routledge.

Iannaccone, L. (1995) 'Voodoo economics? Reviewing the rational choice approach to religion', *Journal for the Scientific Study of Religion*, 34(1): 76–89.

Iannaccone, L. (1997) 'Rational choice: Framework for the study of religion', in L.A. Young (ed.) *Religion and Rational Choice Theory: A Summary and Assessment*. London: Routledge.

Illich, I. (1977) *Limits to Medicine*. Harmondsworth: Penguin.

Inglehart, R. (1997) *Modernization and Postmodernization: Cultural, Political and Economic Change in 43 Countries*. Princeton, NJ: Princeton University Press.

Isaacson, W. (2011) *Steve Jobs*. New York, NY: Little Brown.

Jackson, P. (1995) 'The development of a scientific fact, the case of passive smoking', in R. Bunton, S. Nettleton and R. Burrows (eds) *The Sociology of Health Promotion*. London: Routledge.

James, W. (1900) *Psychology: Briefer Course*. New York, NY: Henry Holt.

James, W. (1956) *The Will to Believe and Other Essays in Popular Philosophy, and Human Immortality*. New York, NY: Dover.

James, W. (1983) *The Varieties of Religious Experience*. Harmondsworth: Penguin.

Jay, M. (2000) *Emperors of Dreams: Drugs in the C19th*. Cambridge: Dedalus.

Jenkins, R. (2000) 'Categorisation: Identity, social process and epistemology', *Current Sociology*, 48(3): 7–25.

Jenkins, R. (2002) *Pierre Bourdieu*. London: Routledge.

Jha, A. (2012) 'Report raises ethical concerns about human enhancement technologies', Guardian.co.uk. Wednesday 7 November.

Johns, J.D. (1999) Yielding to the spirit: The dynamics of a pentecostal model of praxis', in M. Dempster, B. Klaus and D. Peterson (eds) *The Globalization of Pentecostalism: A Religion Made to Travel*. Irvine, CA: Regnum.

Juergensmeyer, M. (2003) *Terror in the Mind of God*. Berkeley, CA: University of California Press.

Kalra, V.S. and Hutnyk, J. (1998) 'Brimful of agitation, authenticity and appropriation: Madonna's Asian Kool', *Postcolonial Studies: Culture, Politics, Economy*, 1(3): 339–55.

Kazmi, N. (2008) 'Why self-flagellation matters for Shias', *The Guardian*, 28 August.

Kerrigan, M.P. (1992) 'Sports and the Christian Life: Reflection on Pope John Paul II's theology of sports', in S. Hoffman (ed.) *Sport and Religion*. Champaign, IL: Human Kinetics.

Kets de Vries, M. (2004) *Lessons in Leadership by Terror: Shaka Zulu in the Attic*. London: Edward Elder.

Kibbey, A. (1986) *The Interpretation of Material Shapes in Puritanism*. Cambridge: Cambridge University Press.

Kim Hy-Young and Yoo Jin Kwon (2011) 'Soulmates, best friends, and casual buddies: The relationship of U.S. college students to retailer brands', *Clothing and Textiles Research Journal*, 29(1): 67–82.

King, A. (2000) 'Thinking with Bourdieu against Bourdieu: A "practical" critique of the habitus', *Sociological Theory*, 18(3): 417–33.

King, R. (2013) 'The Copernican turn in the study of religion', *Method and Theory in the Study of Religion*, 25(2): 137–59.

Klaver, M. and van de Kamp, L. (2011) 'Embodied temporalities in global pentecostal conversion', *Ethnos: Journal of Anthropology*, 76(4): 421–5.

Klein, A. (2008) *Drugs and the World*. London: Reaktion.

Kleinman, A. (1988) *The Illness Narrative*. New York, NY: Basic Books.

Kleinman, A. (2007) *What Really Matters*. Oxford: Oxford University Press.

Klesse, C. (2000) '"Modern primitivism": Non-mainstream body modification and racialized representation', in M. Featherstone (ed.) *Body Modification*. London: SAGE.

Knott, K. (2005) *The Location of Religion: A Spatial Analysis*. London: Equinox.

Knott, K. and Franks, M. (2007) 'Secular values and the location of religion: A spatial analysis of an English medical centre', *Health and Place*, 13(1): 224–37.

Kotarba, J. (1983) *Chronic Pain: Its Social Dimension*. Beverly Hills, CA: SAGE.

Kreuder, F. (2008) 'Flagellation of the Son of God and divine flagellation: Flagellator ceremonies and the flagellation scenes in the medieval passion play', *Theatre Research International*, 33(2): 176–90.

Kripal, J.J. (2001) *Roads of Excess, Palaces of Wisdom: Eroticism and Reflexivity in the Study of Mysticism*. Chcago, IL: University of Chicago Press.

Kristeva, J. (2009) *This Incredible Need to Believe*. New York, NY: Columbia University Press.

Kugle, S. and Hunt, S. (2012) 'Masculinity, homosexuality and the defence of Islam: A case study of Yusuf al-Qaradawi's media fatwa', *Religion and Gender*, 2(2): 254–79.

Kühle, L. (2012) 'In the faith of our fathers? Religious minority socialisation in pluralistic societies', *Nordic Journal of Religion and Society*, 25(2): 113–30.

Kuper, A. (1988) *The Invention of Primitive Society*. London: Routledge.

Kurasawa, F. (2003) 'Primitiveness and the flight from modernity', *Economy and Society*, 32(1): 7–28.

Labrecque, L., Krishen, A. and Grzeskowiak, S. (2011) 'Exploring social motivations for brand loyalty: Conformity versus escapism', *Journal of Brand Management*, 18: 457–72.

Ladkin, D. (2006) 'The enchantment of the charismatic leader: Charisma reconsidered as aesthetic encounter', *Leadership*, 2(2): 165–79.

Lande, B. (2007) 'Breathing like a solider: Culture incarnate', in C. Shilling (ed.) *Embodying Sociology*. Oxford: Blackwell.

Lapidus, I.M. (1984) 'Knowledge, virtue and action: The classical Muslim conception of Adab and the nature of religious fulfilment in Islam', in B.D. Metcalf (ed.) *Moral Conduct and Authority: The Place of Adab in South Asian Islam*. Berkeley, CA: University of California Press, pp. 38–61.

Largier, N. (2006) *In Praise of the Whip*. New York, NY: Zone Books.

Latour, B. (2002) *War of the Worlds: What About Peace?* Chicago, IL: Prickly Paradigm Press.

Latour, B. (2010) *On the Modern Cult of the Factish Gods*. London: Duke University Press.

Latour, B. (2011) 'Reflections on Etienne Souriau's *Les differents modes d'existence*', in L. Bryant, N. Srnicek and G. Harman (eds) *The Speculative Turn: Continental Philosophy and Realism*. Melbourne: re.press.

Lau, R.W.K. (2004) 'Habitus and the practical logic of practice: An interpretation', *Sociology*, 38(2): 369–87.

Lechner, F. (1991) 'The case against secularization: A rebuttal', *Social Forces*, 69(4): 1103–19.

Leder, D. (1990) *The Absent Body*. Chicago, IL: Chicago University Press.

Lee, J. (2010) '(Not quite) beyond belief: Intentionality and materialism in the study of religion', *Culture and Religion: An Interdisciplinary Journal*, 11(2): 147–62.

Lee, M.G. (1982) *Sociology and Social Change in Korea*. Seoul: Seoul National University Press.

Leigh, A. (2011) *Charisma: The Secrets of Making a Lasting Impression*. London: Pearson.

Lenson, D. (1995) *On Drugs*. Minneapolis, MI: University of Minnesota Press.

Levine, D.N. (1995) *Visions of the Sociological Tradition* Chicago, IL: University of Chicago Press.

Lewis, K.M. (2000) 'When leaders display emotion: How followers respond to negative emotional expression of male and female leaders', *Journal of Organizational Behavior*, 21: 221–34.

Leys, R. (2011) 'The turn to affect: A critique', *Critical Inquiry*, 37(3): 434–72.

Liao, L.M. and Creighton, S. (2007) 'Requests for cosmetic genitoplasty: How should healthcare providers respond?', *British Medical Journal*, 334: 1090–2.

Lie, J. (1998) *Han Unbound: The Political Economy of South Korea*. Stanford, CA: Stanford University Press.

Lienhardt, G. (1961) *Divinity and Experience: The Religion of the Dinka*. Oxford: Oxford University Press.

Lindholm, C. (1990) *Charisma*. Oxford: Blackwell.

Louth, A. (1997) 'The body in Western Catholic Christianity', in S. Coakley (ed.) *Religion and the Body*. Cambridge: Cambridge University Press.

Lowrie, W. (1904) *The Church and its Organisation in Primitive and Catholic Times: An Interpretation of Rudolph Sohm's Kirchenrecht, Vol. 1: The Primitive Age*. New York, NY: Longmans Green.

Luckmann, T. (1967) *The Invisible Religion*. New York, NY: Macmillan.

Luhmann, N. (1982) *The Differentiation of Society*. New York, NY: Columbia University Press.

Luhmann, N. (1985) 'Society, meaning, religion: Based on self-reference', *Sociological Analysis*, 46(1): 5–20.

Luhmann, N. (1990) *Essays on Self-Reference*. New York, NY: Columbia University Press.

Luhmann, N. (2000) *Die Religion der Gesellschaft*. Frankfurt: Suhrkamp.

Luhrmann, T.M. (2004) 'Metakinesis: How God becomes intimate in contemporary US Christianity', *American Anthropologist* 106(3): 518–28.

Lupton, D. (1997) 'Foucault and the medicalization critique' in A. Petersen and R. Bunton (eds) *Foucault: Health and Medicine*. London: Routledge.

Lury, C. (2004) *Brands: The Logos of the Global Economy*. London: Routledge.

Lury, C. (2009) 'Brand as assemblage', *Journal of Cultural Economy*, 2(1): 67–82.

Lury, C. (2011) *Consumer Culture*, 2nd edn. New York, NY: Rutgers University Press.

Lynch, G. (2012) *The Sacred in the Modern World: A Cultural Approach*. Oxford: Oxford University Press.

Lyon, D. (2000) *Jesus in Disneyland*. Cambridge: Polity Press.

Lyon, D. (2010) 'Being post-secular in the social sciences: Taylor's social imaginaries', *New Blackfriars*, 91: 648–64.

MacIntyre, A. (2007) *After Virtue: A Study in Moral Theory*, 3rd edn. Notre Dame, IN: University of Notre Dame Press.

Macrae, C. (1991) *World Class Brands*. Workingham: Addison-Wesley University Press.

Maddox, M. (2012) 'In the Goofy parking lot: Growth churches as a novel religious form for late capitalism', *Social Compass*, 59(2): 146–58.

Maduro, O. (1977) 'New Marxist approaches to the relative autonomy of religion', *Sociological Analysis*, 38(4): 359–67.

Maffesoli, M. (1996) *The Time of the Tribes*. London: SAGE.

Magdalinski, T. and Chandler, T. (2002) 'Epilogue', in T. Chandler and T. Magdalinski (eds) *With God on their Side: Sport in the Service of Religion*. London: Routledge.

Mahmood, S. (2005) *Politics of Piety: The Islamic Revival and the Feminist Subject*, Princeton, NJ: Princeton University Press.

Malbon, B. (1999) *Clubbing: Dancing, Ecstasy and Vitality*. London: Routledge.

Maley, T. (2004) 'Max Weber and the iron cage of technology', *Bulletin of Science, Technology & Society*, 24 (1): 69–86.

Mangan, J. (1986) *The Games Ethic and Imperialism*. New York, NY: Viking.

Mangan, J. and Walvin, J. (1987) *Manliness and Morality*. Manchester: Manchester University Press.

Maqsood, A. (2013) '"Buying modern": Muslim subjectivity, the West and patterns of Islamic consumption in Lahore, Pakistan', *Cultural Studies*, 28(1): 84–107.

Marti, G. (2008) *Hollywood Faith: Holiness, Prosperity and Ambition in a Hollywood Church*. New York, NY: Rutgers University Press.

Martin, D. (1966) 'Some utopian aspects of the concept of secularisation', *International Yearbook for the Sociology of Religion*, 2: 87–96.

Martin, D. (1978) *A General Theory of Secularization*. Oxford: Blackwell.

Martin, D. (1990) *Tongues of Fire*. Oxford: Blackwell.

Martin, D. (1991) 'The secularisation issue: Prospect and retrospect', *British Journal of Sociology*, 42(3): 465–74.

Martin, D. (2002) *Pentecostalism*. Oxford: Blackwell.

Martin, D. (2005) *On Secularization: Towards a Revised General Theory*. London: Ashgate.

Martin, D. (2011) *The Future of Christianity: Reflections on Violence and Democracy, Religion and Secularization*. Farnham: Ashgate.

Martin, J.M. (2000) *More Than Chains and Toil: A Christian Work Ethic of Enslaved Women*. Louisville, KY: Westminster John Knox Press.

Marx, K. (1976) *Capital. Critique of Political Economy*, Vol. 1. London: Pelican.

Marx, K. (1978) *Capital. Critique of Political Economy*, Vol. 2. London: Pelican.

Massumi, B (2002) *Parables for the Virtual*. Durham, NC: Duke University Press.

Masuzawa, T. (2005) *The Invention of World Religions*. Chicago, IL: University of Chicago Press.

Mathieu, M. (2009) 'Habitus, freedom and reflexivity', *Theory and Psychology*, 19(6): 728–55.

Mathisen, J. (2001) 'American sport as folk religion', in J. Price (ed.) *From Season to Season: Sports as American Religion*. Macon, GA: Mercer University Press.

Mauss, M. (1969a) *Oeuvres*, Vol. 2: *Représentations Collectives et Diversité des Civilisations*, ed. V. Karady. Paris: Minuit.

Mauss, M. (1969b) *The Gift*. London: Routledge.

Mauss, M. (1973a) 'Techniques of the body', *Economy and Society*, 2: 70–88.

Mauss, M. (1973b) *Sociologie et Anthropologie*. Paris: Presses Universitaires de France.

Mauss, M. (1985) 'A category of the human mind: The notion of person; the notion of self', in M. Carrithers, S. Collins and S. Lukes (eds) *The Category of the Person*. Cambridge: Cambridge University Press.

Maxwell, D. (1998) 'Delivered from the spirit of poverty?' Pentecostalism, prosperity, and modernity in Zimbabwe. *Journal of Religion in Africa*, 28: 350–73.

Mayne, G. (1993) *Eroticism in Georges Bataille and Henry Miller*. Birmingham, AL: Summer Publications.

McDannell, C. (1995) *Material Christianity: Religion and Popular Culture in America*. New Haven, CT: Yale University Press.

McGinty, A.M. (2006) *Becoming Muslim: Western Women's Conversions to Islam*. London: Palgrave.

McGowan, R. (1986) 'A powerful sympathy: Terror, the prison and humanitarian reform in early nineteenth-century Britain', *The Journal of British Studies*, 25(3): 312–34.

McGrath, P. (1990) *Pain in Children*. London: Guilford Press.

McGuire, M. (1990) 'Religion and the body: Rematerializing the human body in the social sciences of religion', *Journal for the Social Scientific Study of Religion*, 29(3): 283–96.

McKenna, T. (1992) *Food of the Gods*. London: Rider.

McKinnon, A. (2010) 'The sociology of religion', in B.S. Turner (ed.) *The New Blackwell Companion to the Sociology of Religion*. Oxford: Blackwell, pp. 31–51.

McLennan, G. (2010) 'The postsecular turn', *Theory, Culture & Society*, 27(4): 3–20.

McNair, B. (2002) *Striptease Culture*. London: Routledge.

McTavish, J. (2004) *Pain and Profits: The History of the Headache and its Remedies in America*. New Brunswick, NJ: Rutgers University Press.

Mead, G.H. (1962) *Mind, Self and Society*. Chicago, IL: University of Chicago Press.

Mellor, P. A. (1993) 'Self and suffering: Deconstruction and reflexive definition in Buddhism and Christianity', *Religious Studies*, 27: 49–63.

Mellor, P.A. (2004) *Religion, Realism and Social Theory: Making Sense of Society*. London: SAGE.

Mellor, P.A. and Shilling, C. (1997) *Re-Forming the Body: Religion, Community and Modernity*. London: SAGE.

Mellor, P.A. and Shilling, C. (2010a) 'Body pedagogics and the religious habitus: A new direction for the sociological study of religion', *Religion*, 40: 27–38.

Mellor, P.A. and Shilling, C. (2010b) 'The religious habitus: Embodiment, religion and sociological theory', in B.S. Turner (ed.) *The New Blackwell Companion to the Sociology of Religion*. Oxford: Blackwell.

Melzack, R. and Wall, P. (1988) *The Challenge of Pain*. Harmondsworth: Penguin.

Merleau-Ponty, M. (1962) *Phenomenology of Perception*. London: Routledge.

Meštrović, S. (1994) *The Balkanization of the West*. London: Routledge.

Meštrović, S. (1997) *Postemotional Society*. London: SAGE.

Meyer, B. (1998) 'The power of money: Politics, sorcery and pentecostalism in Ghana', *African Studies Review* 41(3): 15–38.

Meyer, B. (2004) 'Christianity in Africa: From African Independent to Pentecostal-Charismatic churches', *Annual Review of Anthropology* 33: 447–74.

Meyer, B. (2009) 'Introduction: From imagined communities to aesthetic formations: Religious mediations, sensational forms, and styles of binding', in B. Meyer (ed.) *Aesthetic Formations. Media, Religion and the Senses*. London: Palgrave Macmillan.

Meyer, B. (2010a) 'Aesthetics of persuasion: Global christianity and pentecostalism's sensational forms', *South Atlantic Quarterly*, 109(4): 741–63.

Meyer, B. (2010b) (ed.) *Aesthetic Formations: Media, Religion and the Senses* (Religion/Culture/Critique). London: Palgrave Macmillan.

Miller, D. (1997) *Reinventing American Protestantism*. Berkeley, CA: University of California Press.

Miller, K.E. (2008) 'Wired: Energy drinks, jock identity, masculine norms, and risk taking', *Journal of American College Health*, 56: 481–90.

Miller-McLemore, B. (2001) 'Through the eyes of Mircea Eliade: United States football as a religious "rite de passage"', in J. Price (ed.) *From Season to Season: Sports as American Religion*. Macon, GA: Mercer University Press.

Mitchell, W. (1986) *Iconology*. Chicago, IL: Chicago University Press.

Mitzman, A. (1971) *The Iron Cage*. New York, NY: Transaction.

Monaghan, L. (2007) *Men and the War on Obesity*. London: Routledge.

Mondzain, M-J. (2002) 'The Holy Shroud', in B. Latour and P. Weibel (eds), *Iconoclash: Beyond the Image Wars*. Cambridge, MA: MIT Press.

Moor, L. and Lury, C. (2011) 'Making and measuring value', *Journal of Cultural Economy*, 4(4): 439–54.

Morgan, D. (1998) *Visual Piety*. Berkeley, CA: University of California Press.

Morgan, D. (2002a) 'The body in pain', in M. Evans and E. Lee (eds) *Real Bodies*. London: Palgrave Macmillan.

Morgan, D. (2002b) 'Pain: The unrelieved condition of modernity', *European Journal of Social Theory*, 5(3): 307–22.

Morgan, D. (2005) *The Sacred Gaze*. Berkeley, CA: University of California Press.

Morgan, D. (2010) (ed.) *Material Culture: The Matter of Belief*. London: Routledge.

Morgan, D. and Wilkinson, I. (2001) 'The problem of suffering and the sociological task of theodicy', *European Journal of Social Theory*, 4(2): 199–214.

Morris, D.B. (1991) *The Culture of Pain*. Berkeley, CA: University of California Press.

Morris, D.B. (1993) 'Placebo, pain and belief', in A. Harrington (ed.) *The Placebo Effect*. Cambridge, MA: Harvard University Press.

Moules, T. and Ramsay, J. (2007) *The Textbook of Children's and Young People's Nursing*. Oxford: Wiley-Blackwell.

Mouzelis, N. (2012) 'Modernity and the secularization debate', *Sociology*, 46(2): 207–23.

Mullan, J. (1988) *Sentiment and Sociability: The Language of Feeling in the 18th-Century*. Oxford: Clarendon Press.

Muniz Jr, A. and O'Guinn, T. (2001) 'Brand community', *Journal of Consumer Research*, 27(4): 412–32.

Nauright, J. and Magdalinski, T. (2002) 'Religion, Race and Rugby in "Coloured" Cape Town', in T. Chandler and T. Magdalinski (eds) *With God on their Side: Sport in the Service of Religion*. London: Routledge.

Navaro-Yashin, Y. (2002) *Faces of the State: Secularism and Public Life in Turkey*. Princeton, NJ: Princeton University Press.

Nettleton, S. (1989) 'Power and pain: The location of fear in dentistry and the creation of a dental subject', *Social Science and Medicine*, 29(10): 1183–90.

Nettleton, S. (2004) '"I just want permission to be ill": Towards a sociology of medically unexplained symptoms', *Social Science and Medicine*, 62(5): 1167–78.

Newman, J.I. and Giardina, M.D. (2011) *Sport, Spectacle and NASCAR Nation: Consumption and the Cultural Politics of Neoliberalism*. London: Palgrave Macmillan.

Nixon, S. (1997) 'Circulating culture', in P. du Gay (ed.) *Production of Culture/Cultures of Production*. London: SAGE.

Norris, P. and Inglehart, R. (2004) *The Sacred and the Secular: Religion and Politics Worldwide*. Cambridge: Cambridge University Press.

Norris, R.S. (2009) 'The paradox of healing pain', *Religion*, 39: 22–33.

Novak, M. (1992) *The Joy of Sports*. New York, NY: Basic Books.

Nynäs, P., Lassander, M. and Utriainen, T. (2012) (eds) *Post-Secular Society*. New Brunswick, NJ: Transaction.

O'Malley, P. (2005) 'The undertreatment of pain: Ethical and legal implications for the Clinical Nurse Specialist', *Clinical Nurse Specialist*, 19(5): 236–7.

Orsi, R.A. (1999) *Gods of the City: Religion and the American Urban Landscape*. Bloomington, IN: Indiana University Press.

Orsi, R.A. (2005) *Between Heaven and Earth*. Princeton, NJ: Princeton University Press.

Otto, R. (1958) *The Idea of the Holy*. London: Pelican.

Özyürek, E. (2006) *Nostalgia for the Modern: State Secularism and Everyday Politics in Turkey*. Durham, NC: Duke University Press.

Paasonen, S. (2007) *Pornification*. Oxford: Berg.

Palmer, D.A. (2008) 'Embodying utopia: Charisma in the post-Mao Qigong craze', *Nova Religio*, 12(2): 69–89.

Papoulias, C. and Callard, F. (2010) 'Biology's gift: Interrogating the turn to affect', *Body & Society*, 16(1): 29–56.

Parsons, T. (1960) *Structure and Process in Modern Societies*. New York, NY: Free Press.

Parsons, T. (1968) *The Structure of Social Action*. New York, NY: Free Press.

Parsons, T. (1978) *Action Theory and the Human Condition*. New York, NY: Free Press.

Parsons, T. (1991) *The Social System*. London: Routledge.

Patterson, M. (1999) 'Re-appraising the concept of brand image', *Journal of Brand Management*, 6(6): 409–26.

Peek, L. (2005) 'Becoming Muslim: Development of a religious identity', *Sociology of Religion*, 66(3): 215–42.

Perkins, J. (1995) *The Suffering Self*. London: Routledge.

Pickel, A. (2005) 'The habitus process: A biopsychosocial conception', *Journal for the Theory of Social Behaviour*, 35(4): 437–61.

Pickering, M. (1993) *Auguste Comte: An Intellectual Biography*. Cambridge: Cambridge University Press.

Pickering, W.S.F. (2009) *Durkheim's Sociology of Religion*. London: James Clark & Co.

Pickering, W.S.F. and Rosati, M. (2008) 'Introduction', in W.S.F. Pickering and M. Rosati (eds) *Suffering and Evil: The Durkheimian Legacy*. Oxford: Berghahn Books.

Pincikowski, S.E. (2001) *Bodies of Pain*. London: Routledge.

Pine, J. and Gilmore, J. (1999) *The Experience Economy*. Boston, MA: Harvard Business School Press.

Poloma, M. (1996) *The Toronto Report*. Wiltshire: Terra Nova Publications.

Poloma, M. (1998) 'Inspecting the fruit of the "Toronto Blessing"', *Pneuma: The Journal of the Society for Pentecostal Studies*, 20: 43–70.

Poloma, M. (2003) *Main Street Mystics*. Walnut Creek, CA: AltaMira Press.

Pongsakornrungsilp, S. and Schroeder, J.E. (2011) 'Understanding value co-creation in a co-consuming brand community', *Marketing Theory*, 11(3): 303–24.

Poole, F. (1985) 'Among the boughs of the hanging tree: Male suicide among the Bimin-Kuskusmin of Papua New Guinea', in F. Hezel, D. Rubenstein and G. White (eds) *Culture, Youth and Suicide in the Pacific*. Honolulu, HI: East-West Center.

Poole, F. (1998) 'Aspects of person and self in Bimin-Kuskusmin male initiation', in G. Herdt (ed.) *Male Initiation in Papua New Guinea*. London: SAGE.

Potts, J. (2009) *A History of Charisma*. London: Palgrave, Macmillan.

Priel, B., Rabinowitz, B. and Pels, R. (1991) 'A semiotic perspective on chronic pain', *British Journal of Medical Psychology*, 64: 65–71.

Pyysiäinen, I. (2003) *How Religion Works: Towards a New Cognitive Science of Religion*. London: Brill.

Rahman, S.A. (2006) *Punishment of Apostasy in Islam*. Malaysia: The Other Press.

Ramp, W. (1998) 'Effervescence, differentiation and representation in *The Elementary Forms*', in N. Allen, W.S.F. Pickering and W. Watts Miller (eds) *On Durkheim's Elementary Forms of Religious Life*. London: Routledge.

Rawls, A. (1996) 'Durkheim's epistemology: The neglected argument', *American Journal of Sociology*, 102(2): 430–82.

Reichel-Dolmatoff, G. (1990 [1972]) 'The cultural context of an aboriginal hallucinogen: *Banisteriopsis caapi*', in P. Furst (ed.) *Flesh of the Gods: The Ritual Use of Hallucinogens*. London: Waveland.

Rey, R. (1995) *The History of Pain*. Cambridge, MA: Harvard University Press.

Rey, T. (2004) 'Marketing the goods of salvation: Bourdieu on religion', *Religion*, 34(4): 331–43.

Rey, T. (2007) *Bourdieu on Religion*. London: Equinox.

Richardson, M. (1994) *Georges Bataille*. London: Routledge.

Rieff, P. (2007) *Charisma*. New York, NY: Vintage Books.

Riesebrodt, M. (2000) 'Fundamentalism and the resurgence of religion', *Numen* 47(3): 266–87.

Riesebrodt, M. (2001) 'Charisma', in H.G. Kippenberg and M. Riesebrodt (eds) *Max Weber's 'Religionssystematik'*. Tübingen: J.C.B. Mohr.

Rinallo, D., Scott, L. and Maclaran, P. (2012) *Consumption and Spirituality*. London: Routledge.

Ritzer, G. (1999) *Enchanting a Disenchanted World*. London: Pine Forge.

Robbins, J. (2004) 'The globalisation of pentecostal and charismatic Christianity', *Annual Review of Anthropology*, 33: 117–43.

Roberts, J.S. (1992) 'Drink and industrial discipline in nineteenth-century Germany', in L. Berlanstein (ed.) *The Industrial Revolution and Work in Nineteenth Century Europe*. London: Routledge.

Robertson, R. (1993) *Globalization*. London: SAGE.

Robinson, F. (2004) 'Other-worldly and this-worldly Islam and the Islamic revival', *Journal of the Royal Asiatic Society*, 14(1): 47–58.

Rosati, M. (2008) 'Suffering and evil in *The Elementary Forms*', in W.S.F. Pickering and M. Rosati (eds) *Suffering and Evil: The Durkheimian Legacy*. Oxford: Berghahn Books.

Rose, N. (2007) *The Politics of Life Itself: Biomedicine, Power and Subjectivity in the Twenty-First Century*. Princeton, NJ: Princeton University Press.

Roth, G. (1987) 'Rationalisation in Max Weber's developmental history', in S. Whimster and S. Lash (eds) *Max Weber, Rationality and Modernity*. London: Allen and Unwin.

Roy, O. (1998) 'Naissance d'un Islam européen', *Esprit*, 239: 10–35.

Rudgley, R. (1993) *The Alchemy of Culture*. London: British Museum Press.

Ruel, M. (1998) 'Rescuing Durkheim's 'Rites' from Symbolizing Anthropologists', in N.J. Allen, W.S.F. Pickering and W. Watts Miller (eds) *On Durkheim's Elementary Forms of Religious Life*. London: Routledge.

Ruthven, M. (1997) *Islam: A Very Short Introduction*. Oxford: Oxford University Press.

Sack, D. (2000) *Whitebread Protestants: Food and Religion in American Culture.* London: Palgrave Macmillan.

Saint-Blancat, C. (1997) *L'Islam de la Diaspora.* Paris: Bayard.

Salvatore, A. (2006) 'Making public space: Opportunities and limits of collective action among Muslims in Europe', *Journal of Ethnic and Migration Studies,* 30(5): 1013–31.

Sanders, J.T. (2000) *Charisma, Converts, Competitors: Societal and Sociological Factors in the Success of Early Christianity.* London: SCM Press.

Sandikei, O. and Ger, G. (2010) 'The unveiling in style: How does a stigmatised practice become fashionable?', *Journal of Consumer Research,* 37(1): 15–36.

Sarracino, C. and Scott, K. (2010) *The Porning of America.* New York: Beacon Press.

Sassatelli, R. (2000) 'Body Culture in Fitness Gyms', in M. Featherstone (ed.) *Body Modification.* London: SAGE.

Sayer, A. (2005) *The Moral Significance of Class.* Cambridge: Cambridge University Press.

Scarry, E. (1995) *The Body in Pain.* Oxford: Oxford University Press.

Scharff, R.C. (1995) *Comte After Positivism.* Cambridge: Cambridge University Press.

Scheff, T. (1994) *Bloody Revenge: Emotions, Nationalism and War.* New York: Westview Press.

Schmidt, B., Zarantonello, L. and Brakus, J. (2009) 'Brand experience: What is it? How is it measured? Does it affect loyalty?', *Journal of Marketing,* 73(3): 52–68.

Schmidt, G. (2002) 'Dialectics of authenticity: Examples of ethnification of Islam among young Muslims in Sweden and the United States', *Muslim World,* 92(1–2): 1–17.

Schmidt, V.H. (2006) 'Multiple modernities or varieties of modernity?', *Current Sociology,* 54(1): 77–97.

Schouten, J. and McAlexander, J. (1995), 'Subcultures of consumption: An ethnography of the new bikers', *Journal of Consumer Research,* 22(June): 43–61.

Schultes, R.E. (1990 [1972]) 'An overview of hallucinogens in the Western hemisphere', in P. Furst (ed.) *Flesh of the Gods.* New York, NY: Waveland Press.

Scott, D. and Hirschkind, C. (2006) (eds) *Powers of the Secular Modern: Talal Asad and His Interlocutors.* Stanford, CA: Stanford University Press.

Scourfield, J., Moore, G., Taylor, C. and Gilliat-Ray, S. (2012) 'The intergenerational transmission of Islam in England and Wales: Evidence from the Citizenship Survey', *Sociology,* 46(1): 91–108.

Segato, R.L. (2008) 'Closing ranks: Religion, society and politics today', *Social Compass,* 55(2): 203–15.

Seidler, V. (1998) 'Masculinity, violence and emotional life', in G. Bendelow and S. Williams (eds) *Emotions in Social Life.* London: Routledge.

Seligman, A.B. (1992) *The Idea of Civil Society.* Princeton, NJ: Princeton University Press.

Shamir, B. (1992) 'Attribution of influence and charisma to the leader: The Romance of Leadership revisited', *Journal of Applied Social Psychology,* 22: 386–407.

Sheikh, A. (1998) 'Death and dying – A Muslim perspective', *Journal of the Royal Society of Medicine,* 91(3): 138–40.

Sherry, J. (1998) 'The soul of the company store: Nike Town Chicago and the emplaced brandscape', in J. Sherry (ed.) *Servicescapes: The Concept of Place in Contemporary Markets.* London: McGraw-Hill.

Sherry, J., Kozinets Jr, R., Storm, D., Duhachek, A., Nuttavuthisit, K. and De-Berry-Spence, B. (2001) 'Being in the zone: Staging retail theater at ESPN Zone Chicago', *Journal of Contemporary Ethnography*, 30: 465–510.

Shilling, C. (1993) *The Body and Social Theory*. London: SAGE.

Shilling, C. (2005a) *The Body in Culture, Technology and Society*. London: SAGE.

Shilling, C. (2005b) 'Embodiment, emotions and the foundations of social order', in J. Alexander and P. Smith (eds) *The Cambridge Companion to Emile Durkheim*. Cambridge: Cambridge University Press.

Shilling, C. (2008) *Changing Bodies: Habit: Crisis and Creativity*. London: SAGE.

Shilling, C. (2012) *The Body and Social Theory*, 3rd edn. London: SAGE.

Shilling, C. and Mellor, P.A. (2007) 'Cultures of embodied experience: Technology, religion and body pedagogics', *The Sociological Review*, 55(3): 531–49.

Shilling, C. and Mellor, P.A. (2014) 'Sport as a sacred phenomenon', *Sociology of Sport*.

Shils, E. (1965) 'Charisma, order, status', *American Sociological Review*, 30: 199–213.

Siedentop, L. (2000) *Democracy in Europe*. London: Penguin.

Siegfried, C. (1996) *Pragmatism and Feminism*. Chicago, IL: University of Chicago Press.

Silverstein, P. (2002) 'Stadium politics: Islam and Amazigh consciousness in France and North Africa', in T. Magdalinski and T. Chandler (eds) *With God on their Side: Sport in the Service of Religion*. London: Routledge.

Simmel, G. (1971a) 'The transcendent character of life', in D. Levine (ed.) *Georg Simmel on Individuality and Social Forms*. Chicago, IL: University of Chicago Press.

Simmel, G. (1971b) 'Exchange', in D. Levine (ed.) *Georg Simmel on Individuality and Social Forms*. Chicago, IL: University of Chicago Press.

Simmel, G. (1990) *The Philosophy of Money*. London: Routledge.

Simmel, G. (1997) 'On the salvation of the Soul', in J. Helle (ed.) *Essays on Religion*. New Haven, CT: Yale University Press.

Slack, T. (2005) *The Commercialization of Sport*. London: Routledge.

Smith, C.R. (1956) *The Bible Doctrine of Grace and Related Doctrines*. London: Epworth Press.

Smith, D.N. (1998) 'Faith, reason, and charisma: Rudolph Sohm, Max Weber and the theology of grace', *Sociological Inquiry*, 68(1): 32–60.

Smith, M. (2008) 'Pain experience and the imagined researcher', *Sociology of Health and Illness*, 30(7): 992–1006.

Smith, T. (1992) *Strong Interaction*. Chicago, IL: University of Chicago Press.

Smith, W. (1995) 'From coffeehouse to parlour', in J. Goodman, E. Lovejoy and A. Sherratt (eds) *Consuming Habits*. London: Routledge.

Snow, S. (2008) *Blessed Days of Anaesthesia*. Oxford: Oxford University Press.

Sohm, R. (1970 [1892]) *Kirchenrecht, Bd.1: Die Gescichtlichen Grundlagen*. Berlin: Duncker und Humblot.

Souriau, E. (1943) *Les Differents Modes D'Existence*. Paris: Presses Universitaires de France.

Speck, S. (2013) 'Ulrich Beck's "Reflecting Faith": Individualisation, religion and the desecularisation of reflexive modernity', *Sociology*, 47(1): 157–72.

Spielhaus, R. (2010) 'Media making Muslims: The construction of a Muslim community in Germany through media debate', *Contemporary Islam*, 4(1): 11–27.

Stark, R. (1999) 'Secularization RIP', *Sociology of Religion*, 60: 249–73.

Stark, R. (2001) 'Reconceptualizing religion, magic and science', *Review of Religious Research*, 43(2): 101–20.

Stark, R. and Bainbridge, W.S. (1985) *The Future of Religion*. Berkeley, CA: University of California Press.

Stark, R. and Bainbridge, W.S. (1987) *A Theory of Religion*. New York, NY: Peter Lang.

Starrett, G. (1998) *Putting Islam to Work: Education, Politics and Religious Transformation in Egypt*. Berkeley, CA: University of California Press.

Strati, A. (2000) 'The aesthetic approach to organisational studies', in S. Linstead and H. Hopfl (eds) *The Aesthetics of Organisation*. London: SAGE.

Strenski, I. (2003) 'Sacrifice, gift and the social logic of Muslim "human bombers"', *Terrorism and Political Violence*, 15(3): 1–34.

Strhan, A. (2012) *Discipleship and Desire: Conservative Evangelicals, Coherence and the Moral Lives of the Metropolis*. PhD Thesis, University of Kent.

Sutcliffe, S. and Bowman, M. (2000) (eds) *Beyond New Age: Exploring Alternative Spirituality*. Edinburgh: Edinburgh University Press.

Sweetman, P. (2003) 'Twenty-first century dis-ease? Habitual reflexivity or the reflexive habitus', *Sociological Review*, 51: 528–49.

Szasz, T. (2003) *Ceremonial Chemistry*. Syracuse, NY: Syracuse University Press.

Taylor, C. (2007) *The Secular Age*. Boston, MA: Harvard University Press.

Thomas, S.M. (2010) 'A globalized God: Religion's growing influence in international politics', *Foreign Affairs*, 89: 93–100.

Thrift, N. (2004) 'Intensities of feeling: Towards a spatial politics of affect', *Geografiska Annaler*, 86(1): 57–78.

Tietze, N. (2001) 'Managing Borders: Muslim religiosity among young men in France and Germany', in A. Salvatore (ed.) *Muslim Traditions and Modern Techniques of Power: Yearbook of the Sociology of Islam*. New Brunswick, NJ: Transaction.

Tiryakian, E. (1964) 'Durkheim's two laws of penal evolution', *Journal for the Scientific Study of Religion*, 3(2): 261–6.

Tiryakian, E. (1995) 'Collective effervescence, social change and charisma: Durkheim, Weber and 1989', *International Sociology*, 10(3): 269–81.

Torgovnick, M. (1995) 'Piercings', in R. De La Campa, E.A. Kaplan and M. Sprinker (eds) *Late Imperial Culture*. London: Verso.

Trembinski, D. (2008) '[Pro]passio doloris: Early Dominican conceptions of Christ's physical pain', *Journal of Ecclesiastical History*, 59(4): 630–56.

Troeltsch, E. (1976) *The Social Teaching of the Christian Churches*. Chicago, IL: University of Chicago Press.

Turina, I. (2013) 'Consecrated virgins in Italy: A case study in the renovation of Catholic religious life', *Journal of Contemporary Religion*, 26(1): 43–55.

Turner, B.S. (1974) *Weber and Islam*. London: Routledge.

Turner, B.S. (1984) *The Body and Society*. London: SAGE.

Turner, B.S. (1991) *Religion and Social Theory*. London: SAGE.

Turner, B. S. (1994) *Orientalism, Postmodernism and Globalism*. London: Routledge.

Turner, B.S. (2000) 'The possibility of primitiveness: Towards a sociology of body marks in cool societies', in M. Featherstone (ed.) *Body Modification*. London: SAGE.

Turner, B.S. (2006) *Vulnerability and Human Rights*. University Park, PA: Pennsylvania State University Press.

Turner, B.S. (2010a) 'Religion in a post-secular society', in B.S. Turner (ed.) *The New Blackwell Companion to the Sociology of Religion*. Oxford: Blackwell.

Turner, B.S. (2010b) 'Islam, public religions and the secularization debate', in G. Marranci (ed.) *Muslim Societies and the Challenge of Secularization*. London: Springer, pp. 11–30.

Turner, B.S. (2011) *Religion and Modern Society: Citizenship, Secularisation and the State*. Cambridge: Cambridge University Press.

Turner, B.S. and Rojek, C. (2001) *Society & Culture*. London: SAGE.

Turner, B.S., Possamai, A. and Barbarlet, J. (2009) 'Introduction: States, consumption and managing religions', in J. Barbarlet, A. Possamai and B.S. Turner (eds) *Religion and the State: A Comparative Sociology*. London: Anthem Press.

Turner, S. (2003) 'Charisma reconsidered', *Journal of Classical Sociology*, 3(1): 5–26.

Turner, V. (1969) *The Ritual Process*. Chicago, IL: Aldine.

Tyler, A. (1988) *Street Drugs*. London: Hodder and Stoughton.

Urban, H.B. (1995) 'The remnants of desire: Sacrificial violence and sexual transgression in the cult of the Kapalikas and in the writings of Georges Bataille', *Religion*, 25: 67–90.

Urban, H.B. (2003) 'Sacred capital: Pierre Bourdieu and the study of religion', *Method and Theory in the Study of Religion*, 15: 354–89.

Utriainen, T., Hovi, T. and Broo, M. (2012) 'Combining choice and destiny: Identity and agency within post-secular wellbeing practices', in P. Nynäs, M. Lassander and T. Utriainen (eds) *Post-Secular Society*. New Brunswick, NJ: Transaction.

Van der Veer, P. (1996) (ed.) *Conversion to Modernities: The Globalization of Christianity*. London: Routledge.

Van Gennep, A. (1960) *The Rites of Passage*. Chicago, IL: University of Chicago Press.

Van Klinken, A. (2013) *Transforming Masculinities in African Christianity: Gender Controversies in Times of AIDS*. Farnham and Burlington: Ashgate.

Vásquez, M.A. (2011) *More Than Belief: A Materialist Theory of Religion*. Oxford: Oxford University Press.

Verter, B. (2003) 'Spiritual capital: Theorizing religion with Bourdieu against Bourdieu', *Sociological Theory*, 21(2): 150–74.

Virilio, P. (2000) *The Information Bomb*. London: Verso.

Voas, D. and Crockett, A. (2005) 'Religion in Britain: Neither believing nor belonging', *Sociology*, 39(1): 11–28.

Voas, D. and Fleischmann, F. (2012) 'Islam moves West: Religious change in the first and second generations', *Annual Review of Sociology*, 38: 525–45.

Volpi, F. & Turner, B.S. (eds) (2007) Special issue on Authority and Islam, *Theory, Culture & Society*, 24(2): 1–240.

Von Balthasar, H. (1982) 'Meditation (II): Attempt at an Integration of Eastern and Western Meditation', in M. Kehl (ed.) *The Von Balthasar Reader*. Edinburgh: T&T Clark.

Wale, S. (2001) *Out of It*. London: Hamish Hamilton.

Walseth, K. and Fasting, K. (2003) 'Islam's view on physical activity and sport', *International Review for the Sociology of Sport*, 38(1): 45–60.

Warner, M., VanAntwerpen, J. and Calhoun, C.J. (2010) (eds) *Varieties of Secularism in a Secular Age*. Boston, MA: Harvard University Press.

Warner, R.S. (1993) 'Work in progress toward a new paradigm for the sociological study of religion in the United States', *American Journal of Sociology*, 98(5): 1044–93.

Warner, R.S. (1997) 'Convergence toward the new paradigm: A case of induction', in L.A. Young (ed.) *Religion and Rational Choice Theory: A Summary and Assessment*. London: Routledge.

Wasielewski, P.L. (1985) 'The emotional basis of charisma', *Symbolic Interaction*, 8: 207–22.

Watson Jr, J.B. and Scalen, W. (2012) 'Jesus at Disneyland or spiritual innovation: The enmeshment of consumer culture and U.S. evangelical religious practices', *The 2012 Proceedings of the ASSR-SW*, 16–25.

Weber, M. (1927) *General Economic History*. Glencoe, IL: Free Press.

Weber, M. (1948 [1915]) 'Religious rejections of the world and their directions', in H.H. Gerth and C.W. Mills (eds) *From Max Weber: Essays in Sociology*. London: Routledge.

Weber, M. (1948 [1919a]) 'Science as a vocation' in H.H. Gerth and C.W. Mills (eds) *From Max Weber: Essays in Sociology*. London: Routledge.

Weber, M. (1948 [1919b]) 'Politics as a vocation' in H.H. Gerth and C.W. Mills (eds) *From Max Weber: Essays in Sociology*. London: Routledge.

Weber, M. (1952) *Ancient Judaism*, trans. H.H. Gerth and Don Martindale. Glencoe, IL: Free Press.

Weber, M. (1964) *The Theory of Social and Economic Organization*. New York, NY: Free Press.

Weber, M. (1968) *Economy and Society*. Berkeley, CA: University of California Press.

Weber, M. (1975) *Roscher and Knies: The Logical Problem of Historical Economics*. New York, NY: Free Press.

Weber, M. (1991) *The Protestant Ethic and the Spirit of Capitalism*. London: Collins.

Weber, M. (1993) *The Sociology of Religion*. New York, NY: Beacon Press.

Westerlund, D. (ed.) (2009) *Global Pentecostalism: Encounters with Other Religious Traditions*. London: I.B. Taurus.

Whimster, S. (1995) 'Max Weber on the erotic and some comparisons with the work of Foucault', *International Sociology*, 10(4): 447–62.

Wickström, L. and Illman, R. (2012) 'Environmentalism as a trend in post-secular society', in P. Nynäs, M. Lassander and T. Utriainen (eds) *Post-Secular Society*. New Brunswick, NJ: Transaction.

Wiegele, K. (2005) *Investing in Miracles: El Shaddai and the Transformation of Popular Catholicism in the Philippines*. Honolulu, HI: University of Hawaii Press.

Williams, S., Martin, P. and Gabe, J. (2011) 'The pharmaceuticalisation of society?', *Sociology of Health and Illness*, 33(5): 710–25.

Willner, A.R. (1984) *The Spellbinders: Charismatic Political Leadership*. New Haven, CT: Yale University Press.

Wilson, A. (2011) 'Boots, indecency, and secular sacred spaces: Implicit religious motives underlying an aspect of airline dress codes', *Implicit Religion*, 14(2): 173–92.

Wilson, B. (1985) 'Secularization: The inherited model', in P.E. Hammond (ed.) *The Sacred in a Secular Age*. Berkeley, CA: University of California Press.

Winkleman, M. and Bletzer, K. (2004) 'Drugs and modernisation', in C. Casey and R. Edgerton (eds) *A Companion to Psychological Anthropology: Modernity and Psychocultural Change*. Oxford: Wiley-Blackwell.

Wisse, M. (2003) '*Habitus fidei*: An essay on the history of a concept', *Scottish Journal of Theology*, 56(2): 172–89.

Wittrock, B. (2000) 'Modernity: One, none, or many? European origins and modernity as a global condition', *Daedalus*, 129: 31–60.

Wolf, R. (2007) 'Doubleness, *matam* and Muharram drumming in South Asia', in S. Coakley and K.K. Shelemay (eds) *Pain and Its Transformations*. Cambridge, MA: Harvard University Press.

Wood, M. and Bunn, C. (2009) 'Strategy in a religious network: A Bourdieuian critique of the sociology of spirituality', *Sociology*, 43(2): 286–303.

Wright, T. (1986) *The Religion of Humanity: The Impact of Comtean Positivism on Victorian Britain*. Cambridge: Cambridge University Press.

Zborowski, M. (1952) 'Cultural components in response to pain', *Journal of Social Issues*, 8: 16–30.

Žižek, S. (2002) *On Belief*. London: Verso.

Zizioulas, J.D. (2004) *Being as Communion*. London: Darton, Longman and Todd.

Zola, I. (1966) 'Culture and symptoms: An analysis of patients presenting complaints', *American Sociological Review*, 31: 615–30.

# Index